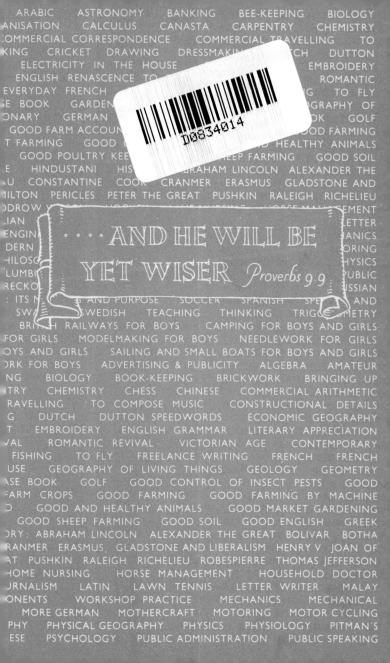

ARABIC   ASTRONOMY   BANKING   BEE-KEEPING   BIOLOGY
ANISATION   CALCULUS   CANASTA   CARPENTRY   CHEMISTRY
COMMERCIAL CORRESPONDENCE   COMMERCIAL TRAVELLING   TO
KING   CRICKET   DRAWING   DRESSMAKIN   CH   DUTTON
ELECTRICITY IN THE HOUSE   EMBROIDERY
ENGLISH RENASCENCE TO   ROMANTIC
EVERYDAY FRENCH   G   TO FLY
E BOOK   GARDEN   GRAPHY OF
ONARY   GERMAN   OK   GOLF
GOOD FARM ACCOUN   OD FARMING
T FARMING   GOOD   HEALTHY ANIMALS
GOOD POULTRY KEE   HEEP FARMING   GOOD SOIL
E   HINDUSTANI   HIS   BRAHAM LINCOLN   ALEXANDER THE
U   CONSTANTINE   COO   CRANMER   ERASMUS   GLADSTONE AND
ILTON   PERICLES   PETER THE GREAT   PUSHKIN   RALEIGH   RICHELIEU
ODROW   HE NURSING   HORSE MA   EMENT
IAN   LETTER
ENGIN   ... AND HE WILL BE   ANICS
DERN   ORING
HILOSO   YET WISER   *Proverbs 9.9*   HYSICS
LUMBI   PUBLIC
RECKO   USSIAN
ITS   AND PURPOSE   SOCCER   SPANISH   SPE   AND
SW   SWEDISH   TEACHING   THINKING   TRIG   METRY
BRI   H RAILWAYS FOR BOYS   CAMPING FOR BOYS AND GIRLS
FOR GIRLS   MODELMAKING FOR BOYS   NEEDLEWORK FOR GIRLS
OYS AND GIRLS   SAILING AND SMALL BOATS FOR BOYS AND GIRLS
RK FOR BOYS   ADVERTISING & PUBLICITY   ALGEBRA   AMATEUR
NG   BIOLOGY   BOOK-KEEPING   BRICKWORK   BRINGING UP
TRY   CHEMISTRY   CHESS   CHINESE   COMMERCIAL ARITHMETIC
RAVELLING   TO COMPOSE MUSIC   CONSTRUCTIONAL DETAILS
G   DUTCH   DUTTON SPEEDWORDS   ECONOMIC GEOGRAPHY
T   EMBROIDERY   ENGLISH GRAMMAR   LITERARY APPRECIATION
VAL   ROMANTIC REVIVAL   VICTORIAN AGE   CONTEMPORARY
FISHING   TO FLY   FREELANCE WRITING   FRENCH   FRENCH
USE   GEOGRAPHY OF LIVING THINGS   GEOLOGY   GEOMETRY
ASE BOOK   GOLF   GOOD CONTROL OF INSECT PESTS   GOOD
FARM CROPS   GOOD FARMING   GOOD FARMING BY MACHINE
D   GOOD AND HEALTHY ANIMALS   GOOD MARKET GARDENING
GOOD SHEEP FARMING   GOOD SOIL   GOOD ENGLISH   GREEK
ORY: ABRAHAM LINCOLN   ALEXANDER THE GREAT   BOLIVAR   BOTHA
RANMER   ERASMUS   GLADSTONE AND LIBERALISM   HENRY V   JOAN OF
AT   PUSHKIN   RALEIGH   RICHELIEU   ROBESPIERRE   THOMAS JEFFERSON
HOME NURSING   HORSE MANAGEMENT   HOUSEHOLD DOCTOR
URNALISM   LATIN   LAWN TENNIS   LETTER WRITER   MALAY
ONENTS   WORKSHOP PRACTICE   MECHANICS   MECHANICAL
MORE GERMAN   MOTHERCRAFT   MOTORING   MOTOR CYCLING
PHY   PHYSICAL GEOGRAPHY   PHYSICS   PHYSIOLOGY   PITMAN'S
ESE   PSYCHOLOGY   PUBLIC ADMINISTRATION   PUBLIC SPEAKING

THE TEACH YOURSELF BOOKS
EDITED BY LEONARD CUTTS

ENGLISH LITERATURE

VOLUME I
Introductory Volume

The Teach Yourself
History of
English Literature

is complete in
six volumes

The Teach Yourself
History of
English Literature

LITERARY APPRECIATION

The Introductory Volume by

PETER WESTLAND

THE ENGLISH UNIVERSITIES PRESS LTD.
LONDON

First printed 1950
This impression 1959

Printed in Great Britain for the English Universities Press, Limited,
by Richard Clay and Company, Ltd., Bungay, Suffolk.

FOREWORD

THE six volumes of *The Teach Yourself History of English Literature* are planned so that they may form one complete work, with each volume complete in itself and yet connecting up with the lines of thought which begin in the first volume and are illustrated all the way through to the end of the series. Thus it is possible for a reader to concentrate on a single volume, for his own purposes, or to read the books in almost any order. The reader who wishes, however, to study the full course should begin with the first volume, since this lays down essential principles of literary appreciation and has been written as the key volume to this account of English literature.

The author of the first and last volumes has prepared the other volumes by condensing the excellent *A History of English Literature* by Dr. Arthur Compton-Rickett, to which summary he has added, both within the text and additionally to it, his own material and comment. In doing this he has tried to preserve as much of the author's style of narrative as possible, with its skilful sketching in of background, lively interest in biographical detail, and that remarkable faculty by which Dr. Compton-Rickett unfailingly interested his readers in the books and authors he discussed. In this last gift he was outstanding among really valuable critics of this century.

The final volume strikes a balance between critical selection of contemporary literature and the recording of works which the reading public and its critics have found notable. By writing it in this way it has been possible to give as much valuation of contemporary work as may be sensibly made, while at the same time indicating to readers books and movements and aspirations which, at this point, each of us must appraise for himself. A general picture of contemporary fiction, non-fiction, poetry, and drama is given in the text; the use of the index brings together the details given about particular authors.

For permission to use Dr. Compton-Rickett's work the kindness of his publishers, Messrs. Thos. Nelson & Sons, is gratefully acknowledged.

The following authors, authors' representatives and publishers are warmly thanked for their permission to use copyright material in this volume.

Miss Rebecca West, The Return of the Soldier ; *W. J. Turner and Messrs. Sidgwick and Jackson,* "*Ecstasy*" *from* The Hunters and other Poems ; *Lord David Cecil and Messrs. Constable,* The Stricken Deer ; *Sir Osbert Sitwell and Messrs. Macmillan,* Sing High, Sing Low ; *Messrs. Burns, Oates and Washbourne,* "*Daisy*" *and* "*The Kingdom of Heaven*", *by Francis Thompson* ; *Miss E. J. Scovell and Messrs. Routledge and Kegan Paul,* "*Alone*", *from* Midsummer Meadow and other Poems ; *Mr. James Stephens and Messrs. Macmillan,* The Demi-gods ; *Mr. Percy Lubbock and Messrs. Jonathan Cape,* Earlham ; *Geoffrey Cumberlege, Oxford University Press,* "*Pied Beauty*", *from* Poems *by Gerard Manley Hopkins* ; *T. S. Eliot and Messrs. Faber and Faber,* The Waste Land, Morning at the Window, The Boston Evening Transcript.

CONTENTS

Chapter One

Intelligent Appreciation

THE purpose of this book is so simple that it can be defined in one sentence. It is to provide an introduction to some of the main facts about authors, readers, and books, so that we may have an intelligent appreciation of what we read.

We all have likes and dislikes which guide our selection from library shelves. Further than this, we all have the right to these likes and dislikes. We should defend that right, unless it is merely a whim to choose something easy to enjoy or a readiness to reject an author because we cannot appreciate him. If we cling to our likes merely because that is an easy way to choose books, we are losing a great deal of pleasure through ignoring books which we do not enjoy on first acquaintance with a few chapters or even a few pages. If we cherish our dislikes we are laying ourselves open to the complaint that we are rather stupid people unworthy of the name of " readers ". Apart from these two exceptions, we should and must read what we like.

The exceptions are the difficulty which this book tries to diminish by examining the principal reasons through which a book or shorter literary composition may be known to be worth liking. Nowhere in these pages is there any suggestion that you *must* enjoy anything. Instead of proposing that useless and indefensible idea, they offer a brief examination of books in general, so that your reading will result in a keen and intelligent enjoyment of authors or a reasoned opinion behind your preference not to make them your companions.

(i) The Approach to Books

The true enjoyment of books requires a certain amount of care. It does not in any way depend on the possession of a large, well-arranged library. It may be that you are reading this while you are in your pleasant reading-room, with its shelves of fragrant cedar-wood, filled with handsome volumes. Perhaps you have near you only a few shelves painted white, and serviceable merely for holding a collection of worn, second-hand bargains, or you may even be one of those whom Arnold Bennett blessed—the enthusiastic beginners whose few treasured books are kept in a biscuit-tin. These circumstances are irrelevant to the fact that you have a wish to read, an enthusiasm to meet authors. Because you have this zeal, you must also acquire care not to accept or dismiss these authors too readily.

You must learn to know why you want to read more of an author's work, why you find it interesting. And you must likewise know why you turn from someone else, assured at least that you are not doing so through laziness or emotional impulse or amazement at his novelty. If you learn to discover why you react in different ways to different books, you will remove the difficulties mentioned above and vindicate your right to choose and reject and doubt as you look over book-titles.

Books are not material things; they are the expressed thoughts and imaginings and feelings of other people. Consequently they stand in the same relation to us as people, even though they are carefully prepared before presentation. Opening an unread book is like meeting someone who has rehearsed all he wishes to say to you. You may or may not be interested in what he tells you; you may or may not like the way in which he tells it. He may prove irritating because of obscurities or mannerisms; he may be unusually attractive but vapid; he may affect you favourably or unfavourably, so exactly as other people do that you may be a considerable time in fully understanding why you like or dislike him.

If you are a good reader, you will deal with books as you deal with people. You will expect to find that, since you do not allow first impressions to harden into unalterable convictions, further meetings with certain books will show you that your early rapture was excessive, or that your distaste is giving way to mild pleasure. Your friends will become acquaintances and the authors to whom you were indifferent will develop into valued and life-long friends. And some, of course, will be what many people are for each of us—a mixture of what we like, when we are in the mood for them, with what we find uninteresting at other times.

If you regard books as people—as they are—you will immediately see why no person or book can tell you whom to like, or why or when you should like them.   In place of a guide to books, you will accept the freedom that the absence of a guide allows.   By this liberty you will sample the books at your disposal, gradually acquiring the familiarity by which a taste for " good " books is formed.   By experience you will gain discrimination, the ability to know what is worthwhile and what is not, the elements of literary criticism, and the ability to take pleasure in the technical perfection of authors.   The building up of a taste for those books which genuinely discriminating readers have decided, generation after generation, are worthy of preservation, is gradual.   As your taste for books and knowledge of them increase, your earlier opinions will in many instances be changed, for this is a process of real development.

Reading books is an intimately personal affair.   It means that you, with your mind and outlook and habits of thought, are meeting Dr. Johnson or Skelton or Cowper or H. E. Bates.   No one has the right or ability to tell you that you must like any one of these authors, but people who have met them may help you to make a surer and quicker acquaintance by speaking of their experience of them.   That acquaintance may ripen into friendship.   It has done so in many instances. If it does not, no one will say that either you or any of these authors is blameworthy.

The similarity between your reading Samuel Johnson and meeting him is clear if, without assuming a pontifical pose, I were to say, " You may find, as I did, or thought I did, that he has a disconcerting habit of using involved, latinised words in a painfully solemn manner. It can be most wearisome, and even discouraging. But let him go on talking. Presently he will say something so striking, and he will say it so perfectly, that your amiability towards him will be generously rewarded. Other people have told me, although I did not experience this myself, that they found him too often remote and cold. Yet they said they loved him for the other times when he is warmly human, heartily amusing, and solid with sound sense."

In this way this book tells you about the authors you meet; suggests what you may find to enjoy or profit by in their writings. If you like to regard it in this way, it is an introduction to authors that tells you how other people have found them, something of the ways in which they express themselves, and nothing of how you " ought " to react to them.

Of course, the introductions cannot be individual. For that you must turn to books about English literature and to literary biographies. The usefulness of seeking personal introductions, with suggestions as to how they may best be sought, will be discussed later in this book.

In short, this book aims at outlining the principal

things to look for in books, and the qualities which, if developed in yourself, will facilitate your pleasure and profit in reading. For instance, a glance at its table of contents will show you that it deals partly with you, partly with authors, and partly with the link between you—your books. It outlines the characteristics of good readers, the nature of authors (their inspiration and art, for instance), and deals with the chief points of the technique authors employ, since an appreciation of " how an author does it " yields enormous pleasure. In this matter the book is not professedly one of literary criticism, but aims at giving the reader an outline of the principles of writing, adequate to his needs if he is to gain the utmost profit from his reading without becoming an expert critic or a literary specialist. The book is an introduction rather than a conclusion. It points to facts which you will, no doubt, take one by one and study more closely as your familiarity with books increases. It shows you ways in which books can be enjoyed. It leaves you free to use any of those ways and to find others it has not space to include.

(ii) Technical Appreciation

As far as literary criticism is included, it is worth pointing out that this aspect of reading is not given undue prominence. At the same time it is not reduced to the niggardly minimum which some readers would wish.

There has been a tendency lately for " lit. crit." to

be depreciated.   Possibly this is a recoil from a time
when its importance was given a formidable priority.
For instance, a glance at examination papers shows that
familiarity with the text of an author is now considered to be of greater importance than a knowledge of
the technical devices he employs.   This is a corrective
tendency, but it is as much a tendency as its opposite,
and therefore, if used as a sole approach to any author,
will result in your missing much of what is to be
gained from him.

For instance, with little critical appreciation of the
play, you may find that *As You Like It*, with its
whimsical Jaques and clowning Touchstone, its
magnificent Rosalind and quietly human Celia, may
become your favourite section of Shakespeare.   Some
day, however, you will know the play almost by heart.
It would be a sad thing if, when intimacy has become
so customary as to be almost unprofitable, you could
not find pleasure in the extraordinarily skilful structure
of the play, the manner in which one scene prepares
you for another, the securing of the desired effect by
a planned juxtaposition of scenes (e.g. Act III Scene i
could have followed Act II Scene iii, but is placed after
Act II Scene vii, so that the ante-plot may reach its
climax close to an Arden scene), or Shakespeare's
deceptively simple use of prosody.

To take another example, we can all enjoy a
moderate use of Alliteration—

> In a somer seson, when soft was the sonne,
> I shope me in shroudës, as I a shepe were—

but what gives effect in

> Now the salt tides seawards flow,
> Now the wild white horses play,
> Champ and chafe and toss in the spray

if we ignore alliteration ? Or, to ask the question in another way, why should it be taken for granted that everyone knows about alliteration but need not know anything about assonance ? Why should it be considered unnecessary to study the elements of literary art at least until we can recognise form or rhythm or unity and more detailed " lit. crit." technicalities ?

When all is said and done, the fact is that authors have expressed themselves in certain ways, both numerous and diverse, varying from word usages to structural architecture. Readers have noticed the means used by writers and have classified them into devices and principles, such as Onomatopoeia, Synecdoche, Heroic Couplet, Unity of Impression, Periodic Style.

To approach this fact from the wrong side is to get the impression that a reader is under some obligation to know what these things are before he may lawfully enjoy a library. Hence arises opposition to an acquaintance with literary criticism. To approach it from the other side is to have a wholly different view of it, a happy and proper view, for it shows us that literary criticism is nothing more than an organised, ordered appreciation of all an author offers us. By it we can enjoy not only what he writes, but also how he writes it. And what sensible reader will object to being given the pleasures of reading which are in the skill of his author's work ?

I suppose that the mild aversion from the inside of literary art which is being encouraged arises from the idea that the slightest suggestion that a reader *must* acquire a small knowledge of literary apparatus interferes with his freedom. And certainly reading is, as I have remarked, a most free and personal activity. It is equally true that great profit from books can be gained by people who have no knowledge of the craft of writing.

These two statements, however, in no way justify a depreciation of literary criticism. In the first place, no one is told that he is obliged to study even the elements of literary craftsmanship. Instead of an obligation the reader is offered only the friendly suggestion that, if he troubles to find out something about how books are written, he will find more interest and pleasure in them.

This point may be debated, of course. Many critics, including some of the most eminent who were also original authors, have said that no one has the right to say " This is an over-rated book " unless he has equipped himself to see and value for himself whatever qualities it has. One can readily see how an author may advance this argument. It need not be elaborated for us to see that a writer, who has given us his best in conception, design, and craftsmanship, may well object to depreciation of his work by readers who are incapable of understanding it save in the utmost limitation. Indeed, Sainte-Beuve objected to approval of books when it is ill-informed, and in this he was logical, for it is surely as stupid to be right for the wrong reasons as to be in error for the wrong reasons.

He is by no means alone in claiming that the real reader will not be content to know what he likes, but to know why he likes it. Whatever we may think of the first argument in favour of a study of literary method, it is scarcely possible to doubt the cogency of this second argument, since it touches each of us personally. However expressed, it amounts to a statement which is valid in application to any art—that learning why a work appeals to you or does not appeal to you gives you not only the right to have an opinion about it, but also the pleasure of having a reasoned opinion. This is in itself a gain, a satisfaction won from reading.

Our conclusion must be that some knowledge of the craftsmanship of writing necessarily opens to us pleasures in reading which its absence inevitably precludes. A balanced view of the dispute is obtained if we see that, in reading, we must neither miss the genius of a work by noticing only its craftsmanship, nor be blind to its technical perfection through inability to see how the genius is transferred to us through the medium of words and the arrangements of literary body.

With this view most writers and readers may be

taken to agree, unless they are prepared to dispute the
statement that an author who is deficient in craftsmanship necessarily fails to give all his meaning to the
reader, together with its imaginative or emotional
background, in the same way that a painter or a
musician cannot possibly give all his conception to his
students if his technical training is inadequate to the
task in hand.   This being so, it is equally clear that the
reader who has some knowledge of critical apparatus
will be so much the better able to receive what the
author has put into his book.

(iii) The Critical Reader

This is the explanation of such particulars of
literary criticism as appear in this book.   They may
be used or not.   A reader who decides to make little
use of them should not consider himself unduly
ignorant or hopelessly crippled in his journeyings in
the land of books.   At most he has cut off from himself certain pleasures of reading for the attainment of
which he may feel he has not leisure to prepare.   No
one can quarrel with him, provided he keeps his self-
imposed limitation in mind when passing judgment on
his authors.

Undoubtedly no one will be disposed to quarrel
with him who reflects on the fact that, as his taste for
reading increases, this too diffident reader will almost
certainly turn to careful consideration of matters he
is at present disposed to neglect.   For reading will
make him observant and sensitive to the finer effects

of what he reads.   He will wonder where lies the magic of

> Charm'd magic casements, opening on the foam
> Of perilous seas, in faery lands forlorn.
>
> (Keats.)

or of

> Dry clash'd his harness in the icy caves
> And barren chasms, and all to left and right
> The bare black cliff clang'd round him, as he based
> His feet on juts of slippery crag that rang
> Sharp-smitten in the dint of armèd heels—
> And on a sudden, lo ! the level lake
> And the long glories of the winter moon.
>
> (Tennyson.)

or of

> " And there was Claverhouse, as beautiful as when he lived, with his long, dark, curled locks, streaming down over his laced buff-coat, and his left hand always on his right spule-blade to hide the wound that the silver bullet had made."
>
> (Scott.)

or of

> " In that dry desert of learning, we gather strength and patience, and a strange and insatiable thirst of knowledge.   The ruined monuments of antiquity are also there, and the fragments of buried cities (under which the adder lurks), and cool springs, and green sunny spots, and the whirlwind and the lion's roar, and the shadow of angelic wings."
>
> (Hazlitt.)

And when he has begun to notice, to savour, to pass sentences through his lips and to let images float in his mind, he will begin to have a growing curiosity to know why words have fascinated him. Disregarding arguments, he will turn to the study of technique with pleasure, and find in it an understanding of his author not far removed from possession of his mind and artistry.

Without further preliminary, we may now take our first step towards close knowledge of books, make our bow to our authors, by looking to see what qualities we require, apart from anything specialised, if we are to read with the maximum of contentment and profit. When we have considered ourselves, we can begin to inspect those who stand behind their books, not necessarily anxious that you or I should read, but certainly requiring that, if we enter into their works, we should offer them the courtesy of being in the proper frame of mind and disposition. For only then can we estimate how those books are to be used, as a prodigious writer and reader has advised :—

> " Read not to contradict and confute, nor to believe and take for granted, nor to find talk and discourse, but to weigh and consider. Some books are to be tasted, others to be swallowed, and some few to be chewed and digested; that is, some books are to be read only in parts; others to be read but not curiously; and some few to be read wholly, and with diligence and attention."
>
> (Bacon : *Of Studies*.)

Chapter Two

The Reader

MEETING someone through the medium of a book is at least as difficult as an introduction and communication by letter. They can understand each other only at second hand in its most remote degrees. That is to say, the reader has one statement to consider, and that is irrevocable; the author has to address himself to someone he cannot know personally but only in so far as he knows men in general.

The inevitable result of these conditions of approach is that the author must take every possible measure to ensure that he evokes in the reader exactly the responses he wishes. Since it would be impractical in this book to suppose otherwise, and since it deals chiefly with the reading of worthwhile books—the "classics" and modern books that may some day attain classical rank—we must take it that he has done so. In other words, we must suppose that he knows his craft and has employed it skilfully.

(i) Amiability

For the reader these conditions imply that he must try to meet the author's careful presentation of what he has to say. He must take his part in overcoming the difficulties that attend their communication. At the outset, then, we must try to obtain a clear idea of what qualities he should cultivate in order to fulfil his part of the joint activity of reading.

Probably the first lesson is that he will benefit by approaching his books with friendliness, with a certain amiable disposition to be interested or pleased.

This does not mean that he should for a moment lay aside his right to disagree or to query or to criticise, or to find a page tedious. It requires only that he should not do any of these things lightly or quickly, if only because he may be to blame rather than the author. For instance, he must be reasonably indulgent to his author's mannerisms, such as Meredith's inverted phrases (" Chimed they in one ", etc.), just as he would not neglect the conversation of someone who occasionally dropped his aitches. Montgomery Belgion deals with the matter roundly by advising us to " always open a good book bearing in mind that we have come into the presence of one of our betters ". That is plain speaking, and no sensible man, recollecting the pains the author has taken in the writing of a book (Belgion carefully confines his remark to " good " books), will resent it. The advice urges us " to go to those actual pieces of writing which are a part of literature in an appropriate spirit of humility ".

It is further necessary that a reader should choose his books according to his temporary inclinations and moods. To take up Hobbes's *Leviathan* when you are tired out and worried is unfair to yourself as well as to Hobbes; it would be more sensible to give yourself a chance of chuckling over Sairey Gamp's taking tea with Betsy Prig. Authors are patient; many of them have waited for centuries to offer you their works; there will be no loss but only gain if you postpone the planned reading of *Vanity Fair* and turn to Law's *Serious Call to a Devout and Holy Life*, or neglect one of Cranmer's *Sermons* for a story by Leonard Merrick. This sensible advice should be followed whenever we find ourselves genuinely out of sympathy with a book. Perhaps the author has gone off into a long digression through which it is wearisome to follow him, or perhaps it is you who have flagged on the journey. Whether the tedium is due to you or to your book, turn to something else for a time and all will be well. Variety in reading is as sensible as variety in conversation, although there are people whose earnestness in the pursuit of " good " books blinds them to the fact. They clench their teeth and stick resolutely to Pope's translation of *The Odyssey* long after they should have paused to take temporary refreshment with John Gilpin or gone to a ball with Elizabeth Bennett.

(ii) Freedom

This necessity for variety in reading brings us to a third suggestion which most readers have found useful —that we should read several books simultaneously. A lecturer whose interest in reading, apart from books his professional duties required him to read, was mainly in informative reading, told me that each

winter he read through one history, one or two biographies, and several works of one fiction writer.
Thus he would read Lingard's volumes, or Trevelyan's
books on the reign of Queen Anne, Boswell's *Life of
Johnson* or the unduly neglected Forster's *Life and Times
of Oliver Goldsmith*, and several books by Dickens.
Of course, he made time for other books also, but he
planned his reading on these lines and found great
enjoyment in it. Others will adapt it according to
their tastes, not necessarily planning by authors but
by subjects. For example, they may wish to have
always available one book of scientific interest, one of
biography, and one of fiction. In addition they will
keep to hand certain old favourites who can be relied
upon to meet the needs of every mood, grave or gay.
Incidentally, it is surprising to find what books people
cherish for their hours of greatest difficulty. A
lawyer told me that his favourite was *Whitaker's
Almanack*, since its contents are infinitely varied
(apart from the history, geography, statistics about
everything, and current affairs, I notice entries on
subjects as diverse as the size of a rising moon, and
fishes' feeding cries and love songs), and a well-known
theologian always relies on *Love and the Ironmonger*,
just as you or I might take up *The Diary of a Nobody* or
something by Jerome K. Jerome.

(iii) Patience

In case this advice may be construed as meaning
that, apart from intervals during which we may law-

fully seek only recreation in our reading, we should conscientiously grind away at books which we find dull, trying to support ourselves by the thought that others have decided they are among the " ought to be read " volumes, I think we may dare to make a further rule or suggestion.   This is that we should read only what interests us.

The rule is not as daring as it appears, although it seems to run counter to the need for persistence in making the acquaintance of authors who are wholly strange to us.   Perhaps it will be clearer if we see why this persistence is necessary, and when it is to be applied.

Patience in continuing our approach to an author is necessary when his manner of writing is wholly unfamiliar to us, as Jeremy Taylor's is to anyone whose previous reading has not taken him farther back than the year 1800, or who is writing of matters of which we are largely ignorant, as we may find in reading some of Watts-Dunton's critical articles.   We cannot expect that a man's wholly personal way of writing, which we may exemplify by mentioning Carlyle, will be immediately acceptable to us.   Nor can we trust that the meaning, the point of view, of a writer who deals with facts beyond our knowledge, or whose way of looking at them has been perceived only in part, will at once engross our whole interest.   In reading him we know that many discriminating people have come to regard him as the author of work with lasting value.   We wish to find out why they came to that conclusion and, even more, to possess ourselves of what is of value in him. In trying to accomplish these aims we find his books dull or irritating or distasteful to us every time we read them.

This distressing fact must be faced and accepted. It does not mean that other people's estimate of the author is wrong. We know that. We ought also to know that it does not mean that we are at fault either. It means nothing more than that, for the time being, we are not sufficiently developed to use these books. Perhaps our familiarity with literary style is too small to enable us to deal easily with this author's mode of expression; perhaps our factual knowledge of his subject is too incomplete for us to follow his line of thought; perhaps our emotions or our imagination are being stimulated in new ways to which they are too unaccustomed to respond. There are other possible explanations of the dullness we find in the author, but no explanation should lead us to suppose that we are incapable of getting the best out of him. The day for doing so has not yet come. This is not to say that it will not come.

The growth of understanding, of the power to feel, of the imagination, of knowledge, which reading causes in us is a guarantee that, sooner or later, we shall return to this disappointing author and find a profitable enjoyment in his works.

From what has been written about this point, two thoughts emerge which will repay consideration, before we pass on to our next suggestion as to the frame of mind which we should develop in order to get the best out of our reading.

The first is that we should be on our guard against suspecting an author of heaviness or obscurity. Although the idea may at first appear unlikely, we must realise that what we suppose to be an author's dullness may be his intentional reticence. It is the equivalent of the deliberate under-writing by which emphasis is secured exactly where the writer intends it to fall. As an example of this, notice the ending of Chapter XXXII of *Vanity Fair* :—

> " All our friends took their share and fought like men in the great field. All day long . . . the lines of the dauntless English infantry were receiving and repelling the furious charges of the French horsemen. Guns which were heard at Brussels were ploughing up their ranks, and comrades falling, and the resolute survivors closing in. Towards evening, the attack of the French . . . slackened in its fury. They had other foes besides the British to engage, and were preparing for a final on-set. It came at last ; the columns of the Imperial Guard marched up the hill of Saint Jean, at length and at once to sweep the English from the height which they had maintained all day, in spite of all : unscarred by the thunder of the artillery, which hurled death from the English line—the dark rolling column passed on. It seemed almost to crest the eminence, when it began to wave and falter. Then it stopped, still facing the shot. Then at last the English troops rushed from the post from which no enemy had been able to dislodge them, and the Guard turned and fled.
>
> No more firing was heard at Brussels—the pursuit rolled miles away. Darkness came down on the field and city : and Amelia was praying for George, who was lying on his face, dead, with a bullet through his heart."

Here Thackeray decided that the best way to shock
us by the news of George's death was to lull us into a
comfortable sense of security by hints that all was well
ended with victory, until the brief announcement of
the tragedy could fall upon us in one decisive stroke.
There is no building up of dramatic detail on dramatic
detail, each forecasting some climax. There is only
the opposite to this method, and a far more effective
means is employed.

Now, writers know well that constant daylight is
wearying, that the unceasing sound of a horn tires and
annoys. They do not, therefore, always write at top
pitch, just as painters skilfully plan their shadows so
as to secure exactly the right effect for their high
lights, instead of using bright colours for every detail
of their pictures. A writer, knowing well what is to
come and balancing it against what has gone before,
may decide that quite lengthy parts of his book must
be subdued in tone and undistinguished in diction.
He may even give us pages of words that are rough
to our tongue, strung together so as to give an
uneven or possibly jerky effect to what is written.
The result may annoy the inexperienced reader,
but the alert reader will suspect a purpose behind
this style. He will not resent being forced to stay
awake while he passes through pages of this prose.
He may even enjoy the fact that he is being
compelled to read slowly and carefully and thought-
fully.

Consequently we should not always take it for

granted that a seeming prosiness in a book is a fault its author could not avoid.

If we should make this mistake, we might also miss the point of the writer's style in another way.   There are times when authors—and some authors are notably expert in this kind of writing—deliberately remove sharpness from their prose.   In it is no crystal clearness, no sharp edged image, no definition of colour, no crispness of phrase, but instead a blend, a mist, an impression, a smoothness almost irritating in its elusiveness.   The mind is attracted by the meaning of sentences, yet finds it impossible to see at once precisely what that meaning is; the imagination moves, but is baffled by the almost wholly shapeless colours that are placed before it; the prose slips by, beautiful but vapid, too quickly for the reader who is trying to halt it and fasten it to certainty of impression.

All this is done with great skill, for various reasons, but usually because the writer wishes to evoke in you the reaction his material caused in him.   He is not unable to tell you succinctly what he has in mind, and it is rash to assume that what he has written is faulty. You will usually find that when a literary craftsman presents you with extensive passages of this kind, he is giving you two things—his meaning and the atmosphere which he wishes should accompany it.   Only a skilled writer can do it and only a tyro would decide that he is wanting in clearness.   You will find many passages of this kind in Henry James—passages often lengthy, which will, when you have become familiar

with them, be pleasurably and appreciatively re-read
many times.

Another occasion for such writing is found when
an author is dealing with matters in themselves obscure.
His mind has seen things which most minds are
too limited to perceive, and which he can view only
in shadowy outline. They are abstractions, perhaps
lightly involved in nature, forms seen as in a glass
darkly, things remote from our material world or
worldly experience. Those things he has been able
to express in words, and can we find fault if what he
writes is shadowed or filled with the brightness that
falls from the air ? A warning against such complaints
is contained in C. E. Montague's reminder that we
must observe the difference between " expression of
obscurity and obscurity of expression ".

To illustrate the meaning of what has been written
is difficult because it refers to passages of some length,
and for such quotation there is no space. But the
kind of thing referred to can be indicated by short
quotations, although the brevity is actually an aid to
their clearness.

Take the centuries-old stanza in which at least the
second line demands thought :—

> Western wind, when wilt thou blow ?
> That the small rain down can rain.
> Christ, if my love were in my arms
> And I in my bed again.

Only by the use of thought and imagination can the
relevance of that line, not to mention the first, to the

last two lines be seen.   Indeed, it may be a hopeless puzzle for some time and the stanza may remain " obscure " through long meditation.   It has a haunting appeal, and will finally soak into the mind, permeating it even as love has saturated the emotions of the speaker. And by doing so it reveals its metaphor. Was there ever a better way by which the author could transfer to you the whole emotion as well as the thought he wished to convey ?   Try to do it in any other way and you find that you have achieved nothing more than a rather bare statement, in no way memorable or really moving. Yet by what seems to be obscure writing, the poet has given it magic.

Now consider these three phrases :—

> (i) Happy eyes.
> (ii) Lovely, shining eyes.
> (iii) Laughing, restless eyes that speak.

The third is far older than the stanza previously quoted.   There is nothing obscure this time;   only the perfect expression of qualities which cannot be captured and imprisoned in words.   You know that the phrase is immeasurably better than the first or second;   you know what it means and you see the eyes for yourself.

Follow it up by a few lines which do exactly the same thing :—

> The brown waves of fog toss up to me
> Twisted faces from the bottom of the street,
> And tear from a passer-by in muddy skirts

An aimless smile that hovers in the air
And vanishes along the level of the roofs.

Again we have an impression and a fact so abstract that they cannot be expressed except by an exaggeration and a fantasy which result in unusual writing. Going farther, into a quotation which may seem both obscure and filled with a too vague suggestion, we turn to

When evening quickens faintly in the street,
Wakening the appetites of life in some
And to others bringing the *Boston Evening Transcript*,
I mount the steps and ring the bell, turning
Wearily, as one would turn to nod good-bye to Rochefoucauld,
If the street were time and he at the end of the street,
And I say " Cousin Harriet, here is the *Boston Evening Transcript* ".

These short quotations, from poems by T. S. Eliot, are concrete expressions of wholly abstract ideas. The more concrete an abstraction is made, the farther it is brought from its own world into ours, the less perfect it is when we receive it. Good writers, whose aim is to give us the gleam or the shadow, the insubstantial thing, take pains to bring it no nearer our world than they must in order to draw it within range of our vision. This implies the stretching of words to the utmost limit of their meaning. That is why stanzas like the above may appear elusive in meaning. The elusiveness is actually the working of our minds in a rarified atmosphere. They are unsteady, hard to concentrate, to make penetrating.

The author is not at fault : rather we are untrained to follow him to the far lands he visits, although those lands may be but the depths of our own selves.

Finally let us take two extracts from Rebecca West's *The Return of the Soldier*, partly for the sake of prose examples and partly because the author characteristically closes each with something concrete which hardens the preceding impressions and suggestions and moods into definite fact. The point about them is that the fact is given only when its significance has been attached to it. Not all authors do this as reliably and definitely as Miss West, but the thing is done and, if we miss the point when they do it, it means only that we have not yet trained ourselves to due alertness.

Writing of Chris and his first love, the author tells us :—

"In the liquefaction of colours which happens on a summer evening, when the green grass seemed like a precious fluid poured out on the earth and dripping over to the river, and the chestnut candles were no longer proud flowers, but just wet, white lights in the humid mass of the tree, when the brown earth seemed just a little denser than the water, Margaret also participated. Chris explained this part of his story stumblingly, but I too have watched people I loved in the dusk and I know what he meant. As she sat in the punt while he ferried himself across it was no longer visible that her fair hair curled diffidently and that its rather wandering parting was a little on one side; that her straight brows, which were a little darker than her hair, were nearly always contracted in a frown of conscientious speculation; that her mouth and chin were noble yet delicate as

flowers; that her shoulders were slightly hunched
because her young body, like a lily stem, found it
difficult to manage its own tallness. She was then just
a girl in white who lifted a white face or drooped a dull
gold head. And as that she was nearer to him than at
any other time. That he loved her, in this twilight
which obscured all the physical details which he adored,
seemed to him a guarantee that theirs was a changeless
love which would persist if she were old or maimed or
disfigured. He stood beside the crazy post where the
bell hung and watched the white figure take the punt over
the black waters, mount the grey steps and assume their
greyness, become a green shade in the green darkness of
the foliage-darkened lawn, and he exulted in that
guarantee."

There is no need for further comment on this
passage, and we come to the next, which will repay
re-reading after we have thought about it.

"It was one of those draggled days, so common at the
end of March, when a garden looks at its worst. The
wind that was rolling up to check a show of sunshine
had taken away the cedar's dignity of solid shade, had
set the black firs beating their arms together and had
filled the sky with glaring grey clouds that dimmed the
brilliance of the crocus. It was to give gardens a point
on days such as these, when the planned climax of this
flower bed and that stately tree goes for nothing, that
the old gardeners raised statues in their lawns and walls,
large things in a subject, mossy Tritons or nymphs—
with an urn, that held the eye. Even so in this unrestful
garden one's eye lay on the figure in the yellow raincoat
that was standing still in the middle of the lawn."

Analysing this short passage reveals its plan. It
consists of four sentences. The first is a plain statement of fact. The second is "difficult" because it

is compact with things that can be perceived instantly, but are most difficult to express. Only genius can do it without a series of statements which leaves us with facts alone, a handful of fingered petals from which the perfume has escaped. In this second sentence the writer has given us four facts descriptive of the garden, only one of which (about the firs) is simple. The other ideas are complex, and the reason for this is easy to understand. Measurably this sentence is three-quarters " obscure " because its writer wishes to give a description mostly in terms which are undefined. The impact on the imagination yields only images whose outlines are uncertain, except under close scrutiny, running over each other's boundaries, so that the whole picture is slightly blurred, seen hazily.

Then comes the third sentence, suddenly snapping into focus the mental images we are receiving—substituting a new idea for the mind to focus upon, but an idea associated with the idea of garden with which it is already dealing. Finally, in the fourth sentence, the fully focused vision of the reader is directed exclusively to one object, *the figure in the yellow raincoat*, whose appearance is a climax in the chapter.

These four sentences are masterly in their technique. Looking back at them we can see how a garden has been described, as it was at a particular moment, and that it was described for a purpose: as a setting to a figure. Almost anyone could have done that necessary work reasonably well without giving us anything valuable or at all memorable. But here we have the delicacy of exquisite perception conveyed in words of great beauty; we have something wholly satisfying in thought and expression; beyond all, we have perfection of the method chosen to secure the desired end —our undivided attention to the right place. In these four sentences alone is the difference between writing of " classic " standard and the competent work of hundreds of other writers who would have been content with

> " The figure in the yellow raincoat stood still upon the lawn, under the grey sky of wind-tossed clouds that cast their shadows after the fitful gleams of sunshine of that wild March day."

(iv) Choice

From our last rule—that we should approach our books with patience, and from the points we have found developing from it—we turn inevitably to a further precept : that we should prefer the original best authors to their imitators. This is by no means the same thing as saying that we should read nothing but the classics of English literature. The opinion has already been expressed that we should read what we enjoy, provided that we do not, for the sake of excitement or mere recreation, read so much of what is worthless in literary value as to vitiate our taste for what is good. The rule means no more than that we should read first the works of those authors who have made an original contribution to literature.

Many of these authors have been followed by others

whom we may hesitate to call imitators, since the word has a connotation of cheapness. It is better to say that they have been followed by writers who have found in them qualities similar to their own. Their reaction to certain authors has included the discovery that they also can express themselves adequately after the manner of their originals. So schools of writers have grown up. The suggestion is that, if you wish to read books belonging to such a school, you ought to go first to its original. To take an example from current fiction, if you want to know what the Hemingway school of writing is, read Hemingway.

It may be objected, not without some reason, that followers have at times improved on their masters, and that the best of a kind is not always the first of its kind. This argument seems to miss the point of the usual purpose for which we read works which can be classified as belonging to one group of writers.

The first approach to such a body is to discern how it differs from what has gone before it, or from contemporary writing. It is not to become acquainted with the most representative or the most valuable work the school has produced. Previously to that, it is wise to sample the flavour of the dish before new and perhaps better ways of cooking it were discovered. By doing this you will be able to perceive more personally how the new form of style or mode of thought, or whatever it may be, appeared to its founder, so that you not only gain a clearer idea of its relationship to its period, but also an idea of how it appeared to its author. For instance, you will find in many books an explanation of Wordsworth's aims in the publication of the *Lyrical Ballads*. Nowhere will you find those aims as convincingly expressed as in the poet's own statement by way of preface to the second edition. His words have a personal quality so strong that it is difficult not to see his point of view. Clearly this must be the starting point, this conversation with the man who began a revolution. From here we can turn to others, to Coleridge or Hazlitt or De Quincey, if we wish to know what they thought about either his theory or practice. Or we may listen to later writers who will point out to us the limitations of the theory enunciated and analyse its merits.

The same principle should guide our reading of any group of authors. If you wish to become acquainted with the Novel of Manners, you may be advised to read what is probably the best of its best representatives, Fielding's *Tom Jones*, the story of the foundling, brought up by the excellent Squire All-worthy, who passes through a thousand scrapes in his hot-blooded career and brings us into contact with people worth meeting, in Squire Western and his daughter and Parson Adams, in the hurly-burly of eighteenth-century England. But to get the best out of all the Novels of Manners it is wise to begin at the beginning with Richardson's *Clarissa Harlowe*. You will probably find the story much too long and frequently tedious. It moves slowly. But it was vastly different from anything that went before it and it has excellence. It is human; it is genuine; it is our greatest novel of sentiment. You will notice that it was not Richardson's first novel, but his best—the best work of a man who brought us a new kind of novel and probably did not realise its full merit himself. That is why we choose it instead of its predecessor, *Pamela*, which stirred Fielding into writing his *History of Joseph Andrews and his Friend, Mr. Abraham Adams*, so continuing the innovations of Richardson.

He surpassed his master—but not in everything. Richardson shows more knowledge of the human heart inside a few pages than Fielding has achieved in his volumes. For his part, Fielding knows more about life. But it was sentiment that began this school, especially feminine sentiment, and a reading of all its examples will not show you the essence of this kind of novel unless you turn to Richardson.

Do not be scrupulous to read every line of every page of *Clarissa*. Do not be so superficial as to skim through its chapters. Give it a reading which will show you why, in its day, it was acclaimed by thousands of readers as a book without which life would be incomplete. It is worth doing this for, in spite of its faults, it has the essential elements of great tragedy.

Next we come to a suggestion which is really a caution.

(v) Order

Above all other dangers be on your guard against promiscuity in reading : I have often wondered how many readers fall by the wayside because they flit to and fro across the road, from field to field and into lanes, in order to collect every flower that pleases or at least tempts them. The symptoms of this light-headedness are sudden, fierce enthusiasms, attacks of disgust, occasional depressions, complete disregard of the difference between the seventeenth century and the twentieth, a persistent tendency to mix Michael Sadleir and Swinburne, Keats and Matthew Arnold, Thomas Hardy and De Quincey. The reader's feverish zeal prevents his realising that his enthusiasm is burning him up and that the excesses to which it drives him are debauching his taste for books. His condition may last for a few years, after which he will cease from reading the literary reviews, turn to some active hobby, and give it as his considered opinion that reading is an impractical affair the value of which is greatly exaggerated.

In other instances readers of tough constitution, in whom the erratic fever burned more slowly, avoid its fatal stroke and carry it with them throughout their lives. They are dissipated in taste, muddled in critical appreciation, drifting from novelty to novelty, filled with enthusiasm for the book of the moment, stuffed with rash conclusions, and unaware of most of the finer or less obvious pleasures of reading. Always talking about books, and ready to plunge deeply into literary discussions, they drift through a world in which everything that is not a valley is a mountain, little suspecting that they have forfeited their right to the name of " reader ".   They are usually to be detected by the fact that their conversation about the giants of literature is almost inexhaustible, but their knowledge of the minor authors, who have immeasurable treasures to offer us, is negligible.   Apart from the fact that they are happy in their unsuspected condition, it is doubtful whether their fate is not worse than that of those who succumbed to their early enthusiasm.

These reflections bring us to the final rule we need to make to ensure steady and reasonably rapid progress in our reading—that it should be ordered.

The plan on which its order is based is of less importance than the fact that there is a plan.   It may be that the reading follows a period of literature, such as the growth of the essay in the eighteenth century or the rise and progress of Elizabethan drama.   By following a plan of this kind, in sections not necessarily chronological in order, a reader gains the advantage of acquiring a sound knowledge of the whole range of English literature.

Of course, it may not be his wish to study English literature, since this is, after all, definitely a study, and not necessarily to be desired by everyone.   Many readers will reasonably be content to follow their personal interests, which may be confined to drama or political writings or lyrical poetry or almost any combination of the classes into which books or authors may be divided.   Since we read to gain, it is reasonable to confine our reading to the kinds of books which are likely to yield us what we are seeking.

Allowing, then, for whatever purposes may govern our approach to books, the fact remains that ordered reading will best assist the fulfilment of those purposes. It is also true that a plan can easily be contrived by which order can be brought into our work and pleasure.

(vi) Biography

For instance, the scope of reading and our understanding of what is read can be greatly increased by a reading which may appear to be unnecessary around the subject. By this I mean that the reading which obviously must be done should be followed up by at least an examination of other books which may be related to the subject already explored. If your interest happens to be Tennyson, seek far and wide for expressions of opinion about his work. This search will take you to literary reviews of his time, the letters of his contemporaries, the monographs and studies which have appeared between his death and our day, and to critical histories of nineteenth-century literature. Even these sources of information by no means exhaust the possibilities of research open to any reader who has access to nothing more specialised than the libraries of our towns and cities. By the time he has got well into his task he will have a large amount of matter collected for consideration. He will have received many sidelights on his subject far more valuable than any one book, however able, could have given him, since he has secured them from their origin.

He has consulted widely.   After carefully evaluating
the opinions he has received and comparing them
with each other, he is in a position in which he can also
pass judgment on the authoritative statements of
biographers and eminent critics.   By following this
kind of plan he has himself slowly acquired the
ability to estimate the worth of the opinions which,
at an earlier stage in his work, were the primary objects
of his inquiries.

The last idea need not be outlined any further.
We turn from it to another way to bring order into any
course of reading.   This is the method of biographical
study.   Every author is the more profitable and
pleasing to us if he is detached from the library index
card and allowed to become a living acquaintance
with whom we may hold conversation wherever we
wish.   When we can see him, with reasonable
accuracy, as he is or was, when we have met his
friends, entertained him to dinner with them, walked
in his garden or climbed into his garret, we have
become accustomed to his atmosphere.   This means
that we have enlarged our capacity to understand him.
The man himself rather than his opinions, or his
friends' views about his opinions, is here the subject
of our interest.   Knowledge of him shows us his
motives, reveals the reasons and emotions which
inclined him to write what he did, and explains his
individuality as a writer.

Through the sympathetic knowledge gained in this
way, even authors for whom we have small affection,

either towards their views or towards themselves, are more readily and accurately appreciated by us. We apprehend something of the black shadow hanging over Cowper, and with it see his delicacy of eager friendship and his thought for others; we read the revolutionary Mary Wollstonecraft, and remember that after she had seen the French king on his way to execution she confessed that, for the first time, she could not extinguish her candle at night; we read the venomous mockery Pope spat at his enemies and recall his infinite patience with his work and with his puny body held together in its ghastly frame; we think of Johnson the pontifical, and then we see him sweating over his meals, with veins standing out on his forehead, and yet again we see him praying to his Maker for forgiveness and atoning for his sins, such as they may have been, by fasting and meditation; we hear the fulsome flatteries of Disraeli and see the fantastic sight of his dress and toilet, and we observe him going home in the small hours to a house brilliantly lit in welcome from his beloved Mary Anne, to whom he pays that most astounding and sincere compliment, that she looked after him as well as if she had been his mistress.

Piece by piece the puzzle that is man, the fragment we know and the more revealing fragment we did not know, come together. Then our authors are ours. Among our books we are not among shelved volumes, but among people, with their oddities and foibles, virtues and vices, courage and fear, their posed exhibitions of self and their indeliberate revelations. Of all this we make free, for we are readers of books and the intimate of their authors whether they will it or not.

Here in capitulation are our principles—an unfeigned friendliness to authors; a resolution to read what we enjoy and are, from time to time, interested to read; a variety of books always to be at our disposal; a decision to read the best of original authors before studying their followers; an ordered method of reading.

Many things have been written about readers and wise counsels have often been offered to them. From them all, the suggestions made here have received a general approval, since they recommend themselves as the most helpful.

Now it is time to end thinking of ourselves and to spend some time in thinking of authors. In doing so we shall find that we become involved in an inquiry into that most vexed problem—Literary Style.

Chapter Three

The Author

BUFFON'S celebrated definition of style, *Le style, c'est l'homme même*, makes an excellent opening to this chapter, for its theme is that *Style is the man himself*. We have spent some time in considering ourselves as readers and in forming a picture of the kind of person a reader should be if he is to become a free and prosperous citizen of the world of books. It is now time to think about authors.

If these chapters were being written for writers as well as for readers, we would take our next step forward by analysing the personal qualities which are likeliest to guarantee success, and the ability they must acquire and the craft they must learn in order to qualify for success. By " success " I mean, of course, the attainment of their purpose, and not mammoth sales figures. These two forms of " success " are in no way similar and often do not coincide, as many authors who desired both have found.

Since this book is offered to the interest of readers alone, however, the aspect of authorship we must examine is the nature of that thing which impels a man to put his thoughts on paper as well as he can, so that others may read them. For most authors certainly write with publication in mind, either by limited circulation among friends or by the organised issue of what is written. The point need not concern us greatly, since we are not trying to form a definition, and therefore need not be anxious because our idea seems to rob Pepys, for example, of the title of *author*. Whether it does or not, he remains a *writer* whose private pages will fascinate and delight their readers for many a generation to come. If we feel any scruple in the matter, we need not accept the intention to publish, even in its most limited sense, as being in the mind of an author. There is much to be said, which it would be irrelevant to our purpose for us to say here, for omitting that part of our original statement. On balance you may eventually decide that it should be included, but this does not matter a great deal, for our essential point is that an author is one who must write his thoughts, and do so as ably as he can. Our interest in this point is to discover what kind of person he is.

At first inspection this interest may appear superfluous to success in reading and possibly impertinent. Yet the longer we think about it, and the more we consider certain fundamental questions which arise about books, the more definitely are we guided back to it, since it seems to be inextricably connected with what is written. Above all, as will be suggested in this chapter, it is essential to an examination of the nature of literary style. We will begin our inquiry at this point.

(i) The First Essential

In spite of the constant assertions, since the earliest beginnings of the literature about books which we call literary criticism, that there is something which we call style, there is an opposite and not so venerably ancient view that the thing does not exist. Clearly this is a point we must deal with first.

If literary style is something we think we see in books but which in fact is not a definable reality, what makes the difference between two kinds of writing ? What is it, essentially, which makes the difference between the following :—

The bubbling wine in the cup.

Beaded bubbles winking at the brim ?

Both images express the same idea as seen by different people. The difference between them is not that one has taken some pains to express himself more vividly and exactly than the other; it is that the writer of the second line saw something different from what the first writer saw. Both looked at the same thing, but only one of them saw something that moved him so deeply that he described it perfectly—transferred it to you and me so as to pass on his reaction to it.

Yet it is the perception that is significant, and more important than the author's ability to convey his idea to us. To make this clear let us concentrate on it for a few minutes.

R. L. Stevenson has related that two lines from

Meredith's nocturne exhilarated and excited him so greatly that he went about shouting them.

> Lovely are the curves of the white owl sweeping
> Wavy in the dusk lit by one large star.

There they are in all their simple beauty, and we can share something of Stevenson's joy in them. We know what he means when he says they excited him, for have we not all been haunted by some line in much the same way ? I remember still, and can easily feel now, the shaking a line gave me when I first heard it in boyhood :—

> On a bare hill raise the dark standard.

Poetry is full of these lines. Othello is about to kill Desdemona :—

> Put out the light, and then put out the light.

Antony to Cleopatra :—

> I am dying, Egypt, dying.

Webster has

> Cover her face : mine eyes dazzle : she died young.

If we allow ourselves more than one line in which to feel this magic, this power to thrill, we find quotations tumbling into our minds, and in every mind is Keats's

> Charm'd magic casements, opening on the foam
> Of perilous seas, in faery lands forlorn.

To passages or even lines of the kind quoted we all respond because there is in us, as in their authors, some complex unity of thought and vision and emotion that responds to what they suggest. Every now and again someone from among the commonalty of us takes his pen and gives us in prose or poetry an addition to our literature. When this happens we realise that this someone, who may be an ordinary-looking and unimpressive person, has the power to perceive what we either do not see or see only in part; we realise that he has also the ability to make us aware of what he has seen or thought or felt. More than this—between his perception and his writing there has been an agitation, or kindling, a spiritual orgasm in him which resulted in the rising within him of a constructive, even a creative, force that has tempted or compelled him, through any labour or weariness, to give written expression to its cause.

He has seen the golden glories of eternity and the light of day in a drop of water, the red glare of lightning in an angry sky, love in a girl's eyes, the shadows of a bird's wing as it flutters in the sunshine, the droop of a head, the fall of blossom; he has heard the running feet of children, the cry of the trapped beast in a wood, the whispering of a stream in the night, the tiny noises that haunt a frosty stillness, the peal of a trumpet, the roar and crash of breakers, the voice that took away hope, the cry of the new-born child; his hands have felt while his nostrils breathed perfume, they have clenched when death and sin and filth came with their stench; he has been down into hell and up into the ecstasy of which not even he can speak in full; he has seen and heard and understood the tears of the world.

Of these things he has been compelled to write when one or more of them has come to him, giving to the task all of himself, perhaps in a short, fierce joy of writing, or perhaps in the slow, infinitely searching work of years.

In giving us his work, he gives us himself. No one else could give us this one thing. Others may pass through his experience; but it will be their experience, even though its cause is the same, and what they give us will be theirs. From each, his own.

This is the author, although our description of him has been as limited as it has been, in a sense, exaggerated. But what is drawn large is better to see and examine, even though its size means that not all of it can be seen in a small space. The picture we have drawn contains the certain truths, however modified they may be in individual applications, that an author is one who has perceived, has responded to what he has seen, and has thereby been compelled to write. This is true whether what he saw was Beatrice in Paradise or Sairey Gamp in a cabriolet.

It is true that his creative force may be drawn out of him in creative action suddenly and by one perception of the external reality, as was the experience of Keats when he wrote his sonnet *On First Looking into Chapman's " Homer "*, or slowly by the gradual fulfilment of his inspired urge, as was the case during the long period in which Gray wrote his *Elegy in a*

Country Churchyard, or it may be that he seeks for external reality which he may use as the material for the working of the power to construct or create. This last case we may take to be that of most authors during most of their active life. Certainly it must apply to novelists.

Whatever classifications or conditions may attach to the emergence of this force, in itself it means that when an author writes he gives us himself, and that what he has seen must come to us as he can give it to us. He can neither perceive reality as any other man could perceive it, nor could he, under the driving energy to which he is subject, consistently express himself as another man would do. Collins may be like Gray, but he is as different from him as he is like him. Shakespeare could not have written in the manner of Marlowe, perpetually suppressing his natural way of writing.

What is this but to say that style does enter into literary composition and that " Style is the man himself " ?

(ii) Its Result in Style

Perception—inspiration, if you wish—the disturbance of constructive force, and the writing done under its influence, are all acts of one process which is individual to every author. As J. Middleton Murry observes in an analysis of this fact, any passage by Shakespeare, if long enough for a critic to feel its influence, could never be mistaken for a passage by Webster.   Shakespeare's peculiarity of vision, his modes of thought, his turn of phrase, are as recognisable as his rhythmical periods, subtlety of harmony, and abundance of fresh metaphor.   Additionally the passage would be markedly without the characteristics peculiar to Webster.   As a brief example of unmistakable style, he expresses the confident opinion that only Marlowe could have written :—

> Sweet Helen, make me immortal with a kiss.
> Her lips suck forth my soul : see where it flies.

In other words, style is found only when something universal, something all can perceive—at least when it is revealed to them at second-hand, as by an author—is expressed through the particular medium of an individual.   Consequently it may be good or bad.   It will be good when a writer who is well endowed with perception, constructive power, and command of words and technique is writing at the best of his ability. Style requires the closest harmony between object, writer, and language.

Further reflections on this matter of style must now be left until it can be dealt with on its own, for much remains to be said, and our immediate concern is the author.   Here we may only add that style is not a quality which is in every author, nor to be found through all the writings of those who possess it. As we have seen, it derives from the rousing of a constructive power by an idea.   If the spiritual alchemy does not take place, there can be no style in the plain writing or verse written. Of course, it is far easier to write prose without style than poetry equally bereft of this lovely quality, but that poetry can be bare of it is possible. Perhaps it should be called merely verse, since it has the form, but not the spirit, as in much of Crabbe. To say this is only to say that its author is uninspired, not that he is incapable of inspiration, and it leaves him many other qualities in which his readers may delight.

We may take it, then, that an author can be said, in the abstract, to have literary style only if his writing shows that he has taken fire, that a kindling has produced, in mysterious ways we cannot pretend to follow in detail, the force and power to construct.

Beyond this point his writing depends on his ability to construct. This is a matter of knowing and being able to practise the mechanics of his craft. In the writing of poetry, and less often of prose, it is scarcely necessary to remark, the whole process of perception and creation may be so inspired that perfection may be reached without the conscious employment of an artistic means. The author is working in a state of intense excitement caused by his act of perception. One result of this exaltation is a heightening of his literary powers. Another is a great and temporary increase in his range of vision, accompanied by an unusually penetrating understanding of what he sees. It is as if he has found happiness developing through joy into ecstasy; as if his understanding has been suddenly illuminated, and goes forward like a beam of white light to catch shapes and significances it has never seen before and may never see so clearly again.

In the fierceness of such activity, rest is impossible. Its subject must write, and it may be that all this happens so instantly and completely that the height of his experience will come to him in words, without effort of his.

A reader can never be sure whether what he reads is the result of writing of this kind or of careful craftsmanship after the inspiration has lessened and let down the author from the heights. Nevertheless there are occasional lines and passages which, we may reasonably believe, have come to their author and not been sought by him.

> Better to reign in Hell than serve in Heaven

has a completeness that suggests it formed itself, as does many a fragment. In the following, for instance, the italicised words are in marked contrast with the deliberate elaboration which follows them :—

> The city cast
> Her people out upon her; and Antony,
> Enthron'd i' the market-place, did sit alone,
> *Whistling to the air*; which, but for vacancy,
> Had gone to gaze on Cleopatra too,
> And made a gap in nature.

In the next quotation one receives an impression that the words were chosen and arranged less easily and automatically. In the beginning they came more directly, the idea was already clothed in words, while almost at once deliberate writing was required to com-

plete the thought—a prick of inspiration, a jet of
thought in words, then a conscious choice of words
and careful arrangement of them while the author was
still influenced by his perception but no longer driven
by its force. Perhaps these lines were so written :—

> Age cannot wither her, nor custom stale
> Her infinite variety : other women cloy
> The appetites they feed; but she makes hungry
> Where most she satisfies.

In choice of examples we are speculating, but there
is no speculation about the point the illustrations are
meant to show—that writing may be a part of the whole
process of creation or construction that follows the
initial perception, and that it is also, and for most of
the time, the endeavour, by deliberate choice and
arrangement of words, to pass that perception, with all
its implications, to others.

Whether you agree with what has been stated here
or not—and you will be in good company whichever
way you make your decision—there is no doubt of
your agreement that the condition of inspiration or perception as described here is not ordinary. It is something that happens and passes, leaving an after-glow of
illumination and warmth sufficient to enable the author
to continue his work still restfully under its influence.
No longer is he in that exalted mood in which matter
and form, meaning and words, come to him together.
Now he must settle down to work on his ordinary level
of mental activity. We may be interested to see how
he works.

That is to say, we may profitably see enough of his work for us to be sure that he has work to do—the work of any craftsman who is also an artist.

(iii) The Craft of Writing

His immediate task is to find words and to arrange them so as to make them convey exactly what he wishes to give his readers. Practice in writing has equipped him to do much of this work without need for considerable revision but, however smoothly and surely his work is done, revision is necessary.

For instance, he must be sure that the words he uses—the smallest elements of his new materials—are those that will secure exactly the desired effect. He must be sure of the evocative value of his words. *Slipping down the slope* may not in itself be vastly different from *sliding down the slope*, but the writer must say precisely what he means. The sibilants may direct the attention to the feet and the ground when the writer wants the reader to be thinking of the poised stillness of the skier—an effect he would better secure by *gliding down the slope*. In *The Demi-gods* James Stephens could have written something like this at his first writing :—

> " It was evening, too early for stars or moon. In the remote west a red cloud lay humped on the horizon. Every moment it grew paler until it was no more than a suffusion of pink light. High above pearly clouds and snow piled up and fell and sailed smoothly away."

Supposing that Stephens had written something like

that, he would certainly revise it.   What he printed
was :—

> "The day had drawn to its close.   The stars had not
> yet come, nor the moon.   Far to the west a red cloud
> poised on the horizon like a great whale and, moment
> by moment, it paled and faded until it was no more
> than a pink flush.   On high, clouds of pearl and
> snow piled and fell and sailed away on easy voyages."

Notice how the picture has become more definite,
brushed in with more certain strokes ; how it has
been given more light and shade ; how its rhythm has
been changed ; notice how *easy* tells something of
speed which is absent from *smoothly*.

Although much laughter has been accorded the
theory of " the right word ", few literary artists have
shared in it.   They have preferred to make certain that
the colour, suggestibility, music, of words enter into
their service.   Perhaps it is significant that one of
the most assured among the amused was Samuel Butler,
one of the most carefully precise of writers.   Others
have preferred in prose or poetry to weave their
patterns of vowels and consonants so that the qualities
of words may deepen and even modify the meanings:—

> But such a tide as moving seems asleep,
>   Too full for sound or foam,

where we listen to the silent swell which is described :—

> The fair breeze blew, the white foam flew,
>   The furrow followed free ;
> We were the first that ever burst
>   Into that silent sea,

where the consonant pattern is as well matched to the meaning as are both consonants and vowels in

> No motion has she now, no force;
> She neither hears nor sees;
> Rolled round in earth's diurnal course
> With rocks, and stones, and trees.

The same care, the same knowledge of how these things are managed, is found if you listen to the subdued whispering that goes on in these two prose passages from Swift and Defoe :—

> "I lay down on the grass, which was very short and soft, where I slept sounder than ever I remember to have done in my life, and, as I reckoned, above nine hours, for when I awakened it was just daylight. I attempted to rise, but was not able to stir; for as I happened to lie on my back, I found my arms and legs were strongly fastened on each side to the ground, and my hair, which was long and thick, tied down in the same manner. I likewise felt several slender ligatures across my body, from my arm-pits to my thighs."

And here is Defoe, also persuasively whispering and wooing our attention :—

> "Much about the same time I walked out into the fields towards Bow; for I had a great mind to see how things were managed in the river and among the ships; and as I had some concern in shipping, I had a notion that it had been one of the best ways of securing one's self from the infection to have retired into a ship; and musing how to satisfy my curiosity on that point, I turned away over the fields from Bow to Bromley. . . ."

Here authors may be seen in their workshop, fashioning prose which will be a perfect medium for their purposes. Look at the pattern of f's and v's in

> From too much love of living,
> From hope and fear set free,
> We thank with brief thanksgiving
> Whatever gods may be

right to the last lines, where another consonant is used to mute the sibilance as a whole :—

> That even the weariest river
> Winds somewhere safe to sea.

And here is what may be the most perfect lyric in our tongue for unity of thought and word :—

> Now sleeps the crimson petal, now the white;
> Nor waves the cypress in the palace walk;
> Nor winks the gold fin in the porphyry font :
> The firefly wakens : waken thou with me.
>
> Now droops the milk-white peacock like a ghost,
> And like a ghost she glimmers on to me.
>
> Now lies the earth all Danaë to the stars,
> And all thy heart lies open unto me.
>
> Now slides the silent meteor on, and leaves
> A shining furrow, as thy thoughts in me.
>
> Now folds the lily all her sweetness up,
> And slips into the bosom of the lake;
> So fold thyself, my dearest, thou, and slip
> Into my bosom, and be lost in me.

It is a wedding of sound to sense, the vowels and consonants being varied in each line to make the verses in every way conformable to their meaning.

The author is equally concerned with the less definable qualities of words. Euphony cannot command his attention exclusively, for he must also consider those other effects of words which prevent any of them being a true synonym of any other. For example, quite apart from the idea of onomatopœia or imitative words whose sound makes their meaning more vivid, a writer can use the suggestibility of words. That is to say, he makes use of the fact that words have a certain significance. The word *white* is always accompanied in our minds, whether we wish it or not, by the idea of smoothness; *pavement* or *paving* has the same effect. Notice the difference between " her *placid* smile " and the same smile described by any other apparently synonymous adjective.

Why words have this virtue of significance is still a subject of inquiry, a fascinating study we can do no more than mention. Our interest in it at present is confined to the fact that it is, with euphony, one of the powers of words an author must keep in mind.

Colour also is at his service. Its meaning may be illustrated by reference to the old lady who used to refer with delight to that blessed word *Mesopotamia*. No doubt the sound of the word was associated in her mind with Scriptural events, so that hearing it gave her a feeling of warmth and happiness and peace.

We all have our Mesopotamias, some of them pleasant and some unpleasant, without reference to their meaning. I am not fond of the word *pallid*, which calls into imagination some reaction to a deed of blood and disgusting cruelty which I can never place. Perhaps if I sat down to let the word work on me, the origin of this curious association might return. I think it is discoverable in some episode of Scottish history, in which the word occurred, which I read when I was a child. This is a personal idiosyncrasy, a false colour attached to a word.

The mental activity which makes it possible for each of us to have similar likes and dislikes is common to us all, with the result that we all have certain reactions to a large number of words. As our vocabulary increases, the meanings of words link up with the meanings of other words. Often we are unaware of the process, but it is none the less effective because of that. Moreover, words take associations from the company in which they are found, and of the impressions we receive in this way we are also usually unaware. Perhaps this explains why *jocund* has a different colour from *joyful*.

Since words convey an impression as well as a meaning, a writer must choose his words so that the impression they convey will be suitable to the meaning he intends the reader to understand. Of course, he may choose his words so as to exclude impression as far as he can. Writers of scientific works or any author who wishes attention to be concentrated on meaning as precisely as possible, with the least chance of misunderstanding, will wisely prefer colourless words, and his manner of writing will be good because it is colourless. He will use many words deriving directly from Greek or Latin, *febrile* instead of *hot*, or *cadaveric* instead of *corpse-like*.

Keeping clearly before him his purpose in writing, an author chooses his manner of writing so that it will be likeliest to fulfil his purpose among the readers for whom he is writing. This matter of choosing words, then, is by no means easy, since it must be governed according to purpose in relation to possible readers.

When deciding the problems about words which follow an attempt to meet the requirements of the work in hand, a writer has also to take into account the rhythm of his prose or the metre of his poetry. Perhaps the words he wishes to use may not fit the rhythmic pattern of his sentence, so that what he has written must be revised. The author may wish to have a smooth alternation of change and recurrence in his sentences or an uneven pattern to convey a particular impression. For instance, from a current novel, notice how you feel the awkwardness, the imitative precariousness of walking about on a day such as the one described :—

> "Mid-town traffic was wretchedly jammed; the cab made barely a block in five minutes. A great quantity of snow from the last storm still lay in the streets like dirty maple sugar; ice from a preceding storm cropped out in dark, slaty veins."

These two sentences bundle you about. Their rhythmic pattern is uncomfortable; it is meant to be so. Equally suitable is the choice of words. If you pay attention to the words you will see why they have been chosen in preference to " synonyms "—partly because they convey an impression of ugliness or discomfort, and partly because they help to form the rhythm scheme planned by their writer.

As a tiny but revealing example of what we have been saying, see the damage caused if you strike out a word and insert *peace* in

> And *calm* of mind all passion spent.

The metre appears to be unaltered, but the impression accompanying *calm* is lost if we substitute for it the quickly slipping *peace*. The grandeur and simplicity of the idea have gone; we are left with a mere fact. Notice, too, how the triple occurrence of the letter P (a letter about which writers have said many harsh things) contributes to the damage.

The study of these matters and of others we cannot find space to mention is among the pleasures of the appreciative reader. Not only what his authors say, but how they say it, is intended for his enjoyment and profit. That is why, at the outset, we have paused to see that he who writes is a busy man who has a craft to learn.

We have not yet mentioned many other technicalities he must know, in which also we can follow him with pleasurable interest. Later in this book we shall be able to pay attention to forms of verse, paragraph structure, plot, characterisation, and other mechanics of writing.

(iv) The Reader's View

In doing this we shall not make the mistake of supposing that writing is wholly mechanical—that if you learn enough about its technique you can write. Writing is an art, and the artistic nature of literary work has been heavily emphasised in previous pages. If it has seemed to you that it has been exaggerated, you will no doubt now agree that, in a book dealing largely with the scientific side of writing, it is wise to stress the art of letters strongly at the opening.

Most of the remainder of the book will correct the mistake people sometimes make, about writing in particular and art in general, of supposing that art and science are completely dissociated. Not so. Every art must have a scientific execution, a set of clearly defined principles to govern the construction of what is being formed. Among the pleasures of reading is an observance of how these principles have been practised and which among them an author has considered the most useful to his purposes.

You will keep in mind that in examining what we read in this way we are not foolishly trying to discover why the rose is perfumed, nor attaching the least importance to the cause of its fragrance. To do that, except for a wholly scientific purpose, would be madness.

The difference between looking into the scientific side of writing and the physical reasons for the scent of a garden lies in the fact that writing is something done by someone to cause an effect in his readers, to do something to their minds or hearts, while the perfume of the rose affects primarily only their senses. It is meant to be breathed in and enjoyed, which is all we can do with it. But the breathing in of literature is an inspiration of another kind, and the full enjoyment of it cannot be had unless we consider its science as well as its art. Knowing why a flower is fragrant does not make it more fragrant; knowing why a page of writing is literature increases our pleasure and profit because—and this distinction is most important—we can really know this only after it has inspired us.

Our aim, then, is to make ourselves as receptive to good literature as possible. For the accomplishment of this purpose we must have some familiarity with its technique. Only when to our growing taste for reading we have added a knowledge of writing can we draw out of books all they contain. Only when we are ready for it can we breathe the fragrance or see the beauty or feel the kindling of written art.

It is time to break off these reflections, to leave the author and turn to a subject we have already opened—this matter of literary style. We have dealt with it only sufficiently for our purpose of getting a picture of an author. Now we must treat it in the abstract.

If you feel you have heard enough about it for the time being, freely omit the next chapter and dip into the book farther on. This kind of book can be read in almost any order of chapters, partly so that it will not become tedious and partly because, as has been said, there is a surprising freedom in reading to be found even in books about books.

To remind you of style, and also as examples of how skilfully science unites with art in literature, we close with these quotations with patterns of vowels and rhythm that neither art nor science alone could have executed :—

> " Nevertheless the dimness shall not be such as was in her vexation, when at the first he lightly afflicted the land of Zebulun and the land of Naphtali and afterward did more grievously afflict her by the way of the sea, beyond Jordan, in Galilee of the nations."

You may find interest, now or when you have read farther, in trying to decide how far inspiration or skilled execution governs that passage from the Authorised Version.

Now we turn to William Butler Yeats :—

And I shall have some peace there, for peace comes dropp-
    ing slow,
Dropping from the veils of the morning to where the
    cricket sings;
There midnight's all a-glimmer, and noon a purple glow,
And evening full of the linnet's wings.

The immediacy of the inspiration is well to the front there—how much of the art was due to its urgency? Contrast it in this respect with a more meditative passage, rising from a different emotion and one expressed in recollection.

When you are old and grey and full of sleep,
And nodding by the fire, take down this book,
And slowly read, and dream of the soft look
Your eyes had once, and of their shadows deep.

Is there style in these quotations ?   Or something that
passes for style ?   Is it only through " knowing how "
that they were written, and that you think they have
style ?

Chapter Four

Literary Style

LEST, going forward rashly in our eagerness, we should run astray, we begin this chapter with a warning from W. H. Hudson, who writes of

". . . the important general principle that though the study of literary technique is in the hands of scholastic critics too often divorced from the study of literature in its personal and historical aspects, it need not be and should not be so divorced. If the art of literature may be taken by itself as a subject matter for analysis and discussion, it can also be connected directly with the substance of human meaning of literature, and indeed treated as supplementary to these. In this way, while, as we have said, everything connected with workmanship —method, treatment, form, style—may be considered for the interest they possess for their own sakes, it is not for their own sakes only that we shall be contented to consider them."

This wholesome advice we have tried to follow so far, repeating, at the risk of tediousness, what Hudson goes on to write :—

" The art of the artist is to hide the art, and the business of the critic is to find it again. But we must be on our guard lest in our search for the art the true results of the art may be lost for us. Analysis must not be allowed to outrun its proper purpose and to become an end in itself; if we are right in considering how a great piece of literature has come to be what it is, it is still with the work as it is that we have mainly to do."

With this principle unmistakably before our eyes, we may turn to this question of literary style—and later to a consideration of literary methods—without misgiving. Our interest in it, following on what was stated about its existence, is in the thing itself and not in what it shows us of an author.

(i) Its Nature

(a) *Platonist View*

The nature of literary style was a problem in the time of Plato, and his opinions about it are wholly different from those proposed by Aristotle. In the Platonist view style is a specific quality which is definitely present or absent. It is not something added to writing nor a mere literary mould into which writing may be cast. It is a quality inherent in what is written, if it is present at all.

Regarding literary style as abstractly as possible, the Platonist argues from the thought which precedes verbal expression. A thought is a spiritual, wholly immaterial reality born of the mind and wholly distinct from the mind. Although distinct from the mind in which it was engendered, it is conditioned by having been born of that mind and not of any other mind.

Thus if you and I think of " horse ", we both think of the same thing, but your thought will be different from mine. This is because of the differences in our mental faculties—my imagination is more colourful than yours, perhaps, and your perception is keener than mine.

If, by a creative act, we each could utter the word " horse ", and thus bring into existence the horse we have mentally conceived, those differences would be apparent.

This, however, is not the point. In order to see the Platonist view about style, we must first be familiar with the idea that a thought is a child of the mind, and a word is the clothing of that child with a garment of flesh. For the Greek philosopher Logos meant both the idea in itself and its external reality in the form of a word. And all this opinion about style is based on what the Greeks meant by Logos. It is in exactly this sense, of course, that the Johannine Gospel refers to Christ—" In the beginning was the Word and the Word was with God and the Word was God ". And later, " the Word was made flesh ".

Word meant idea; it also meant that idea when externally manifested.

You will readily understand how the quick Greek intellect appreciated this thought and saw its implication that every idea can be adequately expressed by only one word. Since every word has a connotation slightly different from even its closest " synonym ", it followed that to use any word but that exactly corresponding to your thought was wrong. It could result only in your putting into someone else's mind an idea different from the idea in your own. The two ideas might be first cousins or even twin sisters, but the fact remained that you had handed over the wrong child.

Since this theory is being unfolded briefly and without much of the cogency it contains, you may feel that so far it is remote and too abstract. Yet a moment's thought will assure you that we are not wasting time in defining what we mean by a word, for, unless we are sure about that, we cannot hope to learn when a group of words can be recognised as good writing.

> Tell me where is Fancy bred,
> In the heart or in the head ?
> How begot, how nourishèd ?
> Reply, reply.

Whatever answer you may wish to make, it is first necessary to know how what is in the heart or head can be expressed, which is the same as saying we must understand all that we mean by words.

For the Platonist there is only one word or phrase which will adequately express one idea. Consequently literary style is that form of expression which perfectly represents the idea in the writer's mind. If the author has a large vocabulary at his command and skill in arranging his words, he will be able to give any idea exact expression—at least in theory. In practice, the better equipped he is the more thoroughly he develops a good literary style, since he has at service all he needs to give perfect expression to his ideas.

It follows from these premises that style is inevitable. Remembering the three factors—that a thought is conditioned by the mind of which it is born, that only one word or phrase can adequately express an idea, and that thus one author has one phrase to express *his* idea—you will see why style is inevitable and inevitably individual. Notice how closely this conclusion, reached from abstract reasoning, fits what we have previously seen to be a fact of experience—that, under the impulse of strong inspiration, an author finds idea and words coming to him together. There is no time lag between inspiration and expression, conception and birth, nor any conscious work by the author. Then we have lines like

> The rest is silence;

> O laith, laith were our gude Scots lords
>   To wet their cork-heel'd shoon;
> But lang or a' the play was play'd
>   They wat their hats aboon;

or (I suggest) the amazingly revealing line in which the physician, having watched the night-walking of Lady Macbeth, realising the crime and the criminal's identity, with a mingling of dread of the knowledge that has come to him, and native caution, and understanding of human nature, makes the comment,

> *Well, well, well.*

O rarely expressive comment!

Now, a logical conclusion to this line of thought is that style is either perfect or it does not exist in any given passage. We have seen that the " right " word

must be found ; we know the struggles of Flaubert
and others (possibly exaggerated slightly in recollection) to find it. We know the approval which many
critics who were also creative writers have given to the
Platonist view which urges the necessity for finding it
and the rights of the idea that it should be found. For
instance, we recall Pater's recommendation of
" the finer accommodation of speech to that vision
within ".

We must not be surprised if the Platonist, after
persuading us to this view, now pushes forward the
advantage he has secured by adding that a word, phrase,
sentence, either perfectly expresses the idea, thus
being style, or it does not, thus being the absence of
style. Imperfection in word means alteration of idea.
Consequently the link between idea and reader is false,
and the transfer of idea to reader results only in the
reader's receiving what the writer does not intend him
to receive. Consequently it would be wrong to talk
about a good although imperfect style. Style is either
perfect or a failure.

This is logical, and we can have no quarrel with it
as abstract thought. We must be excused, however,
from carrying this final dictum forward with us into the
practice of reading or writing. Many perfect, true,
and sound principles of theory must be conditioned in
practice in the same way that an idea is conditioned by
the mind in which it occurs. Even the theologian's
clear line between mortal and venial sin must, when
we judge of individual applications, depend on many

circumstances and personal dispositions that make *a priori* applications futile.

As practical readers, we must admit that there are degrees of success between perfection and failure, that a writer's work may be close to perfect expression of his meaning—so close that we may divine his meaning from a not wholly perfect choice or arrangement of words.   That this is so experience shows us, and we must draw our own conclusion that a good style is possible.   And surely we may talk of a bad style, a faulty style, where the rigid Platonist would insist on finding absence of style ?   If Jonson had written

Queen and huntress, *pure* and fair

instead of *chaste*, we would not have received the same meaning or, more seriously, the suggestion of virginal innocence associated with *chaste*, but the meaning would have been sufficiently present for us to know what he meant.   His style would have been at fault, but style there would have been.   So we refuse to draw our principles to a practical application that would be pedantic and unreal.

Now that we have followed a line of thought which has established the principle that literary style consists objectively of the use of language wholly fitted to express an author's ideas, we must complete it by adding what was said in the previous chapter about the inspiration which prompts an author to write.   Without that our idea of style would be disastrously incomplete.

(b) *Idiosyncracy of Style*

Without it we might be misled into thinking that style is the same thing as manner of writing. If we were to regard style as nothing more than the fitting of words to meaning, it would be possible to say that anyone who writes like Defoe is the equal of Defoe because he has that author's style. If style is the matching of words and meaning, anyone can become an author by playing " the sedulous ape "—a parodist becoming a master. The mere suggestion is too obviously ridiculous, and is based on the mistaken idea that diction is more than a part of style.

It is also based on the mistaken idea that Milton took thought and decided to write in what is recognisable as the Miltonic manner, and that Spenser deliberately chose to express himself otherwise, so that he elected to use a Spenserian manner.

In fact no poet or prose-writer, however much he may have modelled the practice of writing on the examples of masters, was ever able to write original and constructive work in anything but his own manner of diction. The result may have been as artificial as the Euphuistic or as individually natural as the styles of Bunyan or Patmore. Under all similarities and differences, all experiments or modelling, the inspiration that made the author compelled him to write as only he could write. *Style is the man himself*. It is his individual inspiration conditioned by the fact that it is his; it is the way in which that inspiration drove that particular man to write; it is the means he took, whether wholly natural or partly modelled, to express himself. And, as we have seen, his style is good in the degree in which it succeeds in transferring what is in his mind to other minds.

Since style is the whole operation from first to last, revealing itself to us through its result in prose or poetry, it follows that no one can achieve literary style merely by imitating diction or manner of writing. It is possible for a writer to have so clear an insight into another writer's mind, so ready a sympathy with his emotions, such a perfectly imitative knowledge of his diction, that he can write of a thing exactly as his original would have done. But this cannot be maintained indefinitely. Even if it could be, it would lead to no success, for, by the nature of his achievement—the putting on of another's personality—he is making it impossible for himself to have any style at all. Only when two men are born in all things identical and remain so throughout their years will it be possible for their writings to have literary style and still be a source of confusion to enlightened readers.

There will never be another Chaucer, Pope, Wordsworth, or Dickens. Authors are unique. It follows that the style of each is unique.

(ii) Definition

It is now time for us to assemble the ideas we have been considering, to see how they may be briefly expressed in a definition of literary style.

We began with Buffon's dictum that *Style is the man himself*. He also said, *It is a way of seeing*, and this is fully in keeping with the Platonist line of thought we have followed.

These definitions concern the earlier stages of literary style rather than execution. Flaubert endorsed Buffon's view by *It is a way of thinking* or *of feeling*. Tchekov told Gorky that real writing was a *seeing or touching of what is described*. That is, these writers are of one mind.

If we may allow ourselves a parenthesis here, it has seemed to me that Gerard Manley Hopkins throws an interesting light on the problem when we look at it through these definitions. The poem quoted below is remarkable for the way in which Hopkins tries to reach the objects of his perception with the least possible sensuousness. He sees their beauty as fully yet as abstractly as possible, and comes to the only conclusion such an experience could have for him.

Fresh-firecoal chestnut-falls; finches' wings;
   Landscape plotted and pieced—fold, fallow and plough;
And áll trádes, their gear and tackle and trim.

All things counter, original, spare, strange;
   Whatever is fickle, freckled (who knows how ?)
     With swift, slow; sweet, sour; adazzle, dim;
He fathers-forth whose beauty is past change;
       Praise Him.

Here we have an attempt to make the mind see, feel, touch objects of sense as directly as it can by the internal senses. External sensations are almost wholly excluded, except for one of unforgettable brilliance and one of least physical appeal.   For the rest, once these two are given as a key to the meaning of what follows, it is the internal senses, the intellect and a disciplined imagination, that go out to the objects and touch them. Hence the remarkable originality of the style, in keeping with the originality of the idea.

The spiritual part of man is kindled by an idea. So far our definitions take us.   What then ?

Stendhal replies, *Style consists in adding to a thought all the circumstances calculated to produce the whole effect that the thought ought to produce*.   Here he is looking at the outward side of literary style, at the purposeful putting forth of what has been perceived or touched by the internal senses.   I take it, in view of questions that have been raised about the meaning of *ought*, that he means by style the adding to a thought of all that is necessary—words accurately representative of it and their arrangement in forms suitable to such representation—to produce in a reader the full effect intended by the writer.

The definition joins the act of inspiration to the outward act of writing in a way which preserves their unity.   It avoids any occasion for the comment passed on Pope's dictum that style is the *dress of thought*— " he failed entirely to recognise its essentially organic character, for he evidently conceived it as something apart from the man, which he could put on or take off at will ".   The fact that Pope was a thoughtful rather than an emotional poet is probably the reason why

he was less aware of the internal source of style than
he would otherwise have been. An inclination to the
same defect, and perhaps it is attributable to the same
reason, is found in Cardinal Newman's definition of
style as *thinking out into language*.

Our conclusion, at least in so far as we can form
one on this page, is that *Style is the man himself* as
expressed through his work in adding to his thoughts
and feelings and imaginings all he needs to add in order
to convey them to his readers.

The fact that his work, in making this addition,
requires a mastery of an elaborate technique does not
separate this work from his prior inner experience.
Indeed, so far is recognition of the need for technique
from leading us into danger of mistaking diction for
style, the part for the whole, that a realisation of what
inspiration is—the seeing, touching by the mind—
teaches us how complicated and sensitive that technique may be. The statement of this fact was perhaps
the most important part of De Quincey's examination
into the problem of style :—

> "But the more closely any exercise of mind is con-
> nected with what is internal and individual in the
> sensibilities . . . precisely in that degree, and the more
> subtly, does the style or the embodying of the thoughts
> cease to be a mere separable ornament."

(iii) Appreciation of Style

In the study of literary style, then, is a pleasure
every reader should be at pains to secure for himself.

It is a study of the author; it is an intimate sharing in his experience as an author; it is a study of his means of writing. To anyone who gains the ability to detect style there is pleasure in noting how an author's style may change, such as the dying of inspiration in Wordsworth, while he maintained to the end all the devices of expression that had been his when he was most inspired; and the development of Shakespeare from the early plays, delighting in colour of words and cleverness of expression, to the later plays, some with noblest inspiration united with the highest technical skill, and others strained with thought that bursts out in vast sweeping speeches, in prose and poetry, in words no longer handled joyously, but impatiently, because what was coming into mind was almost beyond their capacity to contain. Or it will be to his pleasure and his gain to study the progress of a prose stylist like R. L. Stevenson, to notice not only mastery of word and phrase, not only experiments in expression, but also means of presentation such as we shall study in dealing with fictional prose forms. In doing so he will see the labour behind the apparent ease, the work and incessant practice to secure what Stevenson referred to as the artist's

> " taking up two or more elements or two or more views of the subject in hand so that he . . . combines, implicates and contrasts them; and while, in one sense, he was merely seeking the occasion for the necessary knot, he will be found, in the other, to have enriched the work of two sentences in the space of one ".

Reading *Weir of Hermiston* with that sentence in mind is to increase one's pleasure in the book. Indeed, Stevenson's preoccupation with the mechanics of writing inclined him strongly to regard style as more synthetic than it is. He was more Aristotelian than Platonist—a fact unimportant to one so quickly kindled by a scene, a name, a good story; for it did not prevent his excellence of style. Perhaps the naturalness of intensely quickened interest led him to take it for granted and concentrate his attention on writing, with which he took infinite pains, and on method, of which he wrote that it must attain " the highest degree of elegant implication unobtrusively; and if not unobtrusively, then with the greatest gain to sense and vigour ". Here, too, we have an insight into Stevenson's method which greatly heightens our appreciation of his work.

Putting aside questions of literary execution for the time being, we end our chapter on style with some understanding that style is the quality by which an author perceives something, is interested by it, and moved to write of it; it is, as part of the same unbroken act, a quality which passes from him into his writing, influencing him in the choice of presentment and of language.

If it is present—and there are no real tests by which it may be detected except only the touchstone of intelligent literary taste—it makes literature; if it is absent, there is only writing.

Closing the chapter, getting away from the bare

bones of argument, and desiring to leave them suitably clothed in decent flesh, even as our authors have covered their ideas in suitably expressive language, I think we cannot do better than sum up the matter in the words of Sir Arthur Quiller-Couch :—

"This then is Style. As technically manifested in Literature it is the power to touch with ease, grace, precision, any note in the gamut of human thought or emotion."

Chapter Five

Prose and Verse

(i) Is There a Difference?

A GREAT deal of ingenuity and no small amount of speculation have been employed in evolving theories as to how man first, as a deliberate literary effort, wrote either prose or verse.

I say deliberately because the first efforts to write prose must have been as calculated and conscious as the first making of verse. The reason for this is that prose is no more our natural mode of expression, when we are not with purpose trying to utter our thoughts, than verse is when we are not in a mood of high emotion. Prose is an ordering of the materials of speech so as to secure certain effects in a reader, and the same loose definition is suitable to verse. The following quotation from Edmund Burke will make this point clear.

"I hear on all hands that a cabal, calling itself philosophic, receives the glory of many of the late proceedings; and that their opinions and systems are the true actuating spirit of the whole of them. I have heard of no party in England, literary or political, at any time, known by such a description. It is not with you composed of those men, is it? Whom the vulgar, in their blunt, homely style, call Atheists and Infidels?

If it be, I admit that we too have bad writers of that description, who made some noise in their day. At present they repose in lasting oblivion. Who, born within the last forty years, has read one word of Collins, and Yoland, and Tindal, and Chubb, and Morgan, and that whole race who called themselves Freethinkers? Who now reads Bolingbroke? Who ever read him through? Ask the booksellers of London what is become of all these lights of the world. In as few years their few successors will go to the family vaults of ' all the Capulets '."

A hasty opinion might call this talking, which it is not, or prose, which it is not. A more perceptive reader will realise that something is missing from it—something that would warm it into life and tone and persuasiveness. The one thing missing is a voice.

For this is a passage of rhetoric—of words intended for a hearer, and not for a reader. These words are so ordered as to affect a listener; prose must be ordered so as to affect a reader.

(a) *Rhetoric and Rhythm*

Of course, rhetoric may be read, and excellent reading it provides. Even when Burke was deliberately writing what was to be read and not heard, he often used rhetoric as his medium, addressing himself not to readers but an imaginary audience, as in the extract given from his *Reflections on the French Revolution*. When we read pages of this kind of writing, we feel that we are ourselves delivering a speech; we want to walk about declaiming it; or at least we grow conscious that, if we are merely receiving the work of another man, we would be happy to hear it from him and have it expressed to us not only in words but by gestures, intonations, changes of facial expression, and the compelling influence of an orator's eyes.

We are aware of the absence of the man when we read the next quotation, and we recognise it more easily as rhetoric and not prose.

"Neither party expected for the war a magnitude or the duration which it has already attained. Neither anticipated that the cause of the conflict might cease when, or even before, the conflict itself should cease. Each looked for an easier triumph, or a result less fundamental and astounding. Both read the same Bible and pray to the same God, and each invokes His aid against the other. It may seem strange that any men should dare to ask a just God's assistance in wringing their bread from the sweat of the other men's faces, but let us judge not, that we be not judged. The prayer of both could not be answered. That of neither has been answered fully. The Almighty has His own purposes. 'Woe unto the world because of offences, for it must needs be that offences come, but woe to that man by whom the offence cometh!' If we shall suppose that American slavery is one of these offences which, in the providence of God, must needs come, but which having continued through His appointed time, He now wills to remove, and that He gives to both North and South this terrible war as the woe due to those by whom the offence came, shall we discern there any departure from those divine attributes which the believers in a living God always ascribe to Him? Fondly do we hope, fervently do we pray, that this mighty scourge of war may speedily pass away. Yet if God wills that it continue until all the wealth piled up by the bondman's two hundred and fifty years of unrequited toil shall be sunk, and until every drop of blood

drawn with the lash shall be paid by another drawn
with the sword, as was said three thousand years ago,
so still it must be said, that the judgments of the Lord
are true and righteous altogether."

This makes excellent reading matter, yet throughout
the passage we are aware that something is missing,
that these are words to be spoken and heard rather than
written and read. We recognise this writing as
rhetoric, and not prose. The pauses are odd for prose,
the rhythm strange, the very construction of phrases
and sentences uneasy. The printed word of Lincoln's address has the qualities of rhetoric, but not of
this prose :—

"We came to Ipswich very late, having had to fight
every inch of ground since we were ten miles out of
London; and found a cluster of people in the market
place, who had risen from their beds in the night,
fearful of falling chimneys. Some of these, con-
gregating about the inn-yard while we changed horses,
told us of great sheets of lead having been ripped off a
high church-tower, and flung into a bye-street, which
they then blocked up. Others had to tell of country
people, coming in from neighbouring villages, who had
seen great trees lying torn out of the earth, and whole
ricks scattered about the roads and fields. Still there
was no abatement in the storm, but it blew harder.

"As we struggled on, nearer and nearer to the sea,
from which this mighty wind was blowing dead inshore,
its force became more and more terrific. Long before
we saw the sea, its spray was on our lips, and showered
salt rain upon us. The water was out over miles and
miles of the flat country adjacent to Yarmouth; and
every sheet and puddle lashed its banks, and had its
stress of little breakers setting heavily towards us.

When we came within sight of the sea, the waves on the horizon, caught at intervals above the rolling abyss, were like glimpses of another shore with towers and buildings. When at last we got into the town, the people came out to their doors, all aslant and with streaming hair, making a wonder of the mail that had come through such a night."

(b) *Prose Rhythms*

That passage is not perfect prose; it is disfigured by more than one of Dickens's worst mannerisms. Nevertheless it is unmistakably prose. It is the ordering of words in loose rhythm and without metre for the expression of thought to a reader. Nowhere in it is there a pause because a speaker must take breath, nor a pause because the working of the muscles of speech demands a pause or a slowness of utterance for proper enunciation. Writing of this kind is freed from all the conditions that speech requires, and in that it is different from rhetoric or the prose of plays.

We have discovered the nature of prose without reference to the problem as to whether verse or prose was the first form in which one man tried to convey the fullness of his thought or emotion to others. The case for either cannot be proved by examples from early literature, for this contains what we would expect to find in it—a great amount of poetry. I say we would expect to find this to be so because words in a metrical pattern are easier to remember than those arranged in a free non-metrical rhythm.

She was three years of age

is not memorable, does not haunt the mind, as

> Three years she grew in sun and shower.

Consequently we would expect that metrical composition would be best known and would survive where prose composition would be forgotten, until the time when traditional literature was perpetuated in writing.

For this reason, it seems to me that speculation about this problem is of no help to us when we wish to find the main difference between prose and verse. Probably it will be more profitable to continue a reading of prose until further differences become apparent.

If we must hazard a guess at what was happening in days we cannot explore, it seems reasonable to suppose that the first attempts to do more than talk in ordinary conversation took a rhetorical form. Historically rhetoric as an art is a late arrival. Its principles do not seem to have been enunciated and taught before the fifth century B.C. Yet an *a priori* consideration of the development of conversation to formal expression suggests that rhetoric must have been the first step. Verse may well have been the next, with prose as a later derivative from conversation. A brief consideration of this point will be useful when we come to consider verse, and can be postponed until then.

(ii) English Prose

Continuing to limit our attention to prose in English, let us take an extract from one of our first writers,

Roger Ascham (1515–68), who chose to write his treatise on archery in the vulgar tongue rather than the Latin his predecessors had usually preferred.

"Even likewise can I say of fair shooting, it hath not this discommodity with it nor that discommodity, and at last a man may so shift all the discommodities from shooting that there shall be left nothing behind but fair shooting. And to do this the better you must remember how that I told you when I described generally the whole nature of shooting, that fair shooting came of these things, of standing, rocking, drawing, holding and loosing : the which I will go over as shortly as I can, describing the discommodities that men commonly use in all parts of their bodies, that you, if you fault in any such, may know it, and go about to amend it. Faults in archers do exceed the number of archers, which come with use of shooting without teaching."

This prose is uncertain on its legs. It has force and was a serviceable medium, but it is far from sure of itself. Its very structure is unformed and awkward.

The impetus that Tyndale's translation of the Bible —not the first into the vernacular but the first which can be allowed literary importance—had given to interest in English prose-writing continued throughout the sixteenth century to encourage the use of English as a worthy medium between author and reader. After its brilliant start with Malory (*Morte d'Arthur*) in the fifteenth century and Lord Berners's translations a quarter of a century later, English prose has no pioneer of note except Sir Thomas More, whose *Life of Pico of Mirandola* is sometimes regarded as the first classical work of this kind. But More's influence was negligible, and the prose of Malory and Berners is of the simplest kind of narrative. Within its limits of purpose, their prose reaches a high standard of excellence. Outside those limits, as a generally serviceable means of expression, it was nothing more than our extract from Ascham has shown.

By the end of the fifteenth century many valuable experiments had been made. Lyly had loaded it with euphuistic mannerisms; Sir Philip Sidney had swept these aside, giving strength and melody to his prose. Hooker followed, with longer cadences of rhythm that gave his pages sober dignity. In Hooker prose reached the height of its merit for judicious expression. Later in Bacon it reached the highest point, in Elizabethan literature, for polish of manner. Forty years after Ascham's book on Archery, William Webbe wrote :—

"This place have I purposely reserved for one, who if not only, yet in my judgment principally deserveth the title of the rightest English Poet that ever I read; that is, the author of the *Shepherd's Kalendar* . . . sorry I am that I cannot find none other with whom I might couple him in this catalogue in this rare gift of Poetry : although one there is, though now long since, seriously occupied in graver studies (Master Gabriell Harvey) yet, as he was once his most special friend and fellow poet, so he hath taken such pains, not only in his Latin Poetry (for which he enjoyed great commendations of the best both in judgment and dignity in this Realm) but also to reform our English verse, and to beautify the same with brave devices, of which I think the chief lie in hateful obscurity : therefore will I adventure to set them together as two of the rarest wits and learnedst masters of Poetry in England."

This prose is not yet formed in structure wholly free from Latin models, but it is a freely flowing and melodious writing, sharply contrasting with Ascham's style. You sense that inspiration and execution are now more closely knit together and that this flexible English is a fitter tool for the artist's use.

Setting aside consideration of the several formative influences which were working to this end—for we are not primarily studying the history of English prose— we may notice a point that appears from even the short extracts we have read.

(iii) The Uses of Prose

This is that prose was used almost exclusively to express what men thought. We have volumes on sport, education, theology, biography, history, and a considerable body of literary criticism in prose, and we cannot help noticing that when men wanted to write what they imagined or felt they used verse. That authors should have considered prose an unfit means of " putting forth " anything but thoughts is remarkably significant. For their emotions or fun or romance they turned to verse, in plays or poems, and Ascham was not alone in condemning any attempt to use prose for " romance ". George Puttenham examined the uses of verse, and wrote, in 1589 :—

" And right so our vulgar rhyming Poesy, being by good wits brought to that perfection, we see is worthily to be preferred before any other manner of utterance in prose, for such use and to such purpose as it is ordained and shall hereafter be set down more particularly."

This opinion is important, for it deals with one of the essential differences between prose and verse. When we are emotionally stirred, or when our imaginations are excited, our natural inclination is to move about.   Unless we are utterly overwhelmed by emotion, we seek to express ourselves in some way after the manner of a small boy jumping about because he has been promised a holiday from school, and this tendency leads us to music, dancing, singing.

(iv) Verse Metre

Singing means verse, if not poetry.   It means the ordering of words into a metrical pattern, and not the loosely rhythmical pattern of prose.   David expressed his joy before the Ark of the covenant by singing, dancing, and playing a musical instrument.   He was not so much setting an example as following a natural instinct.   The three main activities by which we order ourselves when we are raised above the normal level of feeling or imaginative perception are all metrical. Indeed, the first need in the immature or more excitable is for the metre first and meaning afterwards—a fact so clear that writers sometimes employ this process, giving us meaningless metre in order to arouse in us the feelings they wish.

> Twinkum, twankum, twirlum, twitch—
> My great grandam—She was a Witch,
> Mouse in Wainscot, Saint in niche—
> My great grandam—She was a Witch. . . .

Sometimes we come across fragments of verse to us so

obscure that we wonder how far their author was in the grip of an emotion or crisis of imagination, and how far he was himself able to grasp the meaning which he has, perhaps only partly, succeeded in putting into words.

> I saw the moon and the moon saw me—
> God help the parson that baptised me.

From wanderings into the dim, far lands of imagination, where Walter de la Mare alone may safely wander and return with intelligible utterances, to the undisguised vocalising of metre with sometimes a vowel pattern, we draw the truth that metrical form is required by communications primarily emotional. Grown-up people understand the singer's

> Tol de riddle, tol de riddle, li ding doh,

and they share

> Hey diddle dinketty, poppety, pet

with their children.

(v) Later English Prose

None of the things these sound-patterns represent can be put into prose, and so emerges a fundamental difference between it and verse. Prose is usually the best medium for thinking in; it is always the best if the thought is entirely factual or abstract. As the author's thought is invaded by the activity of his internal or external senses, as he is moved to feel or to see with the mind's eye, the pitch of his prose rises. The long cadences of free rhythm are broken;

the sober procession of vowels and consonants is interrupted and re-formed in a new plan; traces of metre creep into phrases.

In this passage we find Wordsworth in an exalted mood; in the course of our quotation his excited prose becomes truly more prosaic, and he moves away from the proximity to Nature to an entirely unexciting rhythm. Notice, by the way, how the words I have italicised support the truth we are stating—that verse is the easier and more natural medium for what we feel rather than for what we think.

" The object of the Poet's thoughts are everywhere; though the eyes and senses of man are, it is true, his favourite guides, yet *he will follow wheresoever he can find an atmosphere of sensation in which to move his wings*. Poetry is the first and last of all knowledge—it is as immortal *as the heart of man*. If the labours of Men of science should ever create any material revolution, direct or indirect, in our condition, and the impressions which we habitually receive, the Poet will sleep then no more than at present; he will be ready to follow the steps of the Man of science, not only in those general indirect effects, but he will be at his side, *carrying sensation* into the midst of the objects, of the science itself. The remotest discoveries of the Chemist, the Botanist, or Mineralogist, will be as proper objects of the Poet's art as any upon which it can be employed, if the time should ever come when these things shall be familiar to us, and the relations under which they are contemplated *manifestly and palpably material to us as enjoying and suffering beings*. If the time should ever come when what is now called science thus familiarised to men, shall be ready to put on, as it were, a form of flesh and blood, the Poet will lend his divine spirit to aid the transfiguration and will welcome the Being thus produced, as a dear and genuine inmate of the household of man. It is not, then, to be supposed that any one, who holds that sublime notion of poetry which I have attempted to convey, will break in upon the sanctity and truth of his pictures by transitory and accidental ornaments, or endeavour to excite admiration of himself by arts, the necessity of which must manifestly depend upon the assumed meanness of his subject."

To notice how Wordsworth's prose varies in that short passage is an illuminating study of the effect of emotion on the regularisation of rhythm almost into sustained metre and back again, as thought and awareness of the act of writing make the passage more intellectual than emotional or imaginative.

Now, the idea that romance or anything other than factual writing was unsuitable to prose continued for nearly a century after the period we call Elizabethan. In spite of this misunderstanding, the non-metrical form of writing continued to become more flexible and to be of service to a wider range of thought. Hyde, Hobbes, and Locke carried forward the development until, at the Restoration, a remarkable change occurred. There is little credit in noticing the difference between the prose of Englishmen before, say, 1670 and that which they wrote afterwards. The important thing is to see why the change occurred and what it was that was new in Dryden, Swift, Addison, and the rest.

First, what happened? An extract from Dryden will show us :—

"I take up Chaucer where I left him. He must have been a man of a most wonderful comprehensive nature, because, as it has been truly observed of him, he has taken into the compass of his *Canterbury Tales* the various manners and humours (as we now call them) of the whole English nation, in his age. Not a single character has escaped him. All his pilgrims are severally distinguished from each other; and not only in their inclinations, but in their very physiognomies and persons. Baptista Porta could not have described their natures better than by the marks which the poet gives them. The matter and manner of their tales and of their telling are so suited to their different educations, humours and callings, that each of them would be improper in any other mouth. Even the grave and serious characters are distinguished by their several sorts of gravity: their discourses are such as belong to their age, their calling and their breeding; such as are becoming of them and of them only; some of his persons are vicious and some virtuous: some are unlearned or (as Chaucer calls them) lewd, and some are learned. Even the ribaldry of the low characters is different: the Deane, the Miller, and the Cook are several men, and distinguished from each other, as much as the mincing Lady Prioress and the broad-speaking, gap-toothed Wife of Bath."

You read prose like this and your eyes open in astonishment as you recognise it to be modern English. Indeed, there is early in it a delightful awareness that it is up-to-date—" as we now call them "—and definitely something new. It is so modern, this new prose, that Swift is twisting it here and there into endless new shapes, spirting it in jets or whistling it out in long sentences as his satirical humour skirmishes its way through *The Tale of a Tub* (1704). Shortly afterwards there is Defoe using it with new trenchancy in his superb journalism and, far more marvellously, doing what Ascham would have denounced unceasingly—writing our first novels, the popular *Robinson Crusoe* and lively, human *Moll Flanders*. Material details, pathos, psychological subtlety, the traffic of cities, the conversation of trulls, all come alike to his prose, superbly sure of itself, and thoroughly competent as an instrument of art.

Some day you may perhaps decide to spend a few weeks or even longer in finding out how this development, this breaking of its bounds, this rush into freedom, came to English prose. It is one of the pleasant studies in literary history, and one cannot pass it here without regret that to follow it up for a few pages would be to leave our road and branch off across a specially tempting stretch of country. There are the early novels to explore, and the phenomenon of Swift, the periodical essays of Steele and Addison, opening the way to the amazing variety of eighteenth-century prose—Richardson, Fielding, Smollett, Sterne, the Burneys, Johnson, Goldsmith, Hume, Adam Smith, Gibbon, Paley. The last name reminds us how modern we have become and that at last prose was accepted as a serviceable medium for anything from a tale of horror to theology.

At the end of the seventeenth century men threw away many ideas, some bad and some good, as well as forms of government, and passed into the eighteenth-century talking excitedly. There, I believe, we have two lines of thought which go far towards the explanation of this new prose—a crisis in thought and an eager discussion of it. We come into the period of clubs and coffee-houses and private memoirs and letters and pamphlets. Where there is much talking there is always an increase in more or less formal speech, which men adopt in discourse rather than what we recognise as conversation, as Johnson did. And when that happens they pass more easily into the use of prose. In England men writing prose had approached it, holding it off from themselves as one holds unfamiliar tools; but now it has become part of themselves or, at least, it is nothing more than a new way to use what is fundamentally conversation and speech-making.

The language at their disposal had been immeasurably enriched by the poets of the previous one hundred and fifty years, and its cadences had been rung out as never before by the Authorised Version of the Bible. Now, as they enter the eighteenth century with their keen interest in politics and history and religion and human nature, men rise from conversation to the art of rhythmical self-expression. They are not living on the heights of human experience, in the rarefied air of poetic experience, but much in the streets and in each other's company. Thus prose is the most suitable medium for them, since they are thinking rather than imagining or feeling, and there is difficulty in making poetry out of satire and cynical wit. You will notice how prose invades even their poetry. Their measures become set and increasingly artificial. Pope is formally the most prosaic of poets—this is not to degrade him to the rank of versifier—and could scarcely have been otherwise in his talkative century.

This is as far as we can allow ourselves to go in examining the change that occurred in prose usage at the Restoration and later. Prose became free, not only because men realised what they could rightly do with it, but also because it had been prepared for their demands on it by the pioneers, who had followed a sure instinct by insisting on using it instead of Latin, and by the poets and anonymous revisers of the Bible. From now onwards it becomes increasingly flexible and musical and full of colour.

By way of interest, of comparison in growth, and as a summary of what we have just read, we may read a brief extract by Lord David Cecil, one of the most skilful prose-writers of our day.

"For a happy moment let us shut the door on the modern world and retire in fancy to some Augustan library. The curtains are drawn, the fire is lit, outside the silence is broken only by the faint, crackling whisper of the winter frost. How the firelight gleams and flickers on the fluted mouldings of the book-cases, on the faded calf and tarnished gold of the serried rows of books : the slim duodecimo poems and plays; the decent two volumed octavo novels; the portly quarto sermons, six volumes, eight volumes, ten volumes; the unity of brown broken now and again by a large tome of correspondence, green or plum or crimson, only given to the public in our own time. The whole eighteenth century is packed into these white or yellowing pages; all its multifarious aspects, its types, its moods, its novels, self-revealed; the indefinable, unforgettable perfume of the period breathing from every line of print. For the shortest, dullest passage really written in a letter can bring its atmosphere home to you as the most vivid historian of a later time can never do."

And there we must turn away from the temptation to wander, content to have discovered the birth of modern prose and steadfast in our resolution to stick, at this time, to our task of thinking only about the nature of prose. We have seen that the prose of today came to life in a period when men preferred sense to emotion, distrusted anything mystical, liked the unusual so long as it was material—negro pages, paid hermits, gardening by torchlight—and were thus agile in mind and ideally prosaic. We must deplore the fact that prosaic is given the meaning of dull. The eighteenth century was, in the real sense, prosaic. It was far from dull.

(vi) Definition of Prose

Our attention to the history of prose, as illustrated and discussed, will enable us now to form an accurate idea of what prose is. We may say that it is the ordering of words in loose rhythms and according to vowel or consonant patterns, for the expression of ideas which are not so inspiring as to demand verse as their medium. Many ideas which may be poetical in themselves may be well expressed in prose, provided that the writer does not allow his emotional or imaginative inspiration to hurry him into so-called prose which is disfigured by the presence of metre. If he is so misguided he writes bad prose, as Dickens notoriously did in some of his most moving passages.

The description of the death of Little Nell is often quoted as an example of this fault, since it is almost exactly blank verse.

In reading this passage or others spoilt by this defect, the reader is moved by the author's own emotion, and may not realise that the passage would be more effective if it were written in good prose. If it cannot be written in good prose, it must remain unwritten, since it is either not worth writing or the writer is not sufficiently master of his craft to be able to achieve prose or verse. This remark must not be considered unduly severe, for it does not preclude the future possibilities open to one who is, at least as far as practical experience of his art is concerned, immature. If his inspiration is true, the gaining of executive improvement by honest practice will not only enable him to utter the thoughts rising in him, but will certainly increase the urgency of his inspiration and the vigour of his creative power. By increasing his ability to use verse, his inspiration will declare itself for a prose form or a verse form, and the initial difficulty of his first attempt, in which he wrote bad prose, will be removed.

(vii) Art in Prose

Every author whose inclination is to prose of high pitch, and every reader who enjoys such prose, should watch carefully in case the line between prose and verse is crossed. Where this line lies no one may definitely say. We can say only that it exists and that he who would avoid it may do so, with least trouble to himself, by not wandering too far into the territory which his sense of prose warns him is adjacent to the forbidden land.

Not that he will have great difficulty in knowing when he is in the border country, although the exact boundary through it is uncertain, for he will judge his work by its form rather than by its matter. Prose can be informed by highly poetical ideas, and properly, without ceasing to be prose. It is right that an author should express the most exalted or mystical ideas in prose form; only when he is dealing with ideas which, so to speak, may betray him into an abuse of his medium should he be cautious.

The celebrated verses in the final chapter of Ecclesiastes illustrate this truth.

> "Remember now thy Creator in the days of thy youth, while the evil days come not, nor the years draw nigh, when thou shalt say, I have no pleasure in them . . . because man goeth to his long home, and the mourners go about the streets : or ever the silver cord be loosed, or the golden bowl be broken, or the pitcher be broken at the fountain, or the wheel broken at the cistern. Then shall the dust return to the earth as it was : and the spirit shall return unto God who gave it."

Here we have a highly "poetic" content in excellent prose. In the same way, we can have a content so lowly as to invalidate the verse in which it is given :—

> Something had happened wrong about a bill
> Which was not drawn with true mercantile skill,
> So, to amend it, I was told to go
> And seek the firm of Clutterbuck and Co.

In this case the message is so prosaic in its dull sense that even simple verse metre is deranged. The example is as glaringly defective as it is unworthy of its usually estimable author. Would a passage of prose, equally defective, be equally laughable? It would not, and for two reasons. One is that its emotional intensity would preserve the reader from embarrassment. The other is that, since prose has rhythm and not metre most readers, especially if moved by the passage, would probably not notice the defect. Only the reader who knows what prose should be would recognise it as bad.

> "And still her former self lay there, unaltered in this change. Yes. The old fireside had smiled upon that same sweet face; it had passed like a dream through haunts of misery and care; at the door of the poor school-master on a summer evening, before the furnace fire upon the cold wet night, at the still bedside of the dying boy, there had been the same mild lovely look. So shall we know the angels in their majesty, after death.
>
> "The old man held one languid arm in his, and had the small hand tight folded to his breast, for warmth. It was the hand she had stretched out to him with her last smile—the hand that had led him on through all their wanderings. Ever and anon he pressed it to his lips; then hugged it to his breast again, murmuring that it was warmer now; and as he said it he looked, in agony, to those who stood around, as if imploring them to help her.
>
> "She was dead, and past all help, or need of it."

Dickens found it impossible to shake free from iambic metre; line follows line of it, marring his best passages and losing the effects he could have secured by adherence to prose rhythms.

> " The heavy door had closed behind him on/his entrance, with a crash that made him start./The figure neither spoke nor turned to look,/nor gave in any other way the faint/est sign of having heard the noise."

The iambic pentameters are more hidden in those lines than prose would be among verse, but the error is no less than that of a line of free rhythm if we were to insert it into

> For when the morn came dim and sad,
>   And chill with early showers,
> Quite quietly she closed her eyes because she had
>   Another morn than ours.

These examples serve to show that prose is more subtle than verse. In verse we have metre, which means a measured thing, a variation of stress and pause which is made up of fixed units, of which the principal are the Iamb ($\cup$–), Trochee (–$\cup$), Anapæst ($\cup$ $\cup$ –), Dactyl (–$\cup$ $\cup$). Less often we meet the Amphibrach ($\cup$ – $\cup$) and the Spondee (– –). Thus we can have an iambic line, with an anapæstic foot in it for variation of the metre, or a line regularly measured out between the two kinds of metrical unit or foot.

Not a drúm/was heárd,/not a fún/eral nóte.

As we shall observe more fully later, poets can use the metrical units with a wide range of variation,

> When the hounds of spring are on winter's traces,
>   The mother of months in meadow or plain,
> Fills the shadows and windy places
>   With lisp of leaves and ripple of rain.

Poets often use skilfully planned vowel or consonant patterns as well as variations in feet to disguise the basic metre of their lines. Consequently readers often regard verse as being more rhythmical than prose. In fact it is more metrical; prose is the more rhythmical. It is essential to prose that its rhythm should be free. As far as the ordering of words is concerned, the most fundamental difference between prose and verse is the contrast between unmeasured rhythms and measured metre. Although at least one notable attempt has been made to divide prose rhythms into measurable units, such as the Antispast ($- \smile \smile -$) or the Proceleusmatic ($\smile \smile \smile \smile$), it has yet to be shown that prose is dependent on anything except the freest recurrence and change of stresses. Through this freedom comes the perfection of form in prose, whether of Sir Thomas Browne in 1658,

> "There is nothing strictly immortal, but immortality; whatever hath no beginning, may be confident of no end (all others have a dependent being and with the reach of destruction); which is the peculiar of that necessary essence that cannot destroy itself; and the highest strain of omnipotency, to be so powerfully constituted as not to suffer even from the power of itself"

or of Percy Lubbock two hundred and fifty years later :

" As for the voyage up-stream in the beating sunshine, the later stages are blurred with a luxury of somnolence; it is clear that I have relinquished the rudder; I keep no count of the twists of the river, I lose myself in the rhythmical cluck and splash of the oars. On and on, cluck and splash—and at length we are wheeling and lurching into the cool shadow of the boat house again; and now comes the endless toil of the walk up the park, an almost impossible anti-climax to our adventure."

No doubt it would be easier for the ear that has not been trained by the reading of prose to detect rhythm if the variations of this medium were measurable. But then it would cease to be prose—at least, if prose were to be made of variation of measurable units instead of, as it is, immeasurable alternations of stress and pause—for the freedom essential to it would be gone. The fact is that we cannot state even the nature of these rhythms. Perhaps they are decided by the facility of the muscles of speech and by our breathing. Certainly the rhythms of rhetoric have relation to these, and prose certainly has, of its nature, relationship to rhetoric. Probably one could hazard a guess not too wide of the mark if one were to say that prose rhythms are governed by these controls and by the ear, which checks over the music of both patterns, rhythmical and sound. A writer may achieve prose that is musically suitable, as far as its rhythm is concerned, and yet find that the sound of his words is displeasing or that it does not contribute to the effect he wishes his sentences to have on his reader. So he has rhythm, naturalness (which is governed by the physical factors mentioned), and melody, or at least sound, to consider.

In other words, the writing of prose is the practice of an art. Whether it may be maintained, as some try to show, that prose is more artistic than verse, is a problem into which one must decline to be drawn. At the same time, we must rid ourselves of the general assumption that verse is necessarily a " higher " form of expression than prose. Poor verse is " lower " than good prose. Apart from that obvious fact, there is no reason for saying that, as an artistic medium, verse is any nobler or more beautiful than prose. Admittedly its subject, its content, will often be more exalted than what is usually found in prose, but this fact is apart from consideration of the two forms as forms. In themselves, prose and verse are means of expression requiring considerable skill, and which of them, if a distinction must be made, demands the more perfect craftsmanship for sustained effectiveness is a problem the reader may come to investigate for himself.

In looking into the matter, do not be deceived by the belief that verse has a power to evoke which is absent from prose. Good prose as well as good verse has this mark of being radiant with a quality we cannot define, a power to communicate something outside itself. I think the secret is that its subtleties draw out of your innermost self ideas and impressions that have formed in you unconsciously and emotions rarely blended. And the evocation of these things, their passage from you to meet those of the author, is an experience delicate and delightful. Because what reaches you draws something similar from the depths of your mind—your soul—you are momentarily saturated with content, filled with satisfaction which lingers in the memory like fragrance in a room. How else shall we explain the mystery of passages like this, in which Rebecca West explains how two women made a home for the man whom, in their different ways, they loved ? A plain, factual idea, but here is its reality, drawing from you eager responses :

> "My eye followed the mellow brick of the garden wall through the trees, and I reflected that by the contriving of these gardens that lay, well-kept as a woman's hand, on the south side of the hill, Kitty and I had proved ourselves worthy of the past generation that had set the old house on this sunny ledge overhanging and overhung by beauty. And we had done much for the new house.
>
> "I could send my mind sweeping from room to room like a purring cat, rubbing itself against all the brittle beautiful things that we had either recovered from antiquity or dug from the obscure pits of modern craftsmanship, basking in the colour that glowed from all our solemnly chosen fabrics with such pure intensity that it seemed to shed warmth like sunshine. Even now, when spending seemed a little disgraceful, I could think of that beauty with nothing but pride. I was sure that we were preserved from the reproach, therefore we had made a fine place for Chris, one part of the world that was, so far as surfaces could make it so, good enough for his amazing goodness."

Every word is carefully set in that musical, calm prose, which continues later :

"I could shut my eyes and think of innumerable proofs of how well we had succeeded, for there never was so visibly contented a man : the way he lingered with us in the mornings while the car throbbed at the door, delighting just in whatever way the weather looked in the familiar frame of things, how our rooms burned with many coloured brightness on the darkest winter day, how not the fieriest summer-time could consume the cool wet leafy places of our garden; the way that in the midst of entertaining a great company he would smile secretly at us, as though he knew we would not cease in our task of refreshing him; and all that he did on the morning just a year ago, when he went to the front. . . ."

The best close to this chapter is a slow reading of good prose, possibly a reading aloud, since this is the best way to catch the rhythm. To give a selection of passages for reading is impossible in the space available, but an examination of another passage, also dealing with a house, will provide, from the pen of Sir Osbert Sitwell, an interesting and useful exercise.

"In the winter it is, that all these country places are seen in their best, their most typical, phase. Stout built for cold weather, these houses take on a new quality, upstanding among hoar-frost, glowing warmly through the crisp, grey air. The first impression of the Grove would be, we think, a childlike memory of potting-shed smells, full of the scents of hidden growth; an odour of bulbs, stores, rich fibrous mould, and bass, mingles with the sharp aromatic smell of the bonfire that crackles outside. On the walls of the shed the bass is hung up like so many beards of old men, ritual beards, like those of Pharaoh or Egyptian priest, which, perhaps, the gardener will don for the great occasions of his year. This one he would put on for the opening of the first spring flower coming up glazed and shrill, its petals folded as if in prayer, out of the cold brown earth, beneath the laced shadows woven by the bare branches of the trees; this he will wear for the brazen trumpet-like blowing of the tulip-tree; while that one he reserves for the virginal unfolding of the magnolia, or the gathering up of petals let drop by the last rose. But the gardener himself soon dispels these tender imaginings, as you see his burly form bent over various cruel tasks—the trapping of the soft mole, or in aiming at the fawn-coloured fluffy arcs of the rabbits, as they crouch in their green cradles, their ears well back, nibbling the tender white shoots that he has so carefully nurtured."

We have now formed a reasonably complete idea about what we call prose. In later chapters we shall examine the structure of prose more thoroughly and pass on to review the chief literary forms in which it is used. At present our immediate task is to develop what has been written here about verse, so that we may make a proper approach to the appreciation of poetry.

Chapter Six

Verse and Poetry

On two pages of a book open before me as I write are listed over twenty definitions of poetry; in the books shelved around me are many other attempts, by poets and critics, to catch the nature of poetry and put it into words. Almost all these definitions take for granted—as they must do, since they are concerned with the nature of a thing, and not with its form or literary expression—a knowledge of what verse is.

Consequently we shall be wise to examine verse more thoroughly before trying to discover what raises it to the dignity of poetry. So far as we have dealt with it, we have said that verse is the ordering of words in connected metrical units, which was sufficient for our purpose in distinguishing it from the free rhythms of prose. Also I think we have begun to form the idea that the putting together of words in free rhythms is prose; that both prose and verse are writing; and that when both are given the soul of inspiration they become literature. Thus we may have ordinary workaday prose, such as

"I have ordered fifty chicks and some meal",

or mere verse, such as

> Every time we go to Kew
> We travel on a motor bus.

Here we have the means of expression only. When the writer is inspired, when he is writing under some inner compulsion, his writing is infused by a creative, or at least constructive quality, which elevates his writing to the worthwhile thing we call literature. For instance,

> " Her gates are sunk into the ground; he hath destroyed and broken her bars; her king and her princes are among the Gentiles: the law is no more; her prophets also find no vision from the Lord ",

or

> And laughter, learnt of friends; and gentleness,
> In hearts at peace, under an English heaven.

In those lines we know that the personal part of writing is present and that, whether what we read is in a volume of Collected Works or in a letter from a friend, we have met a fragment of literature.

With this brief recollection of ideas we have formed, and before we go on to meet the personal thing we call inspiration in its most sharply penetrating form, we must make ourselves familiar with the literary form it requires.

(i) Verse Patterns

(a) *Metre*

The feet or metrical units most common in use we have already mentioned; here we illustrate them in the conventional lines. These lines are made up of a fixed number of feet, such as the Monometer, which we may illustrate by the word *Dĕfĕnce*, where it is iambic. The Dimeter line of two feet might be

Līft hĕr ŭp/tēndĕrlў

where the feet are Dactyls, and the Trimeter line might be

Stēalĭng ănd/gīvĭng/ōdoŭr,

where we have a Dactyl and two Trochees. These short lines are, of course, less rarely used than the longer lines, such as the Tetrameter line—

Jŏhn Gīl/pĭn wās/ă cīt/ĭzĕn,

in which are Iambs, or the more dignified Pentameter, and the Hexameter or Alexandrine line, as in the Iambic

He sinks/into/thy depths/with bubb/ling moan,
Without/a grave,/unknelled,/uncoff/ined, and/unknown,

which is a gloomy couplet from Byron. Tennyson was devoted to the long line—too much so—and can generally be relied upon for an example of the longest line to be found, the Octameter, familiar to readers of *Locksley Hall*,

When Ī/dīpt ĭn/tŏ thĕ/fūtŭre/fār ăs hŭmăn/ēyĕ cŏuld/sēe,

which is a syllable short in its Dactyls. You will have noticed that we have omitted the line of seven feet, the Heptameter—which is solemn here with Iambs,

Ăttēnd/ăll yē/whŏ līst/tŏ hĕar/oŭr nŏb/lĕ Ēng/lănd's
    prāise.

Notice that this example is, to the ear, a longer line than Tennyson's immediately above it, although that is actually longer by half a foot.

There are the bare bones of metre, looking odder than notes on a page of music and, to the initiated, as surprising in their patterns of rhythm. Take the sad Tetrameter line of Amphibrachs—

There came to/the beach a/poor exile/of Erin

and listen to Shakespeare's use of this unit in a Dimeter line,

Most friendship is feigning, most loving mere folly :
  Then heigh-ho the holly, this life is most jolly.

Variations are allowed, of course, so that regularity of the metre will not become monotonous, or to provide effects the writer intends to cause :

The red rose cries, " She is near, she is near ";
And the white rose weeps, " She is late ";
The larkspur listens, " I hear, I hear ";
And the lily whispers, " I wait ".

In dealing with these variations and with kinds of feet we are not going into detail. This book is not a handbook on metre; it does not try to tell everything about any single thing, but only to provide an intelligent approach to literature. Every section in it is capable of considerable expansion. We omit, for instance, more than mention of the Spondee (- -), as in Milton's

Rocks, caves/, lakes, fens/, bogs, dens/, and shades/of
  death

or the Pyrrhic (◡ ◡), which often occurs at the end of a
line but rarely in the middle. Here is an exception,
again from Milton :

Ĭn mŭ/tĭny̆/hăd frŏm/hĕr āx/lĕ tōrn

In the same way, many technicalities of verse are
omitted, such as the fact that a line with an accented
final and extra syllable is called Catalectic, but Hyper-
metric if the syllable is unaccented. For our purpose
it is sufficient for us to be able to scan a line of poetry
reasonably accurately.

Accordingly we leave the other elements of verse
Prosody out of consideration, except for the pause
known as the Cæsura. This pause may occur at a
comma or it may occur independently of any punctua-
tion mark. It serves to break the monotony of long
lines of verse, and also to improve the rhythm of a line,
although a pause may not be required by the sense of
the words. Where he uses the Cæsura, Milton prefers
it to fall at the end of the third foot, but he varies its
position with masterly skill, as in

> Of man's first disobedience//and the fruit
> Of that forbidden tree//whose mortal taste
> Brought death into the world and all our woe
> With loss of Eden//till one greater Man
> Restore us//and regain the blissful seat. . . .

As a help to our scansion of verse, especially by
reading aloud, remember that two short syllables
occurring together may be slurred into one, or two
open vowel sounds coming together, even though be-

longing to different words, may be likewise run together by Elision, as in

Mǎy Ī/express/thee ŭnblamed,/since God/is light.

(b) *Rhyme*

With these ideas about metrical pattern, which is essential to poetry, we turn to another kind of pattern which is usual, but not essential. This is Rhyme, by which is meant identity in vowel and consonant sounds, as between *me* and *thee* or *ranging* and *changing*. As you will have noticed in our quotations from Milton, rhyme is not used by all poets all the time; Milton disliked it intensely and considered it an excessive ornament, and therefore a disfigurement of verse.

Most readers prefer poetry with rhyme and—more importantly, since they are the craftsmen—most poets have had the same preference.

Early English poets use what we call Alliteration, and under this name it may seem to be an amusing pastime which quickly becomes tedious. They thought of it, however, as " Head-rime ", and if we look at it in this way we see its usefulness and the beauty it really has. For instance, fourteenth-century Will Langland used it to soften the rugged strength of his verse :—

For all that bereth baselardes, bright sworde, other launce
     (daggers)
Axe, other hachet, other any kynne wepne,
Shal be demed to the deth. bote yf he do hit smythe
In-to sykel other into sithe. to shar other to culter;
Each man to pleye with a plouh. a pycoyse other a spade,
Spynnen, and spek of God and spille no tyme.

This may be paraphrased, " For all that carry a dagger, sword or lance, axe or hatchet, or other kind of weapon, shall be worthy of death, unless he have it smithied into sickle or scythe for share or for coultar; so that each man use a plough, or a pitch, or a spade, spin, speak of God and waste no time ".

This head-rime fashion disappeared, except to remain in alliteration, for special effects, as in *gloomy glade*, or Dryden's

> Deep in a dungeon was the captive cast,
> Deprived of day, and held in fetters fast.

But its most frequent use is in internal alliteration, where it can be used to express an idea of which the sound is in some way suggestive, as in Browning's

> Oh the little more and how much it is !
> The little less, and what worlds away !

Here the *m* sounds suggest bulk and difficulty, the *l*'s have a diminishing effect, and the lines slip away in *w* sounds.

From alliteration it is only a short step in thought, but a remarkable advance in technique, to Assonance and Consonance. Assonance is the rhyming of vowels inside a line, and Consonance is the repetition of consonants. Many poets have made their music far more subtle and their word patterns more suggestive by its aid. Tennyson used it enormously; Shelley, Swinburne, and Francis Thompson are other poets whose work abounds in it.   Alliteration, assonance, and consonance occur in these stanzas of Thompson :

> For standing artless as the air
>   And candid as the skies,
> She took the berries with her hand,
>   And the love with her sweet eyes.
>
> The fairest things have fleetest end :
>   Their scent survives their close,
> But the rose's scent is bitterness
>   To him that loved the rose !
>
> She looked a little wistfully,
>   Then went her sunshine way :—
> The sea's eye had a mist on it,
>   And the leaves fell from the day.

A great deal of the poet's work in thus perfecting his verse is lost on his readers.   To notice even the presence of his subtle cadence requires of the reader a trained appreciation, an ear keyed to the melody, a readiness of perception for which many people are unwilling to prepare themselves, often because they do not realise any necessity for more than a cursory reading of poetry.   This unpreparedness certainly is a breach of one of the fundamental rules about reading either prose or poetry—that it is the work of two people, the author and the reader.   What the one has taken pains to present, the other should be equally prepared to receive.   Every reader of poetry should have been not only diligent enough in studying the craft of this art to know what to notice, but always

alert to see what it offers him.   Its internal arrangement may not be as clear as the

Now the air is hushed, save where the weak-eyed bat
With short shrill shriek, flits by on leathern wing;
     Or where the beetle winds
      His small but sullen horn . . .

of Collins; it may be a hidden beauty as in

     The moving moon went up the sky
      And nowhere did abide;
    Softly she was going up,
      And a star or two beside—

or in

     He came all so still
      Where his mother was,
    As dew in April
      That falleth on the grass—

or in Meredith's

Shy as the squirrel and wayward as the swallow,
   Swift as the swallow along the river's light
Circling the surface to meet his mirror'd winglets,
   Fleeter she seems in her stay than in her flight.
Shy as the squirrel that leaps among the pine-tops,
   Wayward as the swallow overhead at set of sun,
She whom I love is hard to catch and conquer,
   Hard, but O the glory of the winning were she won !

I cannot close this section without quoting a single
line that has always seemed to me to have a remarkable
felicity in its metre, its verbal pattern, and its excellence in suggesting what it does not say.   It tells
us an enormous amount in few words, and those

words sound for us what they leave unsaid. I mean Matthew Arnold's restrained and magnificent

The unplumb'd, salt, estranging sea.

The chiming of sounds being of the greatest use and the crepitation of consonants being of scarcely less value, it is natural that the device of rhyme should come to be employed at the ends of lines. What poets had found excellent as head-rime or as an aid to colour and sound within a line must inevitably be found, sooner or later, at the end of a line, where the reader's attention is usually focused. This is true of English, at any rate, where verse is scanned by accent and not by quantity. It is natural to us to accent the end of every line, even though we should not necessarily do so. Therefore it was natural that poets should see what effects they could secure by rhyming their line endings.

The use of rhyme has a further advantage. By marking definitely the ends of lines and stanzas, even though their sense may run on into the next line or stanza, it emphasises rhythm. It divides each section of rhythm from the next, and has the result of making the poem more musical, if only in the sense that it helps us to notice how musical it is. Those who object to rhyme point out that this is an artificial means of bringing out the melody of verse. They believe that poets should dispense with it and that readers should learn to do without it. While this is a valid argument, in the interests of verse and its readers, against the use of rhyme by every poet, it is

not a reasonable argument against freedom to use it.
For rhyme is natural in itself, and most natural things
are governed by conventions as to their employment.
There is no reason why poetry should not have a convention of rhyme to make verse more interesting to the
majority of readers, to add a natural ornament to it,
provided that it may be discarded at will.

Such a convention has the further pleasure of itself
making verse more musical, apart from its effect on the
rest of a line.   In long poems the echoing of sound
gives unity to the sound pattern of the whole, and also
completeness.   This benefit alone is sufficient to
justify its use.   In shorter poems, it will be noticed,
rhyme has an effect similar to that of a musical chord
which draws together the harmonies of a phrase or
expression of a musical idea.

So the dispute may continue without our feeling
obliged to attend to everything that is said in it.   It is
good, we feel, to be able to appreciate rhyme and also
to be able to enjoy verse music which has no rhyme.
If we can do both things, the pedantry or ruffled
tempers of disputants can pass unnoticed.   Before
turning to the rules about rhyme, let us enjoy two short
extracts from both sides of the argument.   Here is
Carew's poem *Disdain Returned*.

> He that loves a rosy cheek,
>   Or a coral lip admires,
> Or from star-like eyes doth seek
>   Fuel to maintain his fires :
> As old Time makes these decay,
> So his flames must waste away.

> But a smooth and steadfast mind,
>> Gentle thoughts and calm desires,
> Hearts with equal love combined,
>> Kindle never-dying fires,
> Where these are not, I despise
> Lovely cheeks or lips or eyes.

And here are stanzas from a poem by W. J. Turner :

> I saw a frieze on whitest marble drawn
> Of boys who sought for shells along the shore,
> Their white feet shedding pallor in the sea,
> The shallow sea, the spring-time sea of green
> That faintly creamed against the cold, smooth pebbles.
>
> The air was thin, their limbs were delicate,
> The wind had graven their small eager hands
> To feel the forests and the dark night of Asia
> Behind the purple bloom of the bracing air,
> Where sails would float and slowly melt away.
>
> Their naked, pure, and grave, unbroken silence
> Filled the soft air, as gleaming, limpid water
> Fills a spring sky those days when rain is lying
> In shattered bright pools on the wind-dried roads,
> And their sweet bodies were wind-purified.
>
> One held a shell unto his shell-like ear
> And there was music carven on his face,
> His eyes half-closed, his lips just breaking open
> To catch the lulling, mazy, coralline roar
> Of numberless caverns filled with singing seas.

It is difficult not to believe that rhyme adds as much to perfect expression of the first as its absence allows to the other example.

The use of rhyme is governed by rules that are simple and no more numerous or exact than the definition of rhyme requires. The first is that vowel sounds must be identical and, if followed by a consonant, the consonantal sounds must also be identical. Thus, the *share—pare*, *banging—clanging*. The second rule is that there must be difference between the consonants preceding rhymed vowels, as in the examples given. *Spare—pare* or *slanging—clanging* would not be rhyme.

In addition, rhyme requires that the accent of rhymed words should be similar—e.g., *unfórtunate*. *impórtunate*—and that, as in these two words, the syllables following the accent should be the same.

Reflection on these simple rules shows that they are not devices for forming rhyme; rather they are explanations of what rhyme is. The propriety of a rhyme is to be judged by ear alone, not by the spelling of words. By pronunciation, then, we know that *home* and *some* do not rhyme and that *light* rhymes with *indict*.

Most rhyme is single, but double and triple rhymes are not unusual, such as *water* and *daughter*, *enveloping* and *developing*. The shorter rhymes add lightness to a poem, and the longer rhymes usually have the opposite effect, in addition to being useful in poems aiming at a certain grotesqueness of meaning or effect.

(ii) Verse Forms
(a) *Blank Verse*

Everything essential to rhyme may thus be expressed briefly, so that we are able to pass on quickly to notice the principal verse forms used in English poetry. The first of these is Blank Verse, in which the word *blank* means *without* rhyme.

It consists of iambic pentameter lines, and is thus a form of poetry in this extremely popular metre. Blank Verse is found in other metres, such as the trochaic tetrameter of *The Song of Hiawatha*, but the name is popularly associated with the five-footed line of iambs we find in the dramatist Marlowe, who first raised this form of verse to its highest perfection:

> Was this the face that launched a thousand ships,
> And burnt the topless towers of Ilium ?
> Sweet Helen, make me immortal with a kiss—
> Her lips suck forth my soul : see where it flies !
> Come, Helen, come, give me my soul again.

While we may share in the rather thoughtless idea that Blank Verse means this kind of poetry, it is as well to remember that it means any verse without rhyme, whether Tennyson's dactylic dimeters :

> Cannon to right of them,
> Cannon to left of them . . .

or the hotly disputed dactylic hexameter, which we may illustrate from Longfellow's *Evangeline*,

> This is the forest primeval, the murmuring pines, and the
> hemlock,

which some critics object to as the importation of a Latin form into English verse.

(b) *The Heroic Couplet*

The Heroic Couplet is an iambic pentameter metre, consisting of two rhyming pentameter lines.   Here is

a stanza from Waller in this metre; the pronunciation
of his time made rhyme of *home* and *become*.

> The soul's dark cottage, battered and decay'd,
> Lets in new light through chinks that Time has made:
> Stronger by weakness, wiser men become
> As they draw near to their eternal home.
> Leaving the old, both worlds at once they view
> That stand upon the threshold of the new.

Like Blank Verse, the Heroic Couplet has been attached
to one particular form of verse, and in this case the
attachment is particularly unfortunate, for this form of
versification is capable of surprising variation. It
is usually linked with the name of Pope and this kind
of poetry :

> A little learning is a dang'rous thing;
> Drink deep, or taste not the Pierian spring :
> There shallow draughts intoxicate the brain,
> And drinking largely sobers us again.

It is easy to realise that this is exactly the metre of the
extract from Waller. Pope gave it a polish and
rigid completeness of which it is well capable. He and
others used it as a vehicle for biting wit and satire,
as in Dryden's *Absalom and Achitophel* :

> Stiff in opinions, always in the wrong;
> Was everything by starts, and nothing long :
> But, in the course of one revolving moon,
> Was chemist, fiddler, statesman, and buffoon :
> Then for all women, painting, rhyming, drinking,
> Besides ten thousand freaks that died in thinking.

In these quotations the Heroic Couplet has a stop at
the end of each two lines. Moreover, there is a pause

at the end of the first line of most couplets : where there is a " carry-on " of sense it is not strictly between the end of the first line and the beginning of the next.   It is also observable that the metre is rigid.   It allows the writer no liberty for variation.

The Couplet illustrated is of the Classical type perfected after 1660.   Before then it had been practised by poets like Jonson or Chapman, who varied their metre freely and did not aim at self-contained lines or couplets.   Their form of this measure is usually called the Romantic.   It often changes the Couplet so that it resembles Blank Verse.   In the hands of poets the Heroic Couplet ran from the extreme variety of the Romantic form to the equally extreme rigidity of the Classical form.   Where the first became almost something else, the second became monotonous—as verse it was paralysed, and was quickened only by the clarity of the wit and thought glittering in its frozen depth.   A change permitted in its design was the use of a triplet instead of a couplet, the third line being the hexameter or Alexandrine. It is interesting to notice variations in the verse design from the simple *a a* of the Classical form, as in Pope's

> But thou, false guardian of a charge too good !
> Thou, mean deserter of thy brother's blood

to the *a b c b* of Keats' *Endymion*, the *a a b a* of Fitzgerald's *Rubáiyát*, and other patterns.   Alert reading will soon enable you to recognise the Heroic Couplet,

of either Romantic or Classical type, however varied
its metre may be or unexpected its rhyme pattern.

(c) *Stanza Forms*

Not unlike it is the form created by Spenser for his
epic *The Faerie Queen*, since this Spenserian Stanza is
made up of eight lines of iambic pentameters followed
by an Alexandrine.   Its rhyme pattern is *a a b b c b c c*.
In this stanza, as in the Heroic Couplet, you will find
variations, in both metrical and rhyme schemes, as the
result of experiments by other poets.   It is found in
poems as different from *The Faerie Queen* as Burns's
The Cotter's Saturday Night.   Here it is as Keats used
it in *The Eve of St. Agnes*.   The metre is exactly according to Spenser's choice, but the rhyme differs from his.

> His prayer he saith, this patient, holy man;
> Then takes his lamp, and riseth from his knees,
> And back returneth, meagre, barefoot, wan,
> Along the chapel aisle by slow degrees :
> The sculptured dead, on each side, seem to freeze
> Emprison'd in black, purgatorial rails :
> Knights, ladies, praying in dumb oratories,
> He passeth by, and his weak spirit fails
> To think how they may ache in icy hoods and mails.

We will see how fluid this stanza is : how it appears
made to convey melody, music, colour, with a suggestion of languor.   The resonance of the Alexandrine
sums up the stanza, so that each stanza gives us a complete picture as well as a defined piece of melody.
This Spenser effected by using an earlier metre, used
by Chaucer in his *Monk's Tale*, and breaking it into

stanzas by the insertion of the Alexandrine. Beyond this, he allowed the sense of the words to find its delay at a metrical pause. The resulting stanza had a lasting influence on English poetry, and our only caution about it is that it is so musical, so luxuriously restful, that we can be lulled into a reading of the sound alone, a chanting of the music and enjoyment of its accompanying word colour, without due attention to the sense of what we read. Here, from Keats, is a further example of its colour and whispered music.

> Full on this casement shone the wintry moon,
> And threw warm gules on Madeleine's fair breast,
> As down she knelt for Heaven's grace and boon;
> Rose-bloom fell on her hands, together prest,
> And on her silver cross soft amethyst,
> And on her hair a glory, like a saint:
> She seem'd a splendid angel, newly drest,
> Save wings, for heaven:—Porphyro grew faint:
> She knelt, so pure a thing, so free from mortal taint.
>
> Anon his heart revives: her vespers done,
> Of all its wreathed pearls her hair she frees;
> Unclasps her warmed jewels one by one;
> Loosens her fragrant boddice: by degrees
> Her rich attire creeps rustling to her knees:
> Half-hidden, like a mermaid in sea-weed,
> Pensive awhile she dreams awake, and sees,
> In fancy, fair St. Agnes in her bed,
> But dares not look behind, or all the charm is fled.

Another form of stanza was created by a poet whose aim was to secure extreme conciseness, purity, perspicuity, and melody, as he said. This was Thomas Gray, whose *Elegy in a Country Churchyard* is not an

elegy, but is a poem which gives us a new verse form—
the Elegiac Stanza suitable to poetry of reflection
tinged with melancholy.   Once again we have iambic
pentameter lines, four of them, with the simple rhyme
pattern *a b a b*:

> The curfew tolls the knell of parting day,
>   The lowing herd wind slowly o'er the lea,
> The ploughman homeward plods his weary way,
>   And leaves the world to darkness, and to me.
>
> Now fades the glimmering landscape on the sight,
>   And all the air a solemn stillness holds,
> Save where the beetle wheels his droning flight,
>   And drowsy tinklings lull the distant folds. . . .

Pentameter lines are indeed popular with poets and
readers, from the seven-line verses of the Chaucerian
Stanza with a rhyme pattern *a b a b b c c* (also called
rhyme Royal) to the Octava rhyme, which you are more
likely to meet in general reading.   It consists of eight
iambic pentameters with the rhyme *a b a b a b c c*.   This
stanza form, as its name suggests, was borrowed from
Italy, by Sir Thomas Wyatt (1503–42), with other
measures and forms by which English poetry became
immeasurably more musical and richer in verbal
beauty.   Byron used it in *Don. Juan*, Shelley in his
Witch of Atlas, and Keats in his *Isabella*.   Here is
Byron with this form,

> 'Tis sweet to hear the watchdog's honest bark
>   Bay deep-mouthed welcome as we draw near home;
> 'Tis sweet to know there is an eye will mark
>   Our coming, and look brighter when we come;

'Tis sweet to be awakened by the lark,
    Or lulled by falling waters; sweet the hum
Of bees, the voice of girls, the song of birds,
The lisp of children, and their earliest words.

Our review of the chief verse forms can close with
details of these simple plans. One is the stanza
usually named after Tennyson, although previously
used by Sandys in 1626, because it is used by him in
In Memoriam. It consists of four lines of iambic
tetrameter with the rhyme *a b b a*.

Love is and was my Lord and King,
    And in His presence I attend
    To bear the tidings of my friend
Which every hour his couriers bring.

A six-lined stanza of iambic tetrameters, the fourth
and sixth lines being dimeters, is the Scottish or Burns
stanza, with a rhyme pattern of *a a a b a b*.

But, Mousie, thou art no thy lane
In proving foresight may be vain :
The best laid schemes o' mice and men
    Gang aft a-gley,
An' leave us nought but grief and pain,
    For promised joy.

(d) *Ballad Form*

There is considerable spontaneity in this stanza, as
there also is in the Common or Ballad Metre. This
consists of a four-line stanza of iambic tetrameters and
trimeters, often rhyming *a b c b*. The metre was
varied considerably under the vigour of the story-
telling in this primary literary form, which consisted of
story, action, and song.

The king sits in Dunfermline town
  Drinking the blude-red wine;
" O whare will I get a skeely skipper
  To sail this new ship o' mine ? "

O up and spak an eldern knight
  Sat at the king's right knee;
" Sir Patrick Spens is the best sailor
  That ever sailed the sea."

Our king has written a braid letter,
  And sealed it with his hand,
And sent it to Sir Patrick Spens,
  Was walking on the strand.

" To Noroway, to Noroway,
  To Noroway o'er the faem,
The king's daughter o' Noroway,
  'Tis thou must bring her haem."

The old ballad formed a literature in itself, with a
quality later imitations have failed to recapture.
The Nut-Brown Maid, *Helen of Kirconnell*, and many
others are unique. Nevertheless the modern ballad
is full of interest, in its story and technique, and many
poets have been attracted by it, as we see by the names
of Sir Walter Scott (*Rosabelle*), Southey (*Bishop Hatto*),
Keats (*La Belle Dame Sans Merci*), Macaulay (*Lays of
Ancient Rome*), William Morris (*Shameful Death*) and Sir
William Watson, from whose *Ballad of Semerwater* we
take,

Deep asleep, deep asleep,
  Deep asleep it lies,
The still lake of Semerwater
  Under the still skies.

And many a fathom, many a fathom,
    Many a fathom below,
In a king's tower and a queen's bower
    The fishes come and go.

The old ballad was undoubtedly part of oral literature, passed on from generation to generation by people who were illiterate but cherished these old narratives by their firesides or at their inns. The modern ballads are unchanged; the old ballads certainly suffered many changes before they were first gathered into print in 1765. Yet suffered is not the right word, for the changes themselves occurred only because the verses were living among the people, and this may account for the warmth and brightness found in them and missed in many more recent ballads. *Thomas the Rhymer*, *The Battle of Otterbourne*, *The Twa Corbies*, as well as the Robin Hood ballads, are inimitable. Among modern ballads the best loved is, perhaps, Cowper's *John Gilpin*, while *La Belle Dame Sans Merci* and *The Rime of the Ancient Mariner* are notable as being written in the ballad metre.

With this note on ballads, we turn naturally from a review of the metrical and rhyme patterns which are fundamental to English poetry to a summary of the chief forms of poetry, such as the sonnet, ode, or elegy. This we can complete in one chapter before examining the various forms conventional to prose together with the technique they require.

Before doing so, however, we must make sure that the details of versification we have looked at do not

leave us with the impression that English poetry consists mainly of iambic pentameters. It is true that
iambic verse forms a considerable part of our poetry
and that the pentameter line is the basis of most of the
metrical patterns we have considered. From this it
does not follow that every second poem which is
written is iambic pentameter, but only that the iamb is a
standard and the pentameter is a standard.

They are a starting point, that is, for many experiments and variations.

The same truth applies to the verse patterns we
have defined. Many poems have been written in the
Spenserian Stanza; many others have altered either its
metre or versification or rhyme.

Our purpose in listing the basic forms is that a
reader may learn how to detect these variations and
relate them to each other. Our interest in the technical side of poetry may easily be baffled if we have no
knowledge of the models on which poets have been
working. It would be a loss to us, as readers, if we
were unable to appreciate the skill which has been almost invisibly worked into many of the greatest poems.
And the fact is that it is bound to be invisible if we are
without some elementary knowledge of metre, verse
form, and rhyme patterns.

What we learn about these things, together with our
reading of poetry, shows us that our literature is rich
in poetic variation. Almost every conceivable experiment in rhyme has been made as well as in stanza form.
How far the possibilities of metrical experiment have

been worked out it is impossible to guess, but there has certainly been no undue attachment to the iambic foot, which is remarkably suitable to the proper accentuation of English words.

(iii) Free Verse

Of course, in a world as free as that of letters, where the spirit breathes freely on whom it will and in which those inspired to write are free to choose their own forms, it is to be expected that certain writers of prose and poetry will decide to shake off convention. Our comment on this can only be that they have every right to do so. And when an occasional zealot goes farther, by saying that every writer who remains attached to convention is a dunderhead or a traitor to literature, we can admire his zeal and keep patience with his mistakes. For he may, after all, have something worthwhile to contribute to literature; writers do not always make the best critics. So we continue to read our Tennyson or Arnold, and remain willing to try to see what is valuable in new work also.

In poetry this freedom of spirit is expressed in Free Verse or *Vers Libre*, which is poetry written without a recognisable metrical plan. Usually there is no planned stanza either. It is poetry because it is in verse—it uses metre and not rhythm. That is putting the reason bluntly. There are other reasons for admitting it as poetry and not as exalted prose, but technically its verse is the reason for its classification.

Some of it may shock us, dismay us, depress us, make

us fling down our book; some of it will seem to us deeply moving and technically admirable. Whatever our reaction, it is good to remember that the author cannot be reproached merely because he has discarded what is conventional.

I say this because every writer is free to choose either to accept the aid of conventional forms, into which he can weave designs of his own, or to ignore them so that he can design in a wholly original way. Whichever his choice may be, he makes a sacrifice. If he submits to the discipline of stanza form or rhyme or a verse pattern, he gains the advantage of a model on which to work. If he discards a model, he frees himself from the limitations it imposes on him, but assumes the discipline of finding a wholly new way of conveying his thoughts to others by means of verse. If he is so sincere as to do this, he may ask that the reader shall be equally sincere in trying to understand the new modes which result. A display of impatience on either side indicates a misunderstanding of what is happening, and possibly of one's own status as author or reader.

The result of Free Verse may be something genuinely startling to the reader, like E. J. Scovell's

> Nothing will fill the salt caves our youth wore:
> Happiness later nor a house with corn
> Ripe to its walls and open door.
> We filtered through to sky and flowed into
> A pit full of stars; so we are each alone.
> Even in this being alone I meet with you.

or T. S. Eliot's

Here I am, an old man in a dry month
Being read to by a boy, waiting for rain,
I was neither at the hot gates
Nor fought in the warm rain
Nor knee deep in the salt marsh, heaving a cutlass,
Bitten by flies, fought.
My house is a decayed house,
And the jew squats on the window sill, the owner,
Spawned in some estaminet of Antwerp,
Blistered in Brussels, patched and peeled in London.

You may be faced, then, by two things which have to be turned over in the mind until they are understood. One is the problem as to what the poet is trying to convey—this aspect of poetry we shall deal with later—and the other is the means he has adopted for expressing it. His mode may be as surprising as the presence of a tiger in a bedroom, and your consideration of the position may lead you to the conclusion that there has been a mistake somewhere. But you cannot conclude that there is something indescribably wrong with the tiger. After a time it may occur to you that tigers in bedrooms are rather freshly interesting. You may, in fact, become quite fascinated and like your tiger that way. And if you finally come to see why the animal was put in a bedroom, you may enter into a new world of ideas. For you it may be as if a new day of creation has occurred, or perhaps you will decide that what the poet offers is a world you do not care to visit. That is your affair. The point is that you now know what he said, why he said it in a certain way, and why you want or do not want his work.

Apart from the more surprising unconventionality of some Free Verse, there remains a large amount of it which is less luridly revolutionary when judged by what you may have formerly supposed to be verse. For instance, you will find Free Verse handled in a masterly way by Walt Whitman, and you may have no difficulty in appreciating poems like his *The Imprisoned Soul*:

At the last, tenderly,
From the walls of the powerful, fortress'd house,
From the clasp of the knitted locks—from the heap of well-
  closed doors,
Let me be wafted.

Let me glide noiselessly forth;
With the key of softness unlock the locks—with a whisper
Set ope the doors, O soul!
Tenderly! Be not impatient!
(Strong is your hold, O mortal flesh!
Strong is your hold, O love!)

The metre is exceptionally beautiful, the sound cadences no less perfectly chosen; and the structure of the poem amply justifies itself by its proportions as related to the poet's ideas.

Free Verse, then, is not something we should allow ourselves to regard as precocious or undisciplined or strange. It well compensates for whatever initial difficulties we may find in accustoming ourselves to new, quickly changing forms. Above all, we should not conclude hasty judgments about its being irresponsible. It is significant that what many critics consider to be the best composition in Free Verse in English poetry is from the pen of the highly respectable Matthew Arnold, who wrote *Rugby Chapel* in memory of his father. From it we take :

See !   In the rocks of the world
Marches the host of mankind,
A feeble, wavering line,
Where are they tending ?—A God
Marshall'd them, gave them their goal.
Oh, but the way is so long !
Years they have been in the wild !
Sore thirst plagues them; the rocks
Rising all round, overawe;
Factions divide them, their host
Threatens to break, to dissolve.
—Ah, keep, keep them combined !
Else, of the myriads who fill
That army, not one shall arrive;

Sole they shall stray; in the rocks
Labour for ever in vain,
Die one by one in the waste.

Then, in such hour of need
Of your fainting, dispirited race,
Ye, like angels, appear,
Radiant with ardour divine.
Beacons of hope, ye appear !
Languor is not in your heart,
Weakness is not in your word,
Weariness not on your brow.
Ye alight in our van ! at your voice,
Panic, despair, flee away.
Ye move through the ranks, recall
The Stragglers, refresh the outworn,
Praise, re-inspire the brave !
Order, courage, return.

Eyes rekindling, and prayers
Follow your steps as ye go.
Ye fill up the gaps in our files,
Strengthen the wavering line,
Stablish, continue our march,
On, to the bound of the waste,
On, to the City of God !

Chapter Seven

Forms of Poetry

(i) The Ballad

THE ballad form is one of the oldest in English poetry, essentially a product of times we shall not see again. Its name—ballad—indicates a dance-poem, and we find that this form of poetry, while it is sometimes as crude as the society in which it flourished, is by no means artless. The ballad metre we have already noticed. Here is an example of it which is usually dated at about A.D. 1226.

> Sumer is icumen in,
>   Lhude sing cuccu !
> Groweth sed, and bloweth med,
>   And springeth the wude nu—
>   Sing cuccu !
> Awe bleteth after lomb,
>   Lhouth after calve cu;
> Bulluc sterteth, bucke verteth,
>   Murie sing cuccu !

From this beginning the medieval ballad developed into a narrative poetry, distinguishable from the lyrical forms by this habit of telling a story rather than painting a picture or expressing a mood. It is full of vigour, often highly romantic, homely, close to Nature and love of the earth, primitive in feeling and naïve in its simplicity. It is possible only among people who love poetry and are, at the same time, in many ways uncultured and unsophisticated.

This is not to say that it is undeveloped as an art form. On the contrary, its technical development was well able to express its meaning and to fill it with suggestion of mood which gives it a haunting beauty impossible to analyse.

> There was twa sisters in a bower,
> *Binnorie, O Binnorie:*
> There came a knight to be their wooer,
> *By the bonnie mill-dams o' Binnorie.*
>
> He courted the eldest with glove an' ring,
> *Binnorie, O Binnorie:*
> But he loved the youngest abune a' thing,
> *By the bonnie mill-dams o' Binnorie.*

The tragedy develops through another twenty-six stanzas. The ballad formed its own conventional refrains, its own diction, its tricks of repetition. It celebrated great events, such as *Chevy Chase*, well-known people, like *The Bonny Earl of Murray*, gathered many poems around Robin Hood, and its wandering gleemen and minstrels, who eagerly sought noble patronage, indulged the taste of their audiences for romance and often stark tragedy. Here is a refrain characteristic of the best in English and Scottish ballads, from *Clerk Saunders*:

> In hosen and shoon and gown alone,
> She climbed the wall and followed him,
> Until she came to the green forest,
> And there she lost sight o' him.

" Is there ony room at your head, Saunders ?
  Is there ony room at your feet ?
Or ony room at your side, Saunders,
  Where fain, fain I wad sleep ? "

" There's nae room at my head, Marg'ret,
  There's nae room at my feet;
My bed it is full lowly now,
  Among the hungry worms I sleep.

" Cauld mould it is my covering now,
  But on my winding sheet;
The dew it falls nae sooner down
  Than my resting-place is weet.

" But plait a wand o' bonnie birch,
  And lay it on my breast :
And shed a tear upon my grave,
  And wish my soul gude rest."

By the time we come to *The Nut-Brown Maid*, about
the year 1500, the conditions which inspired and
favoured the true ballad were passing. It died
quickly. We take no notice here of the Political
Ballad, e.g. *A Son of the Husbandmen*, which was chiefly
satirical, and more self-conscious than the more
spontaneous ballad loved by the people, and of the
Satirical Ballads, of which *Hudibras* was the most
famous, which appeared in the seventeenth century and
derived rather from Skelton than the old ballad. In
the nineteenth century there was a revival of the ballad
by way of revolt against the formal classical poetry of
the eighteenth century. It was a desire to restore the
ballad rather than a true revival, for most of the poems

written were completely cut off from the spontaneity of the old ballad impulses or were too deliberately trying to recapture, by repeating old devices, a charm which only genuine simplicity can give. Macaulay's *Lays* and *English Ballads*, Aytoun's *Ballads of the Scottish Cavaliers*, poems by Kingsley, William Morris, Sir William Watson, admirable in many ways, have necessarily failed to revive a form which cannot be modernised. The most notable poems of the revival, written in ballad metre, are Keats's *La Belle Dame Sans Merci* and Coleridge's *Rime of the Ancient Mariner*.

> I saw pale kings and princes too,
>   Pale warriors, death-pale were they all !
> Who cried—" La Belle Dame sans Merci
>   Hath thee in thrall ! "
>
> I saw their starved lips in the gloom
>   With horrid warning gapéd wide,
> And I awoke and found me here
>   On the cold hill's side.
>
> And this is why I sojourn here
>   Alone and palely loitering,
> Though the sedge is withered from the lake,
>   And no birds sing.

(ii) The Lyric

From the ballad we turn to the enormous body of poetry which is composed of various forms and is called Lyrical. Under this title we shall consider the Lyric itself, the Ode, the Sonnet, the Idyll, and the Elegy.

We must not be surprised if we find, in anthologies, that the early ballad, *Sumer is icumen in*, is classified as a Lyric, for a lyric proper is a song. It is written so that it may be sung. It is not limited to any basic pattern of metre or rhyme or form of stanza. Because of its sole purpose—that it should be a song—the lyric covers a bewildering variety of poems, among which are *Who is Sylvia, Cherry-ripe, Drink to me only with Thine Eyes, Go, lovely Rose, Sally in Our Alley, Lament for Flodden, The Land o' the Leal, The Last Rose of Summer, The Sands of Dee, Home Thoughts from Abroad, Sweet and Low.*

Knowing what is a lyric is, then, easy. Not so easy to know, unless it is pointed out, is the way in which the purpose of the lyric has made it an exceptionally beautiful form of poetry. This point is worth careful attention.

Because it is intended to be sung, a lyric must be restricted in metre. That is, the accent must fall regularly so that the metre is regular. As a rule, too, the same metre must be retained throughout the lyric. A further requirement is that the open vowels must coincide with long notes. This last rule implies that a lyric must not be written with too few open vowels— so that something which at first seems only to interest anyone listening to the sung lyric really interests the reader. For, no less than the other two rules, this has its effect on the poem's diction. These three principles have guided the lyric to firmness of metre and openness of melody.

The demands which its purpose makes on the lyric, however, are more detailed than those principles suggest. Because it is primarily a song, formerly intended to be accompanied by lyre or harp, a lyric poem must make little use of close sounds, like the *i* in *hit* or any sound that is uttered through almost closed teeth. The placing of such sounds in relation to the notes is interesting, but does not concern us here. Our interest lies in the fact that these vowel sounds are used as little as possible.

Where consonants are concerned, the same need for an open mouth must be met, so that *f, p, s, v, w, z* are undesirable unless they precede an open vowel, as in *sound* or *father*. Other consonants are found to be useful because they give smoothness or fluidity. For instance, notice how often *l, m, n,* or *r* are used in lyric poetry. The aim which these are used to achieve is defeated by hissing sounds, so these are reduced to a minimum.

In the following stanza by Waller, notice how skilfully these guiding ideas are carried out. For example, closed sounds are tied to helpful consonants, as in *seems* or *sweet*.

> Go, lovely Rose,
> Tell her, that wastes her time and me,
> That now she knows
> When I resemble her to thee,
> How sweet and fair she seems to be.

Burns runs this lyric through by the use of the letter

l, which is in six words of its vocabulary of only seventeen :—

> O my Luve's like a red, red rose,
>   That's newly sprung in June :
> O my Luve's like the melody
>   That's sweetly played in tune.

Of the eleven words without an *l*, including the definite or indefinite articles, the open vowel *o* is one and *m*, *n*, or *r* occurs in seven. Thus, only three words—*a*, *the*, *that's*—are not ideally suited to lyrical use. In the stanza succeeding only seven words are without an effective, *l*, or *n* or *r*, and four of these seven are the open sounds *as*, *thou*, *so*, *I*, so that again we find only three words less than perfectly suitable.

The skill of the diction is completely hidden. It is rarely equalled by any other lyrical poet, although Dibdin has a claim to exceptional mastery of this form. Taking the first verse of his most popular lyric, we find that the most suitable consonants occur in twenty-nine words in a vocabulary of forty-four, while five of the remaining words have open vowel sounds.

> Here, a sheer hulk, lies poor Tom Bowling,
>   The darling of our crew;
> No more he'll hear the tempest howling,
>   For death has broached him to.
> His form was of the manliest beauty,
>   His heart was kind and soft.
> Faithful, below, he did his duty,
>   But now he's gone aloft.

With these notes we must be content to leave the best of a most musical form of poetry. It was followed

by the " literary " lyric, which aims at being read and
not sung.   Obviously the whole technique of lyrical
poetry is altered by the change of purpose.   No longer
is the lyric bound to concentrate on one idea, one
clearly painted picture, emotion rather than thought.
Now it can deal with shades of feeling and complexi-
ties of thought, since a reader can go over it as often as
he wishes.   The " literary " lyric includes Kipling's
Recessional, Dobson's *Song of the Four Seasons*, Austin's
When Runnels began to Leap and Sing and other successes,
but for many readers it has not the appeal of the true
song lyric.

(iii) The Ode

A lyric form of great diversity is the Ode, a majestic
poem usually addressed to someone, generally rhymed
and of no fixed stanzaic pattern.   Based, in England,
on the Odes of Pindar, the Anglo-Pindaric Ode is
divided into Strophe, Antistrophe, and Epode (of which
form Gray's *Progress of Poesy* is the finest example) or
is composed of regular stanzas.   In this second form
our best odes were written—Wordsworth's *Ode to
Duty*, Shelley's *Ode to the Skylark*, and Keats's three
odes *To Autumn*, *To a Nightingale*, *On a Grecian Urn*.
In these last three this form of ode reaches perfection.
From the *Autumn* ode, we take :

Who hath not seen thee oft amid thy store ?
　　Sometimes whoever seeks abroad may find
Thee sitting careless on a granary floor.
　　Thy hair soft-lifted by the winnowing wind;

Or on a half-reap'd furrow sound asleep,
Drowsed with the fume of poppies, while thy hook
    Spares the next swath and all its twinéd flowers :
And sometimes like a gleaner thou dost keep
Steady thy laden head across a brook;
   Or by a cider-press, with patient look,
    Thou watchest the last oozings, hours by hours.

Our Irregular Odes are usually rhymed and are written in stanzas of unequal length. Metre and versification often change abruptly. These odes were written on a mistaken notion of the structure of Pindaric odes and gave place, as Pindar's complicated measures were understood, to odes of the kinds we have already mentioned. In reading Irregular Odes, always watch the metre, since their authors aimed at matching it with their ideas. Thus a change of metre accompanies a change of emotion or thought, however subtle or brief. The greatest skill and beauty is to be found in them. Wordsworth's *Immortality* ode, Matthew Arnold's *Philomela*, and Dryden's *Alexander's Feast* belong to this group. Dryden's ode is probably technically the most perfect.

Soothed with the sound, the King grew vain;
    Fought all his battles o'er again;
And thrice he routed all his foes and thrice he slew the
    slain !
   The master saw the madness rise,
   His glowing cheeks, his ardent eyes;
  And while he Heaven and Earth defied,
  Changed his band and checked his pride.
    He chose a mournful Muse
    Soft pity to infuse :

He sung Darius great and good,
  By too severe a fate,
Fallen, fallen, fallen, fallen,
  Fallen from his high estate,
And weltering in his blood;
Deserted, at his utmost need,
By those his former bounty fed;
On the bare earth exposed he lies
With not a friend to close his eyes.
With downcast looks the joyless victor sate
    Revolving in his alter'd soul
      The various turns of Chance below;
    And now and then a sigh he stole
      And tears began to flow.

(iv) The Sonnet

The unity which marks the lyric necessarily distinguishes its sonnet form. Since the Earl of Surrey published poems of this form, based on the Italian *Sonnetto* of Petrarch, Dante, and Michaelangelo, in Tottel's *Miscellany* (1557), English poets have rejoiced in its fourteen iambic pentameter lines. In its normal form known as Italian, Classical, or Petrarchan, these lines are divided into eight and six (*Octave* and *Sestet*). Between them occurs a change of thought (*Volta* or "turn"). Further, the *Octave* may be divided, in rhyme pattern, into two *Quatrains* and the *Sestet* into two *Tercets*. The *Tercets* may follow one of three rhyme patterns. The *Volta* is of great importance. A quotation of Milton's sonnet *When the Assault was Intended to the City*, accompanied by a diagrammatic note of the form, will illustrate these details. It will be noticed that the *Tercets* follow the second of the rhyme patterns.

OCTAVE	QUATRAIN	a	Captain, or Colonel, or Knight in Arms,
		b	Whose chance on these defenceless doors may seize,
		b	If ever deed of honour did thee please,
		a	Guard them, and him within protect from harms.
	QUATRAIN	a	He can requite thee; for he knows the charms
		b	That call fame on such gentle acts as these,
		b	And he can spread thy name o'er land and seas
		a	Whatever clime the sun's bright circle warms.

Volta

SESTET	TERCET	c	c	c	Lift not thy spear against the Muses' bower:
		d	d	d	The great Emathian conqueror did spare
		e	c	e	The house of Pindarus, when temple and tower
	TERCET	c	d	d	Went to the ground: and the repeated air
		d	c	c	Of sad Electra's poet had the power
		e	d	e	To save the Athenian walls from ruin bare.

After several experiments, Henry Howard, Earl of Surrey, evolved an English form of the sonnet, changing the rhyme scheme and abandoning the division into *Octave* and *Sestet* in favour of three *Quatrains* and a *Couplet*. This form of the English sonnet is usually named after Shakespeare, with whom it reached its most perfect expression. Notice that, although the *Volta* has gone, there is often a slight change of thought between the second and third *Quatrains*, as in this example:

QUATRAIN	A	That time of year thou may'st in me behold
	B	When yellow leaves, or none, or few, do hang
	A	Upon those boughs which shake against the cold—
	B	Bare ruin'd choirs where late the sweet birds sang.
QUATRAIN	C	In me thou see'st the twilight of such day
	D	As after sunset fadeth in the West,
	C	Which by and by black night doth take away,
	D	Death's second self, that seals up all in rest.

QUATRAIN
E In me thou see'st the glowing of such fire
F That on the ashes of his youth doth lie,
E As the death-bed whereon it must expire,
F Consumed with that which it was nourish'd by.

COUPLET
G This thou perceiv'st, which makes thy love more strong,
G To love that well which thou must leave ere long.

This *English* or *Shakespeare* form of sonnet increased the rhymes from five to seven. Spenser introduced a sonnet in which it was reduced to the five of the Classical sonnet; in structure also he returned towards the Classical model, evolving the following type :

QUATRAIN
A Most glorious Lord of Life ! that, on this day,
B Did'st make Thy triumph over death and sin;
A And having harrowed hell, didst bring away
B Captivity thence captive, us to win ;

QUATRAIN
B This joyous day, dear Lord, with joy begin;
C And grant that we, for whom Thou diddest die,
B Being with Thy dear blood clean washed from sin,
C May live for ever in felicity !

QUATRAIN
C And that Thy love we weighing worthily,
D May likewise love Thee for the same again;
C And for Thy sake, that like dear didst buy,
D With love may one another entertain !

COUPLET
E So let us love, dear Love, like as we ought,
E —Love is the lesson which the Lord us taught.

It will be noticed that the rhyme pattern links the *Quatrains* together.

For about a century after Milton's death the sonnet languished, and returned to its former glory with Wordsworth, Keats, Matthew Arnold, and other poets who use it with distinction. Like Wordsworth, they introduced irregularities into both metre and structure, although adhering mostly to the Classical model.

(v) The Elegy

In marked contrast to the clearly defined form of the sonnet is Elegy, which, at least in English poetry, has no prescribed structure. It is a poem of yearning, always plaintive, mourning the loss of someone or something.

Unless this quality of repining is present there is no true elegy. Thus Gray's celebrated *Elegy* is not an elegy at all.

There is no prescribed metre, no fixed length, no required stanza form—nothing but the quality described above, to tell us what poems are truly elegiac in character. Consequently this form of poetry embraces Milton's *Lycidas* and Tennyson's *Break, break, break*. Quotation does not do justice to this beautiful kind of poetry. To sample it, turn to an anthology and read, besides those two poems, Spenser's *Astrophel*, Ben Jonson's *To the Memory of Mr. William Shakespeare*, Cowper's *On the Receipt of My Mother's Picture*, Arnold's *Rugby Chapel*, and *Southern Night*, and *Thyrsis*.

(vi) The Idyll

The meaning of Idyll, " a little picture ", is the best definition of what is essential to the form of poetry bearing that name, for it tells us that it must be short and it must be a picture. This form has neither set structure nor pattern of rhyme. It may be narrative or lyrical or almost anything else, provided that it fits the definition of its name.

The conception of the Idyll formed by poets is that it should represent a scene, a mood, an imagined vision, a landscape, a romance or incident marked by pathos, and that this should be expressed as the poet saw it. That is to say, it should be tinged by some reflection, not necessarily formally stated, of the poet's mind. It should be simple and direct. At the same time, its brevity and simplicity exact every skill of craftsmanship from the author. The Idyll is a small, highly finished form of poetry, a miniature of exquisite workmanship.

For all its apparent formlessness and apparent ease, the Idyll is quickly recognisable, and is also extremely artistic in technique.

The Pastoral Idyll is a convention. From the earliest Latin idylls of Theocritus, there has always been a tendency, arising from the simplicity of the Idyll, to represent the incidents of the poems as belonging to the lives of Shepherds. Marlowe's

> Come live with me and be my love,
> And we will all the pleasures prove
> That hills and valleys, dale and field,
> And all the craggy mountains yield !

is its spirit. It has been a highly suitable form for some of our finest idylls, e.g. Milton's *Lycidas* and *L'Allegro*. Yet there has always been the danger that, in England, this convention might be too artificial. As a result it has, at least for the time being, died out.

The range of the ordinary idyll, its descriptive, romantic, imaginary, real, and meditative " pictures," may be gathered from a selection of titles—Milton's *Il Penseroso*, Dyer's *Grongar Hill*, Marvell's *Emigrants in the Bermudas*, Wordsworth's *Solitary Reaper* and *Ruth*, Coleridge's *Kubla Khan*, Tennyson's *Mariana* and excellent *Dora*, Arnold's *The Forsaken Merman*, Longfellow's *The Village Blacksmith*.

Two notes should be added to this outline of the Idyll.

One is that some poems which appear by their considerable length to be ineligible for inclusion in this form will be found to consist of a series of little pictures, and may therefore be admitted among the shorter idylls.

The other is that Tennyson's *Idylls of the King* are difficult to reconcile with the necessary idea of a " little picture ". On the whole, however, opinion has been in favour of their being admitted as idylls, even if the title must be stretched to cover them. Various reasons can be given for the good sense of this extension. For instance, the poems are essentially simple, dealing with various emotions in their simplest forms. Further, the people in the poems are not real people, nor intended to be so; Sir Galahad is Chastity, Vivien is Wantonness, and King Arthur is only an incarnate Manliness. And the poems are presented as " little pictures ", even if lengthened by descriptive passages. The use of *Idyll* in their title may be exceptional, but it is true enough to be acceptable.

In this chapter we have examined a number of the literary forms we are likely to meet most often in reading poetry and their characteristics, e.g. Romantic, Allegorical, Narrative, Didactic. Our interest has been confined to structure and pattern, since these forms underlie more superficial classifications. They are, moreover, lessons we might not for a long time see unaided, and are therefore worth attention.

Now that we have made ourselves familiar with these forms, let us turn to poetry itself, to the invisible power, the inspiration which uses these forms to raise us to levels of thought and feeling far higher than those of ordinary experience.

Chapter Eight

Reading Poetry

SINCE we have already spent some time in considering the nature of inspiration, we are not now going to ask what we mean by the word poet. Once we understand the main truths about his inspiration, and when we have seen the forms he uses as his patterns, we incline to ask only one other question—exactly what does he do?

Although this question might require a solid volume set in small type by way of answer, only certain pages in it would interest us, for we ask the question only as preliminary to another—how can we get the best out of reading his work?

(i) The Nature of Poetry

With this in mind, then, we may be content with the brief answer Shakespeare gives to our first question:

The lunatic, the lover, and the poet
Are of imagination all compact. . . .
The poet's eye, in a fine frenzy rolling,
Doth glance from heaven to earth, from earth to heaven;
And, as imagination bodies forth
The forms of things unknown, the poet's pen
Turns them to shapes, and gives to airy nothing
A local habitation and a name.

This tells us so much and no more. That is the way with every inquiry into the nature of poetry. Shakespeare or Francis Thompson or Sir Philip Sidney or Shelley or some other great poet begins to tell us what poetry is, and after a while we find that he has stopped short. Shelley says it is the expression of the imagination; Wordsworth defines it as emotion recollected in tranquillity; Matthew Arnold is content to describe it as the most delightful and perfect form of utterance; Edgar Allan Poe calls it the rhythmic creation of beauty. And so it goes on, this list of attempts to tell us what poetry essentially is.

Each attempt is like the kindling of a spark and its sudden extinction. We learn something new about poetry with each statement, and almost immediately perceive that the little illumination has gone again. There is the flicker of eager hope and the darkness of disappointment.

This is because every definition of poetry is an aspect from a different point of view. To try to form an idea of what poetry is by studying definitions is a slow, useful way of becoming familiar with the subject. But it will not give us a direct approach—the sort of approach we want here and now—to the beauty we wish to possess. It is like our being offered fifty snapshots of a vast palace, with its gardens, so that we may understand the whole of its architectural plan and perfection at once. When all our study of poetry is over we realise that we still want to know why a man can write,

Bare, ruin'd choirs where late the sweet birds sang.

or

> A noise like of a hidden brook
>   In the leafy month of June,
> That to the sleeping woods all night
>   Singeth a quiet tune,

or

> The moon shines bright !   In such a night as this,
> When the sweet wind did gently kiss the trees,
> And they did make no noise. . . .

or

> The fair breeze blew, the white foam flew,
>   The furrow followed free;
> We were the first that ever burst
>   Into that silent sea,

or

> While birds of calm sit brooding on the charméd wave,

or

> Three April perfumes have I seen
> In three hot Junes burned,

and can momentarily catch us out of ourselves into a brief ecstasy.   When we read lines such as these we realise that our definitions are all concentrated on the versification of poetry rather than on its source.   The magic of poetry has not been found, and its black letters are spread out on a page for us to see without revealing their secret.   The fierce and happy exultation that is in the quietest of these lines has run away, a mysterious quicksilver that flashed and vanished as we tried to grasp it.

We feel that definitions begin at the wrong end of poetry, as if we would explain a waterfall by painting its spray, or account for a flash of lightning by talking about electricity. As long as we do this sort of thing no one will ever know why falling water is a thing of wonder or a flame of lightning anything more than a possible source of danger.

The only way to get near to the heart of poetry—for we shall never so possess the heart of it as to be able to dissect it—is to find out when a man is a poet and when he is not. For instance, sitting above Tintern Abbey, Wordsworth heard

> the still sad music of humanity,

and, on a less favourable occasion, he wrote :

> Jones ! as from Calais southward you and I . . .

Milton wrote :

> His servants he with new acquist
> Of true experience from this great event
> With peace and consolation hath dismist,
> And calm of mind all passion spent.

He also described a gardening anxiety of Adam and Eve as flat-footedly as possible :

> what we by day
> Lop overgrown, or prune, or prop, or bind,
> One night or two with wanton growth derides,
> Tending to wild.

Here we have instances of poets giving us lines that are intimately effective and lines that, in immediate contrast, cause a revulsion of feeling and an embarrassment as if the writer had done something shameful.

Obviously the man who wrote one line is not the man who wrote the other. The writer of the first was lifted above himself at some time, and either wrote in a mood of exaltation or in its resulting clearness of mind. He was like a man who has dreamed dreams. He was like a lover whose whole being is enraptured by the beloved. He had seen something, understood something, felt something, not normally within his range of experience—that is to say, more accurately, something his normal powers of experience could not reach without stimulation. When he was stimulated, however, he became the man who, according to Shakespeare,

> bodies forth
> The forms of things unknown, the poet's pen
> Turns them to shapes, and gives to airy nothing
> A local habitation and a name.

Once his mind is functioning in its ordinary, uninspired way, he is incapable of writing more than verse, perhaps shockingly bad verse. He uses his accustomed literary form to express factual statements that can scarcely be bodied forth in prose, but require mere writing. Hence his fall into bathos. Where you or I would be content to send a note to a friend, the poet not-at-the-moment poet may write in poetic form, iambic pentameter and sonnet structure automatically included, and write the ill-advised *Jones! as from*

Calais. Presently he falls to musing on certain experiences of childhood; is roused by their recollection; turns over a page or two written several years before and, his spirit radiant with the returning inspiration they restore, picks up his pen, and adds the fifth stanza to his greatest Ode. So it was with Wordsworth, and doubtless with many another.

(ii) The Nature of Inspiration

Now, this fact means one thing which is perfectly in harmony with what we have earlier decided about style and inspiration. This is, that the beginning of the whole matter, both in prose and in poetry, is inspiration. Plato, whose views we followed in Chapter Four, calls it *enthusiasm*, by which he means the access of some emotion or perception so overwhelming as to cause almost madness. The whole of the writer is caught up in this enthusiasm; his faculties are roused to intense activity, so that they seem to act without effort. They even seem to drive him to express what is happening inside.

Thus there can occur a certain inevitability between what is experienced and its expression. In these moments or hours of feverish preoccupation are forged those immortal lines which are the only way a *particular* idea could have been expressed—the lines that haunt us as long as we live. A poet could express himself in that way only; his inspiration gave it to him together with the thing his line " bodies forth ".

This is not to say—for we must keep our feet on the

earth by reminding ourselves of this—that such lines may not be subject to revision. Now and again the perfect line may come in all its perfection. Often it will come rough cast, the material on which the craftsman will later labour, filing and polishing or even remodelling, until he recognises it as the line towards which he had been guided.

The essence, however, is the inspiration, the enthusiasm, the ardour, or whatever else you may choose to name this kindling of the whole man and elevation of his faculties. Here is poetry in itself, and anyone who looks at verse, however perfect, to find poetry in it, or round heaven or earth, will never find it. Poetry is something that happens to a man; *his* poetry is the way he communicates it to us. It is only by looking into him that we can find it.

How do we know this? Because all of us who read are poets in a limited way. The qualities of spirit which enable a poet to be inspired are so far in us as to make us receptive of his poetry and enable us to be inspired by it. To understand poetry we must understand the poet; to know him we must look into ourselves. The world of poetry is in the soul, the spirit, the mind. There we find it and nowhere else. We can say of it what Francis Thompson wrote of the Kingdom of God:

> O world invisible, we view thee,
> O world intangible, we touch thee,
> O world unknowable, we know thee,
> Inapprehensible, we clutch thee!

> Does the fish soar to find the ocean,
> The eagle plunge to find the air—
> That we ask of the stars in motion
> If they have rumour of thee there ?
>
> Not where the wheeling systems darken,
> And our benumb'd conceiving soars !—
> The drift of pinions, would we hearken,
> Beats at our own clay-shuttered doors.
>
> The angels keep their ancient places ;—
> Turn but a stone, and start a wing !
> 'Tis ye, 'tis your estrangèd faces
> That miss the many-splendoured thing.

Now, this theory as to what poetry is does not rest upon conjecture nor only upon the shrewd reasoning of Plato. Remarkably rarely do poets talk about poetry ; when they do, they yet more rarely try to tell us what it is or how it happens. What has always appeared to me to be the clearest description of the genesis of poetry occurs in a poem by Andrew Marvell, *Thoughts in a Garden*. If I may be allowed a personal remark, it is with unusual pleasure that I quote Marvell here, for these pages are being written near the centre of the city which he represented in Parliament and almost in sight of the street in which he was born.

I quote a preliminary stanza, since it helps to make clear his meaning in the opening lines of the second stanza :

> What wondrous life is this I lead !
> Ripe apples drop about my head ;
> The luscious clusters of the vine
> Upon my mouth do crush their wine ;

> The nectarine and curious peach
> Into my hands themselves do reach;
> Stumbling on melons, as I pass
> Ensnared with flowers, I fall on grass.
>
> Meanwhile the mind, from pleasure less,
> Withdraws into its happiness;
> The mind, that Ocean where each kind
> Does straight its own resemblance find;
> Yet it creates, transcending these,
> Far other worlds, and other seas;
> Annihilating all that's made
> To a green thought in a green shade.

No mystic ever made a more determined attempt to describe his spiritual experience than Marvell here makes to tell us what poetry, in itself rather than in its expression, really is. And his final line, at once mysterious and revealing, surely means that his mind conceives that which it has perceived—that which, by its nature, it has been fitted to conceive from the world without and re-create in a new form.

The Puritan poet now gives a simile Biblical in its simplicity and beauty, expressing the poet's delight in poetry when it comes to him.

> Here at the fountain's sliding foot,
> Or at some fruit-tree's mossy root,
> Casting the body's vest aside,
> My soul into the boughs does glide;
> There, like a bird it sits and sings,
> Then whets and combs its silver wings,
> And, till prepared for longer flight,
> Waves in its plumes the various light.

Poetry is the enthusiasm which descends on a poet, takes possession of him, and compels him to the activity of writing. I suggest that our first test of poetry should be whether it contains this unmistakable inspiration. If it does, it is poetry of a high order. It is this quality of ardour to follow what has been seen—an ardour so compelling as to supply its own motion to the faculties—which makes the poetry of

> One impulse from a vernal wood
> May teach you more of man;
> Of moral evil and of good,
> Than all the sages can,

and

> They shall not grow old as we that are left grow old;
> Age shall not weary them nor the years condemn;
> At the going down of the sun and in the morning
> We will remember them.

(iii) The Test of Inspiration

There is no need to labour the point, especially as our answer to our first question—what is poetry?—has quickly brought a further question. We see it as soon as we apply our answer to any of these quotations from Pope and Prior:

> His garden next your admiration all
> On every side you look, behold the wall.
> No pleasing intricacies intervene,
> No artful wildness to perplex the scene;
> Grove nods at grove, each alley has a brother,
> And half the platform just reflects the other.

> When I am weary with wandering all day,
>   To thee, my delight, in the evening I come;
> No matter what beauties I saw in my way.
>   They were but my visits, but thou art my home.

There is no marked enthusiasm here. What we find is considerable skill in versification by which a real thought or a mild emotion is pleasingly conveyed to us. And of this art and craft there is an abundance in English literature. The more finished the poetic form, as a rule, the less the degree of enthusiasm observable. Pope has a quite breath-taking acuteness of thought and cleverness to express in

> Damn with faint praise, assent with civil leer,
> And, without sneering, teach the rest to sneer;
> Willing to wound and yet afraid to strike,
> Just hint a fault, and hesitate dislike.

It would be difficult to write that as effectively in prose. Metrical expression makes words more penetrating, which is one reason why it is the natural vehicle for conveying things as personal as emotions or imaginations when they are intense or highly wrought. Yet suppose we have a perfectly suitable metrical arrangement accompanying a perfect choice of words —are we to say it is not poetry because it is " uninspired " ? Are we to say that we find poetry in the first stanza of Gray's *Elegy*,

> The curfew tolls the knell of parting day,
>   The lowing herd wind slowly o'er the lea,
> The ploughman homeward plods his weary way,
>   And leaves the world to darkness, and to me.

because it contains this curious quality of the inspired statement of an emotion, and deny it to the last stanza,

No farther seek his merits to disclose,
  Or draw his frailties from their dread abode,
(There they alike in trembling hope repose),
  The bosom of his Father and his God.

because the verse contains nothing but a stale platitude ?

There cannot be any doubt that we must give an unqualified " Yes " to both questions. If we have been accustomed to regard poetry as the expression of ideas in verse, this answer will be surprising and almost shocking.   Before deciding that a conclusion so profane must indicate that our argument has taken a wrong turn somewhere, let us examine this passage by Crabbe (Horace Smith's " A Pope in worsted stockings ") and one of the most lovable of our writers :

The few dull flowers that o'er the place are spread
Partake the nature of their fenny bed;
High on its wiry stem, in rigid bloom,
Grows the salt lavender that lacks perfume;
Here the dwarf sallows creep, the septfoil harsh,
And the soft shiny mallow of the marsh;
Low on the ear the distant billows sound,
And just in view appears their stony bound;
No hedge nor tree conceals the glowing sun;
Birds, save a watr'y tribe, the district shun,
Nor chirp among the reeds where bitter waters run . . .

What is wrong here ?   It would be foolish to say that Crabbe was uninspired.   It would be truer to say that, where Nature is concerned, he is more genuinely inspired than Pope and, where human sympathy with men and women is concerned, he has a passion Pope never felt.   Yet we acclaim Pope and smile at Crabbe. Why is this ?

Quotations may aid us in answering this.   Let us take one of the simplest, from Francis Thompson.

> Where the thistle lifts a purple crown
>   Six foot out of the turf,
> And the harebell shakes on the windy heath—
>   O the breath of the distant surf !—
>
> The hills look over on the South,
>   And southward dreams the sea ;
> And, with the sea-breeze hand in hand,
>   Come innocence and she.

Here the description is far less than in the passage from Crabbe and, although it is intended to be no more than incidental as an introduction to a poem about a girl, it is far more effective than Crabbe's.   Apart from an evocativeness we can ignore for the present, the lines appear to us to be the joyful cry of a man immediately responding to a sudden inrush, through his senses, of the colour and smell and life of the Downs.   They are, that is, the cry of a man lifted out of himself, a man inspired.   And this inspiration they pass on to us.   They are poetry.

Unfortunately, Crabbe was, like many others, incapable of inspiration of the kind and degree that makes poetry.   His powers of perception may have been greater than those of Francis Thompson ; his feelings may have been deeper and more passionate than those of Pope.   One gift was fatally lacking— the mysterious quality by which a man can be kindled by inspiration.   That Crabbe was inspired is evident. Because he was inspired he glowed, he smouldered ;

unhappily, at times he smoked a good deal. All too rarely he burst into the sudden illumination, the burning, flickering fire that gave us

> Rough winds do shake the darling buds of May.

In Crabbe is the power to see and to be moved; not the power to see an instant's significance and catch the flame of poetry as it flashed in him. Only when a man has the gift, although transiently yet reliably, to experience this change from the normal and to be able to cause something similar to it in us, has he poetry. There was poetry when a man looked at the soundless heave of the sea in a bay and wrote :

> Where the green swell is in the havens dumb,
> And out of the swing of the sea.

We must come to the conclusion that much "poetry" is verse. That it attracts us, that it has admirable technical perfection, that we are in many ways better for our acquaintance with it—these facts do not make it poetry. We have used the name Pope in connection with this distinction between poetry and verse because his lines often give us great pleasure, through the excellent delicacy and sureness of his choice of words and the polished finish of his metre. His craftsmanship is such that we are often unable to see, unless we keep the point in mind, that he is writing marvellously artistic verse, and not inspired poetry. He does in verse what Bacon does in prose. He gives us a wonderful shell to hold to the ear, a shell which is involute and iridescent. We turn it over and over in our hands, admiring its exquisite beauty. Only if we remember to raise it to our ears do we notice that it is silent.

Our first test of poetry, then, is to see whether it has genuine inspiration, and as our perception is increased by the reading of poetry the test becomes easier to apply. As we grow accustomed to the sometimes thin and heady air of the world of poetry, we are the more able to perceive whether what we read gives us what Matthew Arnold called " a wonderfully full, new, and intimate sense " of whatever poetry deals with, so that we feel we have a new relationship with its subjects. A poet cannot give us this sense of a new personal attachment to something unless he has a unique relationship to it himself and the ability to pass it on to us. If he is gifted in these ways, what he writes will unmistakably be, by the test outlined, poetry.

For poetry appeals primarily to the emotions and the imagination. It may tell us certain things which we did not previously know. The point is that its first purpose is not to teach, but to inspire, to pass on " enthusiasm ", to reveal things to us in such a way that they will possess us.

Another way of saying this is to say that poetry has a quality to evoke, as we mentioned in connection with an illustration a few pages back. It is able to awaken in us instincts and emotions and imaginative perceptions which, apart from the inspiration of poetry, rarely come to us. We are aware of excitement within us, and of a sudden and great increase in what C. E. Montague calls "penetrative sympathy", as if what we are reading brings us nearer to the nature of things. Beyond this we find in ourselves an experience remarkably difficult to define. Sometimes on waking we recall fragments of a dream, and accompanying the memory of them is a vivid sense that, if we had dreamt on, some marvellously beautiful and wholly satisfying thing would have happened to us : something understood, some great truth seen whose apprehension would have made life altogether happier, or some event would have occurred almost ecstatic in its power to make every fibre of our being radiantly and finally joyful. Occasionally we have a similar experience in our waking hours—short periods of such earnest and confident longing that we want to say, " Something wonderful has just got to happen today ".

At rare intervals the vast waters of the deep within us stir mysteriously, as if restless for the glitter of the moon and the stars on their dark surface. For many people these are wholly inexplicable experiences which they attribute variously to the weather, the Spring, the new doctor, or a glass of whisky.

To go into any detailed explanation of them would lead us into two fields, one psychological and the other theological. This we cannot do, nor is it of particular use to our present purpose that we should. Man is, ultimately, a pilgrim to ecstasy, and we can find no really conclusive reason for many of his virtues and vices unless we recognise that fact. He may accept heroic self-denial in order to gain the final possession of the beatitude in which he believes. On the other hand, he may follow some noble or some ignoble means of trying to find, here and now, such measure of it as is obtainable through material pleasures. If we see that, a great deal of the sickening disgust we feel for certain evil things—evil in the sense that they are the opposite to real or good—drains away, for we see these things for the mere deformities, distortions, or mistakes that they are.

Within us is an abyss that calls to an abyss. Sometimes we are aware, in the form of an aching, longing happiness, that it is there. As to why it is there we need say no more than we have just said; as to how it calls we may say nothing without wandering too far. It is important only that we should realise that it is there—this Ocean of Andrew Marvell's poem, this counterpart of some external reality which we need.

The need is complex : its forms are numerous; here we can satisfy now one, now another. There is our hunger for what is beautiful, our need for knowledge of some ultimate good, which we call the thirst for true knowledge and wisdom. And there is our great need of love. There is our need to give love, too. If we go no farther than these, we can see how immeasurably powerful our wants are, the more powerful because they cry for abstract things—not this rose nor that idea nor these eyes, but for what those things give us. Thus we find ourselves looking for the material things, because their immediate gift is some alleviation of our need, and more necessarily for the immaterial things that are shut up in them.

This complex need the poet, who is inspired because he can give voice to the same want and conjure up some of the things by which it can be partly satisfied, can awaken to life. And its very stirring, the renewal of the old call of nature, is itself pleasurable, since it evokes from ourselves and our experience accompanying thoughts of what we desire.

Here is a test of verse. If a poet can effect this change in us, he writes poetry, since he cannot do so unless his verse contains what we have called enthusiasm or inspiration. We know his verse is poetry because we detect, through its effect on us, that it is written by one of whom Mangan wrote:

> Tell thou the world, when my bones lie whitening
>   Amid the last homes of youth and eld,
> That once there was one whose veins ran lightning
>   No eye beheld.

Or, as Coleridge expresses it, indicating a cause rather than an effect:

> For he on honey-dew hath fed,
> And drunk the milk of Paradise.

If you are so far unfamiliar with poems other than those usually studied in every school, what has been written here about real poetry might mislead you into thinking that it is easily recognisable. The fact is that poetry is rarely distinguishable from verse at a glance or even at one reading. For instance,

> For when thy folding-star arising shows
> His paley circlet, at his warning lamp
>   The fragrant Hours, and Elves
>   Who slept in buds the day,
>
> And many a Nymph who wreathes her brows with
>   sedge
> And sheds the freshening dew, and lovelier still
>   The pensive Pleasures sweet,
>   Prepare thy shadowy car . . .

from Collins's *To Evening* may appear attractive in many ways, but not to be inspired. Perhaps its semi-classical allusions hold it remotely from you; the atmosphere of its century may make it slightly unreal. Yet it is from a poem assuredly to be ranked among the best work of a poet whom all discriminating readers judge to be a poet in the best sense of the title. No doubt if you were to read the whole poem your first impression might be less definitely in favour of the view that it is made up of highly finished verse rather than poetry. On the other hand, it is at least probable that your opinion would remain unchanged.

The example serves to mark a warning that inspiration is not always as easy to see as it was in the quotations given earlier in this chapter. They were mostly distinguished by high emotional tension or irresistible appeal to the imagination. More often the inspiration of a poet is not found at the white heat in which immortal lines are forged, but in its later glow and warmth, in which poetry flows rather than jets out self-formed. This quieter poetry will not force itself upon you. It presents itself quietly, perhaps in a manner deliberately chosen for its restraint. Before this chapter closes we shall consider how we may read it to our best advantage. At present it is enough for us to realise that inspiration is by no means always to be associated with impact or haunting images or exceptionally melodious verse.

Before we can go on to deal with the second question with which this chapter opened—as to how we may most profitably read poetry—we must delay to minimise an exaggeration, possibly a deception, which you have no doubt already questioned in your own mind.

In making a distinction clear it is useful to exaggerate the contrast between its alternatives. A difference may be confusing if it is a matter of inches; there can be no confusion between a giant and a dwarf.

For this purpose I have deliberately minimised the importance of what I have too lightly called verse. I have suggested that unless verse is evidently charged with " enthusiasm ", it is verse and nothing more. And now this mis-statement must be corrected.

We do not make this change by denying the validity of what has been said, about inspiration being the certain division between verse and poetry, for it is true. What must be adjusted is the impression that much of the verse which attracts us is not poetry. No doubt you queried that in your own mind. Perhaps you re-read some favourite poems, and then doubted still more what you had read in this chapter.

You doubted it because you found that the verse you read was moving as well as in various ways attractive. For instance,

> The poplars are fell'd; farewell to the shade
> And the whispering sound of the cool colonnade;
> The winds play no longer and sing in the leaves,
> Nor Ouse on his bosom their image receives.

These lines of Cowper's are sweet and pleasant. They skilfully suggest the whispering of the wind in the tall, rustling poplars. Much more mysteriously they somehow convey an impression of sunlight spreading thinly over the field, the trees, and the river. Perhaps they do this by a pattern of thin vowel sounds interwoven with the open sounds. Or perhaps they do so because they paint such a scene as we respond to by adding the cool, bright sunshine for ourselves— they evoke this reaction from us.

However this may be, they are unmistakably fine verse, and you may instinctively feel that the poem from which they are taken is really poetry.

In this you are certainly right, although there is nothing turbulent or compelling in the gentle lines. They do not reveal any vision, stir any high or intimate emotion, nor fill us with a sense of " heaped-up anguish and despair ". Equally certainly the poem does move us. It is not a merely mechanical exercise in metrical composition nor is it only the expression

of a thought in perfectly finished verse, as much of
Pope's work is found to be. The poem is the expression of regret, of a mild and bearable sorrow, seen
through the after-glow of much happiness Cowper
had enjoyed in that poplar field by the quietly flowing
Ouse. It arose from an emotion, and is so written
as to play on our imagination and emotion, too. It
gives us a share in Cowper's happiness and wins our
sympathetic communion in the loss of the beauty which
gave it to him. It does this by words in a metrical
arrangement. That is to say, it fulfils our idea of
poetry.

I would say the same, less certainly, about the
opening lines of Cowper's fifth book of *The Task*.

> 'Tis morning; and the sun with ruddy orb
> Ascending fires the horizon; while the clouds
> That crowd away before the driving wind,
> More ardent as the disc emerges more,
> Resemble most some city in a blaze,
> Seen through the leafless wood. . . .

Here the appeal to the imagination is upset by a
convention of language to which we are now unaccustomed, so that the phrases appear more artificial
than they actually are. Moreover, the emotional
content of the lines has nothing compelling about it;
if we read hastily we may miss it. Nevertheless, the
fiery splendour and loveliness of the morning scene
come to us clearly enough to stir our sensibility and
rouse our imagination, so that this tiny fragment is
poetry. It is as poetic as the more immediately

identifiable tossing plumes of perfumed lilac, of Coventry Patmore, or Wordsworth's daffodils that fringed the wooded lake, fluttering and dancing in the breeze.

To have a true idea of poetry we must recognise not only the work of the masters at their best, but also the less exciting and overwhelming stanzas which they and many others use to give us part in their perception of that other world strangely compact of eternity and ourselves. We may not, since to do so would be to distort the fact, reserve the name of poetry for the resounding line, the emotion that scorches like lava, the image that haunts the senses and the inward eye. We must see that poetry covers all metrical expression of what succeeds in drawing readers out of their everyday habit of mind to where there is purified experience which it helps us to share.

Fortunately, and naturally, there is good company and gaiety there, for the times when we need it, perhaps in the company of Burns or, to stick to Cowper, in the company of certain immortals who give us the laughter that is one of the most amazing gifts of man.

> John Gilpin was a citizen
>   Of credit and renown.
> A train-band captain eke was he
>   Of famous London town.

That, I suggest, opens an excellent poem. If it does not, comedy can have no place in literature, and literature must be limited to writings that appeal only to certain of the qualities that make us little less than the angels. If ever we come to that conclusion we must close our library doors and go out into the world to find some material thing that, from one year's end to the other, is better than literature.

(iv) Appreciative Reading

Now that we have our idea of poetry, we must deal with our second question—how are we to read so that we may gain the utmost benefit from this wonderful art? The question arises because the least experience of poetry reading shows us that we cannot pick up a book of verse and draw from it all that it contains.

One reason why we cannot do this is that we must be able to distinguish between poetry and the skilled verse of which our poetry books contain a great amount. Indeed, it would be surprising if they did not, for no writer of any considerable body of verse can sustain unending or uninterrupted poetry. It must inevitably be that some poets are never more than versifiers, while others rise from and fall to a generally held level, while a few are more at home in the world of poetry than out of it, giving us almost always rich gifts exquisitely wrought.

How, then, are we to dispose ourselves so as to receive these gifts, to know where to find them?

(a) *Critical Knowledge*

Obviously anyone who reads poetry as anything more than an occasional pastime must acquire some knowledge about its source, its forms, and technique. This book aims at supplying readers with adequate knowledge for their first travels in what are sometimes irritatingly called " realms of poesy ". When any-one who has thus equipped himself has made his explorations and formed his own tentative opinions, he will want to learn more. No doubt he will wish to know more about certain poets or forms of poetry; he may want to accompany a poet in a poet's examina-tion of poetry, as he may do by reading some of Edith Sitwell's anthologies; he may wish to become more familiar, under specialised tuition, with metre or diction. There are many paths he can follow, for there is always more to be learnt and revised as the mind's capacity to receive poetry increases. That is all in the future. At present we may be content that we have substantially met the first contribution the ex-perience of poetry requires.

(b) *Method*

Then there is the need for methodical reading. This does not mean an hour a day with the Carolines until they have been faithfully and perhaps wearily read, nor an evening a week with Shakespeare until Tragedies, Comedies, and Histories have been painstakingly plodded through. It means something half-way be-tween that extreme and the other extreme of anthology dipping. The first deadens the mind; the second dissipates it.

Under this heading one can give only general advice

on the assumption that the reader has so far no formed taste, at least no taste sufficiently developed as to be a reliable guide through a course of reading.

For such readers the best course to follow is first to allow yourselves a certain amount of rambling about. From this your inclinations will become apparent. Perhaps Rupert Brooke will appear wholly delightful and John Donne mainly formidable; you will enjoy Blake's *Songs of Innocence* and be seriously perturbed by his prophetic poems. Well, you have made a beginning.

It might be a good thing to find out something about Rupert Brooke's life and about what other people think of his poetry. And before that line of inquiry absorbs you too fully, there is some investigation to be made into what sort of a man Blake was and what was going on in the amazing mind his poetry reveals.

Your interest in literature is widening. In one of the biographies or books of literary criticism you refer to, there will be references to other poets in some ways similar to those in whom you are immediately interested. This is a further step, to be taken at your leisure. And you know that, whatever your own reaction to a poem may be or whatever others may tell you about it, you are never supposed to like it or admire it or disregard it. You are free to do any of these things, but there is no *must* about it. One of the minor pleasures of reading is pushing a book away and thinking, " Well, I still can't see why that's so specially good.

I'll come back to it some day. . . ." Some day you find another pleasure in reading—the pleasure of a discerning and a pensive self-examination as to why you once doubted that this book has riches.

Any more exact rule as to how you should organise your reading would be rash. A suggestion, together with the advice that you should read methodically, is sufficient to preserve you from the wasting delights of too constant rambling. If you do not follow the way pointed out you will find another, possibly one more personally suitable.

These two ideas—that reading poetry should be accompanied by knowledge and method—seem to me to be two of the three important guides to intelligent poetry reading. The third but not least in importance is that we should, in our reading and in our whole conception of poetry, leave ourselves as open as possible to influence.

(c) *Response to Poetry*

Poetry is meant to work upon us. It is intended to enter us through our feelings, to dwell in our imagination, to work upon our highest aspirations. Furthermore, it is used by poets to convey to us complications of response, not single or necessarily simple emotional designs. The force of "enthusiasm" is converted into a constructive power whose finished work we are to receive. And we can receive it only if we are completely passive to its influences. We must not at first offer it an intent scrutiny, for our very effort may distract us from the refinements—we may not see the wood for the trees. Rather we should try to read easily, quietly, without anxiety or impatience. Do not try to see what you are told to see or be worried because your reaction is not what some eminent critic says it should be. Critics are shocking people, usually because they are rather higher up the road, and occasionally because they are the self-confident people who have done no more than set foot on the road and taken a searching glance along it. On the whole, they do a good work for us readers, and not one of them, if he is a sane, honest critic, would try to make us see things his way.

Whether you know what other readers have found in poetry or not, come fresh to your reading, without any particular mood and without intellectual blinkers. Art is a highly personal affair. If you want to know what a poet is doing, leave yourself entirely in his hands. You are his instrument; his verses are the means by which he plays on it. Perhaps there will be, for a short time or a long time, some ill adjustment between them and you. The remedy for that is patience and a willingness to re-read what you believe to be worth reading once. Sooner or later you will know why the poet wrote; you will realise what he tried to do; you will respond either wholly or in part to his work, or you will at least know what responses he expected to cause in you. Then you may move in judgment. Before then your humility must equal the humility of all great artists, arising from the recognition of something in their art that is greater than they.

Other rules for reading you will formulate for yourself according to your needs and opportunities. Some of them will be important, although none will be as essential to poetry reading as this principle of leaving yourself open to the work poetry has to do. Perhaps one ought to suggest that you should not plan your reading on too narrow a scale. Do not, for instance, sketch out a course of reading which will cover most of English literature by assuming that you will ever read all of it. It is quite possible to read, as a matter of bulk, all the important poetry it contains, but you cannot read it all in the sense of exhausting it.

Poetry is as inexhaustible as the mind of man from which it comes. It will always have more to give you as your familiarity with it increases. It will draw you past its symbols and conventions and periods of time, so that your spirit approaches closer communion with the aspirations and joys and sorrows and questionings which have stirred the soul of man, and have been resolved into poetic expression, for a thousand years.

You must plan generously, so that you may enter into the vastness of your heritage and into its depth—into the inner place which is the soul of the poet, so that you may share in the things even he finds difficult to give. For in the centre of poetry there is an ultimate something we cannot grasp, and may not even suspect to exist, unless we come to it through the minds of others. Is it a perfection—some absolute and final perception, of which in this life we can obtain only rare glimpses?

Whatever it is, it is there. It is your goal, lying at the end of various paths opening before you. It is the thing poets themselves seek, as Francis Thompson said, with silent lips and climbing feet. Shelley wrote of it, too, in the second line of

> The desire of the moth for the star;
> Of the night for the morrow:
> The devotion to something afar
> From the sphere of our sorrow.

And Marlowe wrote, in *Tamburlaine*,

> If all the pens that ever poets held
> Had fed the feeling of their masters' thoughts,
> And every sweetness that inspired their hearts,
> Their minds and muses on admired themes;
> If all the heavenly quintessence they still
> From their immortal flowers of poesy,
> Wherein, as in a mirror, we perceive
> The highest reaches of a human wit;
> If these had made one poem's period,
> And all combined in beauty's worthiness,
> Yet should there hover in their restless heads
> One thought, one grace, one wonder, at the least,
> Which into words no virtue can digest.

There it is objectively stated. We have already seen it subjectively stated, from the experience of the poet himself, in the earlier quotation from Andrew Marvell. Here it is again, the goal, the nearest possible approach to what Thompson says lies beyond the fosse of death, the source of poetic inspiration, caught into words by Gerard Manley Hopkins :

> Elected Silence, sing to me
> And beat upon my whorlèd ear,
> Pipe me to pastures still and be
> The music that I care to hear.
>
> Shape nothing, lips; be lovely—dumb :
> It is the shut, the curfew sent
> From there where all surrenders come
> Which only makes you eloquent.

For the end of the highest poetry is perception and contemplation. The object and the nature of that contemplation you, in the company of poets, are to discover for yourself.

Chapter Nine

Prose Structure

THE pleasure of reading prose is considerably increased
if we observe the author's handling of his material.
As an introduction to the appreciation of literature,
this book would be remarkably incomplete without
notes on the structure of prose similar to those given,
necessarily in greater detail, about the structure of verse.
This necessary minimum is given here, and it excludes
quite important considerations, such as choice of
words, because they are fully dealt with in many other
books.

We take for granted your ability to notice an
author's skill in selecting the word which will express
both his meaning and the background he wishes to
provide for it; his economy in the use of words; his
preference for the clear word and avoidance of phrases
which are smudgy, such as *nice view*, *good soup*, *quaint
walk*, *marvellous car*.

Instead of reviewing any large number of the factors
which are included in sound prose, we may best use
the space available by reminding ourselves of the way
in which such prose is constructed.

We shall be better able to judge the excellence of a
prose writer if we have clearly in mind the principles of

writing, since writing cannot be effective unless it is ordered towards its author's immediate purpose. He must order his words into a sentence which will adequately contain and deliver all he places in it for the reader's benefit. The sentence is the unit of prose by which meaning is wholly and intelligibly written.

(i) Sentence Structure

Consequently every well-ordered sentence must be constructed so that it has unity, coherence, and emphasis.

Unity means that a sentence contains only one main thought. It is present in

> "The common people of England first showed their power in the Revolt of 1381, coming together for one purpose, acting with discipline, and giving resolute support to their chosen leader, Wat Tyler."

This unity is destroyed if you add to it the clause *whose murder filled them with dismay*, since this idea is not indicative of the power the sentence purposes to describe. Unity will be impaired if a sentence is continued beyond its natural close, as in the example given, or if its theme is changed, as in

> "The wreck of the ship caused me to be marooned on an island, alone and ill, where I could hope to speak to none, and eat nothing except the nuts that grew on the palm trees whose grace and slender strength pleased me."

It will also be destroyed if the sentence has too many parentheses, as in:

> " John said to his brother, who was his junior and he resented the fact, that he would in future manage his own affairs."

You will notice that not only does the second parenthesis destroy the unity of the sentence but it also makes the obvious meaning clash with the grammatical meaning—which brother does *he resented* actually indicate ?

Coherence means only—it is a great only—that parts of a sentence should be arranged in logical order. Apparently simple, this principle is often frustrated through some violation of syntax, the separation of words which should have been close to each other, or want of balance. When this happens the sentence is found to be wanting in clearness of reference, as in each sentence of :

> " Boiled cows' milk is a safe food. To cool it, pour it into a saucepan and put it on a floor, preferably of stone. I have rarely drunk it, as I often do in summer, without pleasure."

Emphasis is necessary so that a sentence may secure its full effect. The best means of securing it is to place the important part of the sentence at the beginning (*Great is Diana of the Ephesians*) or at the end (*The wages of sin is death*). Sometimes the effect may be secured by dividing the emphasis between both ends of the sentence (*Home they brought her hero dead*).

Every sentence must be written according to the requirements of those three principles, which you will find elaborated in any book on English syntax. There you will be able to see the rules by which words are arranged to secure the greatest clearness of meaning— e.g. rule of proximity.   Our concern is with principles and forms rather than with grammar or syntax, so we go on to a brief revision of the kinds of sentence at an author's command.

(ii) Kinds of Sentence

The simplest and most natural is the Loose Sentence, since it closely resembles conversation.   It is particularly suitable to narrative writing.   There is no suspense secured by special arrangement.

> "The next morning we left the inn at the first light of the sun, determined to have a whole day in the open."

By contrast the Periodic Sentence withholds its most important statement until suspense has been built up to secure effect for it.   The meaning is not complete until the grammatical structure is also complete.

> "At the first light of the sun, determined to have a whole day in the open, we left the inn."

Each of these forms has its advantages, according to the writer's purpose.   Each also has its dangers—the Loose Sentence can become slipshod and the Periodic may easily be artificial.   If prose is to be fresh and interesting, each form requires considerable skill.

The Balanced Sentence is best defined as one in

which parts similar in thought are also similar in structure. Macaulay provides examples almost too balanced for complete success, as in

> "The work which had been begun by Henry, the murderer of his wives, was continued by Somerset, the murderer of his brother, and completed by Elizabeth, the murderer of her guest."

Whether using the simplest statement as a sentence or piling up clause on clause, phrase on phrase, in periodic solemnity, or balancing his sentence's components, the prose writer uses the short or long sentence according to his requirements. If he wishes to stab home his ideas in quick thrusts or to heighten his effect by antithesis, he uses short sentences; if he wishes to produce suspense and a cumulative effect, he uses long sentences.

(iii) Writing and Prose

To conclude from this that prose writing is artificial —a mere selection of means to secure the end of the moment—is to misunderstand the use of both structure and form. Prose may be technically more complicated than verse; it is often a medium for less exalted or volatile thoughts than those which elevate verse to poetry. Nonetheless, it is by no means mechanical. A writer uses staccato sentences because what he has to say impels him to their use, or he builds up sentences half a page in length because his instinct, as well as his literary technique, tells him that only by a cumulative sentence can the whole aspect of his thought be satisfactorily presented.   Prose is as inspired as poetry, and its methods are selected under the guidance of inspiration in the first instance and of technical knowledge in the second.

This point must be understood.   Just as there is verse and poetry—a distinction we all realise immediately—there is also writing and prose. Unfortunately the term prose is generally used to cover any writing which is incapable of metrical division or at least of a regular rhythmic division.   The distinction between *English writing* and *English prose* is blurred in our minds, although in fact it is sharply defined.

The writing of English means the expression of ideas in non-metrical language which is grammatically and syntactically correct.   English *prose* means the arrangement of the *writing* by such technical means as will convey to a reader not only an idea with its imaginative or emotional accompaniment, but will do this as its author wishes.   In other words, by the principles of prose mere writing is elevated to an art.

This cannot be done unless a writer is inspired. His inspiration is of the same nature as a poet's.   The style of prose, like that of poetry, is essentially spontaneous, the outcome of constructive power flowing from " enthusiasm ".   Only the fact that, at its highest pitch of intensity, prose appears more deliberate than poetry at the same level leads to the general assumption that prose is a less inspired art than poetry.

(iv) Paragraph Structure

With this in mind, we leave the basic unit of prose structure, the sentence, and consider its only other unit, the paragraph. Its structure may be remarkably variable, from the brief statements of Bacon to the massive architecture which Thackeray sometimes shows in sentence and paragraph alike. Underneath its variety, however, are discernible the unchanging principles which govern the sentence, Unity, Coherence, and Emphasis.

In the paragraph Unity requires that there shall be only one main theme and one main idea. This idea is usually placed, in the Topic Sentence, either at the beginning or end of the paragraph. At the beginning, it allows the reader to grasp it and relate the rest of the paragraph to it. At the end, it comes after suspense of some kind. Every thought in the paragraph must develop this main idea and every significance shown must be in keeping with its theme as they appear in the Topic Sentence.

> "Michael died, after a lingering illness, alone and in poverty. He had for many weeks endured slowly increasing pain and there had been no one to advise him of its grave import. For several months he had been in need of skilled medical aid and nursing, during which time his dwindling resources had compelled him to most strenuous efforts to earn his livelihood."

Here we see the relation of idea and theme as both are developed from the Topic Sentence with which the paragraph opens.

Coherence means, as in the case of a sentence, that every part of a paragraph must lead on to the next in such a way that the relationship between the parts, as well as between them and the topic sentence, shall be clear. Sometimes called the Principle of Explicit Reference, Coherence may be secured by various methods, such as inversion, repetition, or a suitable use of conjunctions, adverbs, or relative pronouns. Notice not only the unity of the example given from Dr. Johnson's *Life of Joseph Addison* but how easily the sentences cohere to each other and to the opening sentence.

> " The necessity of complying with the times, and of sparing persons, is the greatest impediment of biography. History may be formed from permanent monuments and records; but lives can only be written from personal knowledge, which is growing every day less, and in a short time is lost for ever. What is known can seldom be immediately told; and when it might be told, it is no longer known. The delicate features of the mind, the nice discriminations of character, and the minute peculiarities of conduct, are soon obliterated : and it is surely better that caprice, obstinacy, frolic and folly, however they might delight in the description, should be silently forgotten, than that, by wanton merriment and unreasonable detection, a pang should be given to a widow, a daughter, a brother or a friend. As the process of these narratives is now bringing me among my contemporaries, I begin to feel myself ' walking upon ashes under which the fire is not extinguished ', and coming to the time of which it will be proper rather to say ' nothing that is false, than all that is true '."

In that quotation you will no doubt have observed

the principle of Emphasis also at work.   Since Unity is often made to centre round the placing of a Topic Sentence in one or other of the more emphatic parts of a paragraph—the beginning and the end—it may be assumed that it is scarcely to be distinguished from Emphasis.

This is not so, for, as in the last example, emphasis may rightly be placed not on the main idea but on one connected with it.   In the example given, Johnson states a fact in the first sentence and quietly stresses an application of it in the last.   It is highly suitable that he should have done this in a passage relating to Addison, whose prose is remarkable for the subtlety of its emphasis.   Addison is constantly ending his sentences and paragraphs with apparently trivial detail. Yet it is by these apparent irrelevances that whole characters are drawn with delicious humour and innuendo.   Waiting upon a lady early one morning, he is asked to pass the time in her library :

> " The very sound of a lady's library gave me a great curiosity to see it; and, as it was some time before the lady came to me, I had an opportunity of turning over a great many of her books, which were ranged together in a very beautiful order."

The main idea is the lady's collection of books, but the detail seemingly thrown in at the end gives us the tiniest suggestion that the lady enjoys the appearance of the books more than their contents.

> " At the end of the folios (which were finely bound and gilt) were great jars of china placed one above the other

in a very noble piece of architecture. The quartos
were separated from the octavos by a pile of smaller
vessels which rose in a delightful pyramid."

So the passage goes on, describing the books but,
stroke by stroke carefully placed, leading us to its
final sentence :

> " I was wonderfully pleased with such a mixed kind of
> furniture as seemed very suitable both to the lady and
> the scholar, and did not know at first whether I should
> fancy myself in a grotto or a library."

Notice how undue emphasis on the point of the whole
passage is avoided by the last five words, which a less
sensitive writer might have presented as " a library or
a grotto ", thereby making his emphasis finally thump
home the point, instead of insinuating it with the quiet
skill which makes the whole passage eminently
successful prose.

In dealing with Emphasis, the structure known as
Parallel Construction must be mentioned. It does not
necessarily secure Emphasis nor should it be confused
with it, since its purpose is to give a passage force and
lucidity. Parallel Construction is the method by
which successive sentences which repeat the same line
of thought should be similar in construction. For
example :

> " The wind rose in the night and howled wildly. It
> sent great trees crashing in the park where it did great
> havoc in the darkness. It flung the clouds by in ragged
> masses as the sun rose. It raised up and hurled down
> mighty masses of water onto the beach as the first
> anxious hours of day passed. It nothing abated but

grew even more furious and dangerous about the hour of noon."

The balanced sentence is a manner of writing : Parallel Construction is a device used in occasional passages. Here it is evident that the construction increases not only the emphasis of the paragraph, but also its unity and coherence.

A fact also evident is that, if sentences or paragraphs are modelled rigidly according to any few forms, they will ruin any writing by making it stiff and monotonous, robbing it entirely of the cadence of free rhythms essential to prose. Variety of structure in both sentence and paragraph is required by the artistry of good writing. Sentences should be varied in construction and length : paragraphs should be built up according to plans in keeping with their purposes : in both, the three principles we have reviewed should always be observed.

Beyond this point it is useless to look for literary style, for, as Addison remarks, you cannot go beyond the paragraph. It is the final unit of construction, and nothing remains beyond it except that paragraph should be joined to paragraph by explicit links. Inexperienced or careless writers often overlook the fact that connections cannot be seen by a reader if they exist only in the writer's mind. The transition from paragraph to paragraph should be shown to the reader as he passes from one to the other.

If the principles of prose structure and the right connection of paragraph to paragraph are observed, the whole composition will acquire the unity and coherence essential to any artistic work, and due proportion be gained from first to last. For the whole work must have unity, coherence, and emphasis. These will be present in completed prose in the degrees in which they are found in its parts.

A study of the exact means by which the principles of prose construction are executed is not essential to a reasonable enjoyment of prose, for which it is necessary only to be so sufficiently familiar with the principles themselves as to be able to recognise their presence in what we read. Anyone who wishes to examine them in greater detail may do so by studying the English language itself under those aspects uninvitingly called grammar and syntax. For our purposes, however, we may now pass from the structure of prose to the chief forms of literary expression for which prose is the usual medium.

Chapter Ten

The Essay

Of all literary forms, the Essay is probably the most indefinable, and this for two reasons.   One is that no one knows exactly what it is.   The other is that it has no prescribed or conventional literary form : it may as rightly be written in verse as in prose.

In spite of this vagueness about its nature and form, the essay makes definite demands of its authors.   We know when a prose composition is not an essay, even if we cannot give an abstract and indisputable definition of what an essay is.   In thinking about it, then, it is wise to deal with its recognisable qualities rather than with its nature.   This chapter suggests a definition, and thereafter confines itself to the qualities of this elusive and delightful kind of reading.

(i) Its Nature

The word Essay came into use on the publication, in 1580, of the " Essais " of Montaigne, who is described as " the first to say as an author what he felt as a man ". In this description we find a characteristic of the essay : its personal approach to its subject.   Montaigne's essays would now be called reflections, for they contain little of what we now admit, in its present form, to be an essay. Yet this personal element was present, which may be why Montaigne's essays are more acceptable than those of Bacon, who, writing in 1612, called his pieces " dispersed meditations ". His essays were notes on things outside himself, whereas Montaigne's give us himself. This relationship between the author and his writing has survived to become an accepted canon of essay-writing. As W. H. Hudson writes, " The central fact of the true essay, indeed, is the direct play of the author's mind and character upon the matter of his discourse ".

An essay is also distinguished by its brevity. Formerly authors wrote at great length, in verse or in prose, under the title of *Essay*, but the fact is that, as the " direct play of the author's mind and character ", an essay must be either voluminous or brief, and length converts it into a treatise. Consequently the essay is limited in length; it does not attempt to cover all the facts or ideas connected with its subject, as does Locke's *Essay on the Human Understanding*, but chooses one or only a few aspects of it for consideration. Herein lies its art, for the author must choose such aspects of his subject as he can present to his readers in an interesting way. This involves not only skilful selection of precise subject and careful choice of material belonging to it, but also craftsmanship adequate to the placing of the right degree of emphasis on the right places in the essay, so as to secure the desired response from the reader. Before the significance of the essay's brevity was realised, it was supposed that the

essay was written by authors who had ability to handle
a subject only in a limited way.   Hence comes Johnson's definition, "a loose sally of the mind, an irregular,
undigested piece, not a regular and orderly composition ".   Coming from an essayist in the century of
Addison, Steele, and Goldsmith, this interpretation
shows us how extremely fluid opinion has been, between that time and our own, as to what the essay is.
The idea that the brevity of the essay imposes restrictions on it, that it makes selection and grouping of
material a task requiring the finest skill, and that an
essay must fit all its material between an interesting
opening and a formal conclusion, has developed
during two hundred years.

Accompanying a realisation of those essentials, however, has been acknowledgment of the fact that the
essay must enjoy considerable freedom of treatment.
For from doubts and arguments has emerged the fact
that the only legitimate aim of the essay is to give
pleasure.   If it has any other aim it becomes a moral
lesson, or a sketch, or a story, or some other definable
and established kind of literature.   Essentially it is
none of these things, being more like a lyric than anything else.   Because it is the free, spontaneous reaction
of its author to his subject, it resembles the idea of the
true lyric in being the song of a single voice.   It gives
us as much the author as his subject.   Consequently it
must arise directly from his mood.   It may be grave or
gay, imaginative or soberly factual, nostalgic or hope-
ful.   It may be whatever a man may be when he lets

his emotions and imagination and wit respond to a thought.

This idea leads us close to the heart of the matter—that the essay is the expression of a mood. As Alexander Smith wrote, " Give the mood, and the essay from the first sentence to the last grows around it as the cocoon grows around the silkworm ". It is the author's response, fashioned for our sharing, to a disaster, a fan, a social custom, a daily habit, a person, a singing bird, an attack of influenza, a play, or a tramp over a twilit moor. It is the mood that makes the essay.

By now you may have perceived how elusive the essay is of definition, but you will also have noted the qualities by which it may be recognised. Presently we shall cast these ideas together so that our conception may be complete. Before doing this, there are further characteristics to be noticed.

Since the essay consists of the play of an author's mind and character upon a subject for the purpose of pleasing a reader, his essay must " have the appearance of casual and unpremeditated ease ". There must be no forcing of a point of view, no argument, no direct teaching, no cautionary moralising in the essay as we at present receive it. It has been all things in its time—a time extending over two thousand years in the world's literature, but the modern essay must be graceful, allusive, charming, amusing, stimulating, individual, and nothing more.

Or should we not say, *nothing less* ? To show these

qualities the essay is necessarily a work of consummate skill. It must be as carefully wrought as an intricate pattern in ivory, with all the inflections of the author's thought and mood perfectly in accord with each other, showing each other's perfections.

(ii) Technical Qualities

Of the technical qualities necessary to such craftsmanship as the essayist must have the most important is unity of design. Every thought or allusion or epigram must be directed towards the main impression the essay is planned to effect. We have already seen that the essay should be based on one idea only or one aspect of a topic. Between the introduction of this subject and the conclusion to which the essay leads, every word must openly or imperceptibly direct the reader's mind. No doubt you are familiar with at least one large theatre or cinema so designed that, in spite of its size and decoration, every line guides the eye to the stage or screen. The architecture and ornament of the essay must be planned according to the same principle. Here all is unity, coherence, and emphasis. These features should mark every sentence and paragraph and the whole composition.

And all this is to be done with " the appearance of casual and unpremeditated ease ". Stevenson said of the novel that " it's the length that kills ". Allowing for this, one wonders whether it may not be far easier to write the eighty thousand words of a novel than a book of good essays.

To summarise, then, we see that an essay is the play of an author's mind and character on a subject, limited in scope, for the pleasure of his readers. It must be artistically whole; coherent in the logical order of its thoughts; proportioned according to the relative value of its facts; skilfully introduced and unobtrusively designed in every part to lead to a conclusion following naturally from the main part of the essay; written so that every word is exact, every sentence clear, rhythmical, and serviceable to its paragraph, every paragraph ordered towards the central idea of the essay as well as to its immediate need; ornamented by nothing away from the essay's unity, but digressing, whether by a word or at some length, with charm and purpose. All these things are included in the idea of the essay.

Evidently it is a form of literature in which artists can delight, and from which readers also can derive great pleasure, since the essay requires both literary skill and unusual gifts both of mind and heart. Without consulting biographies, I cannot think of any first-rate essayist who was not also distinguished among his friends as a man. This is a curious fact and by no means unimportant.

(iii) The Reader's Approach

To which of the many essayists you should turn in order to gain a real appreciation of this form is difficult to decide because the form has itself changed

considerably. Today it is under the influence of the
daily Press. In following the course of the essay you
will notice how daily journalism, now serving a vast
number of readers of varied tastes and capacity for
appreciation, has in many ways limited its tone and
range. Since the essayist writes to please the reader,
this is an inevitable result of writing for people who
find something over twelve hundred words as much as
they can attend to in a train or after the wearying
business of the day.

Perhaps it will be as well to suggest that, with the
names of E. V. Lucas and Robert Lynd in mind, you
should find your own way among contemporary
essayists. When you go back to earlier writers, Bacon
awaits attention, with Abraham Cowley at his elbow.
Then you come to the work of Addison, Steele, with
Johnson not to be omitted, and Goldsmith, Lamb,
Hazlitt, Leigh Hunt, De Quincey, Jefferies, Max
Beerbohm, R. L. Stevenson, Chesterton, Belloc . . .
whom have we omitted unlawfully ? Well, the list
will at least give you familiarity with the English essay
in all its variety of form. One thing intimately belonging to the essay it will certainly give you—the
essayists themselves. And this is the purpose of the
essay.

Anthologies are useful to readers of essays, but they
are not good guides. Your taste must form itself,
and not be influenced by the number of essays appear-
ing under any one name in an index of contents. If
you have not the liberty to roam at will in the company

of essayists, and must accept a suggestion with which you may later quarrel, you may find you will gain the greatest profit among the older and more recent essayists by reading Oliver Goldsmith and Max Beerbohm. Goldsmith blended in his work the excellences which had appeared in the essay up to his time; Beerbohm gives you delicacy of thought, imagination, and humour. In that personal quality which distinguishes the essay both writers give something unique and consistently of the best.

It is to be hoped, however, that you will find opportunity to read the other essayists whose names are in our list, and to look further for the occasional and worthwhile essays of Cowper, Gosse, Birrell, and Alexander Smith.

I would like to close this chapter by quoting from a lecture by Virginia Woolf on *The Modern Essay*, for her words sum up perfectly the reason for the essay in our literature. Early in her lecture Mrs. Woolf says, " The essay must wrap us about and draw its curtains across the world ". It must be our companion in quiet half-hours when we can be at peace to enjoy quiet, good company. It is a sharing in someone else's pleasantness of thought, goodness of nature, tolerant understanding of our foibles, and witty comment on our pretensions. It is a peaceful listening to the exquisitely fashioned talk of the best of company who wants us to be interested. That is important, the desire to interest us and the exertion to do so. That is integral to the essay, so that at the end of her talk Mrs. Woolf recalls her simile by wisely remarking, " . . . a good essay must have this permanent quality about it; it must draw its curtains round us, but it must be a curtain that shuts us in, not out ".

Chapter Eleven

Plot Structure

(i) Definition of Plot

THE behaviour of bees in a hive, complex though it is and pursuant to design, cannot be said to indicate plot, since this arises only from the conflict of interests between people. Pattern and activities arising from it are not sufficient to form the complication we call a plot; for this the design must be made up of incidents occasioned by the clash of human emotions, passions, or interests. Without intelligence in its characters, a chain of events would be uninteresting as fiction. Any interest it might have could arise only if it were not fiction, since only then would such linked events be wholly and rationally inevitable. Similarly, defect of conflict between the interests of the characters means that a record of the incidents forms only a chrono-logical narrative, offering nothing that can stir or arrest us. It is only when the characters causing and sharing in the interests are in conflict, and are able to make decisions and decide on courses of action, that plot is formed.

Real life complications of this kind can be tediously involved and, indeed, can be centred on issues so obscure that the resulting action is highly unsuitable to fictional narrative. For the purposes of the novel or short story a plot must have a certain form which keeps it in order. Most readers do not see the form of what they read, but some knowledge of form and an interest in observing it is certainly one of the pleasures of reading.

(ii) Plot Structure

Essentially form consists of the pattern in which the action lies between two points—the purpose and the result—in the conflict of the plot. If A aims to marry B, in spite of the rivalry of C and the prohibition of D, he will either succeed or fail. His success or failure is the result, in moving towards which he will at times reach several crises of near-success and near-failure. These crises may be imagined as standing above and below the straight line running between the two points of purpose and result, and the line of action in the story crosses it several times as it passes from success crisis to failure crisis. Finally it joins the straight line at its end or finishes below it, according to the ultimate attainment or loss of the main purpose behind the story's action.

This method of visualising a plot has its disadvantages, but it is useful for separating the incidents important to the plot without regard for their apparent value to the narrative. It enables you to see exactly what plot the story is built around, and may be called the anatomy of plotting.

Coming closer to the subject, to see how a plot

works, we see that it can be divided into sections: Introduction, First Incident, Growth to Crisis, Denouement, Resolution, and Catastrophe. We will consider each of those in turn.

The Introduction gives us all the information we need for understanding what is to follow. It may be supplied by dialogue, in which characters refer to past incidents or to other people's desires or purposes. Again, it may be supplied by the description of an incident, such as a marriage or death, presented in such a way that we realise that action in the plot will follow from it. Whatever the method used, the purpose of the Introduction remains unchanged.

Once we have this information we are able to appreciate the First Incident, in which the action of the plot begins. The incident may be an event; it may be anything, subjective or objective, provided that it commences the action by making further action inevitable.

From this follows Growth to Crisis. That is to say, the action becomes complicated so that the purpose of the action is either almost attained or is almost lost. In bringing the action to the first of its crises, the author will base the development on the nature of his characters and will make clear the motivation that leads to the first incident and on to the first crisis. He will also give to each incident in the action an appearance of naturalness. All that happens must appear to come spontaneously from the characters and aims of the people in the story. However exciting a crisis may be

in itself, such as a murder during a thunderstorm, it
will fail in merit unless it follows logically from both
character and previous incident. This is the great
law of Crisis, and must be observed throughout the
story.

After a succession of crises, by which the action of
the story's conflict develops, the moment comes when
the various elements of the conflict reach a supreme
climax. The approaches to success and the descents
towards failure all exert their conflicting influences;
the motives of the characters, ardently pursued in
action, involve the plot in increasing complication;
the characters themselves develop towards a climax of
self-expression. All these factors must meet, and they
do so in the Denouement, so that they may resolve
into some sort of conclusion. In the main, you will
find that the Denouement of " happy ending " stories
consists of the removal of the obstacles which impede
that attainment of the main object towards which the
plot has developed. In tragic stories the Denouement
consists of the opposing of at least one insuperable
obstacle to the attainment of the main purpose.

This might appear to be the end of the plot, but a
moment's thought shows that it is not. When a war is
over so many things are changed that the victors face a
new set of problems. A war is fought, we say, to
achieve certain aims. Actually it is discovered that the
victors do not secure those purposes by winning the
war. They merely remove the chief obstacles opposing their purpose. They must now discover how to

obtain possession, under the new circumstances, of what they want.

In the same way, the Denouement of the plot opens alternative ways to the real end of the story. If it has facilitated attainment of purpose, we still have to see how that attainment actually occurs; if it has prohibited this success, we must know what is going to happen to the people who have met the misfortune.

The progress of the plot from Denouement to its real end, technically known as Catastrophe, is the Resolution. It is a stage of the plot which demands considerable skill of the author, for it is at this point rather than any other that a reader's interest is most easily lost. From Exposition to Denouement there has been no serious difficulty in maintaining suspense. The reader has continued to turn the pages, asking himself " And then . . .? " Now that he knows or believes he can foresee the end of the plot, he relaxes and is quickly distracted. The author's problem is how to maintain suspense from the Denouement to the final act of the plot. Many writers keep the Denouement until as late as possible and pass through a brief Resolution. However, where this is not done, the Resolution is handled in the case of the " happy ending " by crises which appear to threaten the favourable outcome forecast by the Denouement. If the hero finds, for instance, that nothing now stands in the way of marriage, the Resolution may reveal that the bride-to-be has been so affected by earlier plot incidents as to turn, not from the hero, but into doubt as to whether she should not remain unwed. The opposite course is followed in the tragic story—the hero, thwarted of his aims, may not pass into immediate defeat, which would be an event of no particular interest or significance, but may move through a Resolution in which he realises that he would not have found what he sought if he had obtained the object of his pursuit.

We are here dealing with plot structure in its simplest form. Almost always it is complicated and its interest heightened by subsidiary plots or by more complication in the stages of the plot than we have suggested in our outline. If we follow the structure of stories and novels, we will be surprised to notice how effectively the Resolution is handled. For instance, let us suppose that A wishes to marry the girl B, and also to discover her father's murderer. The discovery of the murderer is, under the aspect of the incidents followed by the author, his main purpose in the story. He achieves it at the Denouement by learning exact particulars of the murderer's identity, which reveals that B is the guilty person. The Resolution consists of his further discovery that she had committed the crime because her father had forbidden her marriage to A. In a plot such as this the Denouement rests on two dramatic incidents, and the resolution contains even more suspense than any previous stage of the story, since it has in it two possibilities to exercise the reader's mind as he reads on to the end of the plot.

This conclusion is known as the Catastrophe, a term which does not necessarily signify any connection with misfortune, but means only the real end of the plot. The main purpose suggested in the book will be here fulfilled or defeated. Here also the effects of the end will manifest themselves in subsidiary plots. The all-important principle that each stage of the plot must grow out of character and previous incident must be observed here, where it is in greatest danger of being violated. An author, unwilling to face the logical outcome of his plot, may twist it out of shape so that his heroine may not die; unable to unravel it successfully, he may invoke the *deus ex machina*, the rich uncle who leaves the hero a large legacy, or some other intruder who intervenes to bring a conclusion not fitting to the plot; he may rely on coincidence to remove his difficulty, possibly in the form of the identical twin for whose crimes the heroine has been blamed : under the influence of an idea extraneous to the plot, he may pull the strands of the plot into a new shape in conformity with it. In this last way Dickens inflicted most extraordinary contortions on his plots in his efforts to get all his characters into happiness and security under the guidance of his busy pen. In the Resolution the author's aim must be to sustain interest; in the Catastrophe it must be to draw all the elements of his plot to an ending that is formed naturally from all that has gone before.

(iii) Methods of Construction

To this outline of plot structure we can add little, for what has been omitted belongs not to an introductory survey but to more specialised study. Three points, however, must be mentioned.

The first is that the plot of a book may not follow the exact order of Exposition, First Incident, Growth to Crisis, Resolution, and Catastrophe, and one of our interests in studying fiction plots will be to see how an author has adapted this order so that he may increase the significance or interest of his story. For instance, the First Incident may precede the Exposition, thereby relieving the monotony which would arise if every story we open were to begin with a statement of what happened before the novel commences, and also gaining our immediate attention by the occurrence of an event curious or difficult to understand. It has been said that a dramatic story " always starts half-way through ".

A second feature of plot construction worth noticing is that the Denouement of incident may be followed by a Denouement consisting of the significance of that incident. Thus, if A murders his wife at the Denouement to free himself from her possessiveness, he may in the Resolution find that her will deprives him also of her possessions which he wished to enjoy alone; he may also realise that, because of his crime, he has not only stripped himself of what he wanted to have, but has also made his wife a memory which daily haunts him more cruelly. His first discovery may well make his crime appear useless; but it is the second—the extension of the Denouement—which really makes it utterly futile and exerts a determining influence on the

Catastrophe.   This fact of dispersed Denouement is a highly interesting and effective method of structure worth studying.

Finally, we cannot omit from our outline of fiction plotting the two other means by which the main action may be made more interesting or significant. The first is by the introduction of parallel plot, character, or incident.   In *As You Like It*, for instance, we have a good-natured Duke who is persecuted by a Duke of wayward disposition : their two daughters fall in love with brothers, one of whom is of generous character, while the other is envious and vindictive : two " philosophers " are respectively half wise and half foolish; there are two marriages; there are two Courts, one the artificial ducal Court and the other the forest of Arden.   The contrasts set up by these dual sets numerously and diversely illustrate both the characters and incidents of the play as it evolves its main plot and five subsidiary plots.

The other means by which chiefly the significance of a plot may be increased is the introduction of occurrences, which may include dialogue or event or characterisation only, not vitally necessary to the incidents of a plot, but indeed valuable to full expression of their significance. Thus we may find characters acting in ignorance of some incident known to the reader.   For example, Romeo returns to marry Juliet, finds her dead, and drinks the poison he has by him, while we know that she will shortly awake from her death-like sleep.   The incident is not necessary to the

Catastrophe of *Romeo and Juliet*, but it wrings out the last drop of emotion which, less significantly, is contained in the words " two star-crossed lovers " with which the play opens. The meaning of the phrase has been well established before we meet Romeo in Juliet's tomb. The action of the play would have been suited if Paris had killed Romeo outside the mausoleum, and if Juliet had woken to find Paris awaiting her. But in fact the play deals not so much with life's tragedy as with its irony, and it is to reveal this in its most poignant way that Shakespeare has Romeo poison himself at the moment when complete attainment of his purpose is at hand.

This short statement of the theory of plot structure, and the few notes on method, are sufficient to increase our profit in the reading of fiction. They also enable us to pass on to consideration of the two chief forms of prose fiction in English literature, the novel and the short story.

Chapter Twelve

The Theory of The Novel

MUCH that is in this chapter applies to fiction forms other than the novel, and may be taken as introductory to the chapter on the theory of the Short Story. The chapter must also be prefaced by the remark that only such parts of the theory are dealt with as will enable readers to get the best out of fiction. It is not intended as instruction to writers, for, although a knowledge of the points dealt with is necessary to writers, the chapter says *what it is* rather than *how it is done*. Its purpose is to help readers of fiction to enjoy more than the story or characters in broad outline and to be able to assess the literary value of what they read. The novel is taken for special reference, since it is our latest and most important form of fiction. Chaucer's *Troilus and Cressida* may be reckoned as the first novel in modern English literature, but our remarks deal only with such prose works as are reckoned to be novels according to the technique of the past two hundred years.

With so much by way of premise, we begin by stating that fiction is based on the interest each of us has in other men and women and in what happens to them or within them. It consists of events (plot) done or suffered by people (characters) who reveal something of themselves and of what happens by the third customary constituent, which is dialogue.

It will be for us shortly to see how these elements are combined into a story. At present one must pause to notice two facts already emerging.

(i) The First Essentials

One is that narrative concerning people and events cannot interest us unless it is solidly based on things that concern us. The events should be things that can happen to real people at least on the plane of existence chosen by the author. This does not mean that fiction should be documentary in truth to life; it does mean that it must be concerned with the ideals and beliefs, the passions and emotions, the instincts and impulses which do really fashion what we are pleased to call the destiny of men and women.

The second is that even in this case our interest will not be maintained if it meets with a bare chronicle of events. A kills B because he loves C, and he is acquitted of murder. This is in itself uninteresting. Interest is gained and held only if the author gives his story significance (interpretation). Thomas Hardy wrote, " As in looking at a carpet, by following one colour a certain pattern is suggested, by following another colour, another; so in life the seer should watch the pattern among general things which his idiosyncrasy moves him to observe, and describe that alone ". The author must choose as his subject certain events concerning certain characters, both seen in a certain significance. It is this perfection of choice that makes Hardy's *Tess of the D'Urbervilles* superior to his *Jude the Obscure*.

From this fact follows a further condition of excellence in fiction, that an author should confine himself to those matters which are, externally in the world or internally in his mind, within his experience. His artistic experience may not be the same as his experience as a man. By this I mean that much that he has himself experienced may leave him unmoved and without perception of any unusual significance, whereas he may have in him the faculty not only of appreciating the significance of the experience of others, but also of assimilating it as if it had been his own. Thus Defoe was able to write *Moll Flanders* and *Robinson Crusoe* because his experience of their lives, in the sense I have defined, was greater than that of the people who lived those lives. Jane Austen, however, was far more restricted in experience, since for her it was almost synonymous with personal experience. In the result each author was a supreme artist through working inside the individual range of artistic experience.

By the way, please do not imagine that we are going to be pedantic about the theory of fiction. We know that some of the great works of fiction were, in theory, gravely defective, and we are not going to deny their due merit for that reason. We can appreciate excellence however it may appear. Here and now our task is to learn what may yield the best fiction, as it has actually often done, so that we may read with intelligent appreciation, thus seeing good qualities we would otherwise miss and also knowing why a book is good and why it is in any way defective.

(ii) Plot

With this much by way of insight into the conditions of fiction, we feel ready to pass on to appreciation of plot. Immediately we face a complication we can deal with briefly only by taking its main strands and examining each separately.

The first is the plot of miscellaneous incident, such as we find in *Humphrey Clinker*, *The Pickwick Papers*, *Vanity Fair*, or *Nicholas Nickleby*. There is no unity by which the incidents acquire significance; there is merely a succession of incidents experienced by the characters. As they occur they may surprise the author as much as the reader. This kind of loosely knit plot is a favourite of English writers, to the amazement of classical French writers such as Flaubert.

The second kind of plot is a pattern of incidents, each event causing or affecting at least one other event in which the characters are involved. *Tom Jones* or *Bleak House* stands out among the many novels in which there is the interest of following the pattern of the plot.

Some novels have a combination of both kinds of plot. In *David Copperfield*, for instance, are many incidents highly pleasurable to the reader but unnecessary to the plot pattern. In many ways novels of this kind turn out to be more interesting than those of either the loosely or tightly organised plot.   This is because they combine the advantages of both kinds of plot, while avoiding the danger that a series of incidents may lose our interest or a pattern spoil our pleasure by giving us a sense of planned inevitability or even of improbability.

It would be a mistake, however, to judge any of these three plot methods as superior to the others.   In itself each is a lawful and highly useful means of writing fiction; it succeeds or fails according to the author's ability to handle it.

Your reading will have reminded you that our un-ravelling of plot has left one important strand to be picked up.   This is the complication of plot with plot into one large design.   From my own reading ex-perience I choose *Bleak House* as an example of this kind of plotting.   For a number of years I read this novel every winter.   Only when I began to study the technical side of writing did I realise why it caught me up and carried me away unfailingly each time.   The reason was that the novel has three stories—those of Jarndyce and Jarndyce, of Esther Summerson, and of Lady Dedlock.   These three are woven into one over-all plot, drawing you into its design chapter by chapter.   In this the novel is in marked contrast with *Vanity Fair*, where the stories of Becky Sharp and Amelia Sedley remain apart all through the book.   Not the least pleasure in reading fiction is an observance of how the author combines plots and sub-plots to explain why his characters are what they are and how they become involved, as we ourselves do, in everyday life.

Incidentally, who will say that *Bleak House* is a better novel than *Vanity Fair* ?   Its plot is sounder and more skilfully contrived but, apart from personal likes or dislikes which may make us prefer one to the other, we cannot say infallibly that one is superior.   In all novels we may find ourselves drawn by the plot of one and the characters of another; if one fails in one essential it compensates by excellence in another; we rightly acknowledge the qualities which, perhaps un-evenly, have carried it to the mountain top, while lesser works, of theoretical perfection but practical mediocrity, remain abandoned among the foothills.

(iii) **Theme**

The complication of events into a plot is not in itself sufficient for the making of good fiction, since, as we noted at the beginning of this chapter, a pattern of activities is not interesting unless it shows forth the significance of human emotions in relationship to each other.   This essential interest an author might supply by placing a note at the beginning of his story : " This tale will show you that greed can turn the sweetest fruits to ashes in the mouth."   Indeed, in primitive forms of fiction the significance which the author wishes us to see in his plot is sometimes stated almost as baldly as that.

Since, however, art is the concealment of art, writers

have devised various methods by which the aspect under which their plots are to appear become clear to us more pleasantly. The sub-plot, for instance, can show us the main plot in a new light—e.g. the main plot may concern the efforts of a married couple to provide a Christmas surprise for their daughter which will induce her to stay at home more often in the evenings; a sub-plot may show us the girl arranging to be married before Christmas, so as to escape from the otherwise inescapable tyranny of good parents for whom children never grow up. The conclusion, which is nowhere stated, is that it is wiser to please people in their way rather than in our own. The more the main plot develops the better is this point seen, since our view of the plot has been fixed by the sub-plot.

A favourite method of supplying the significance required by a plot is to give the story a theme. In itself a theme is nothing more than something which gives meaning or human interest to the plot's events. Let us suppose a plot in which a soldier, responsible for leading his men out of an encircled position and across dangerous country back to their regiment, is planning a way to win back his wife's affection. The situations with which he finds himself called upon to deal in handling his men are, we notice, repeatedly made worse through his faults of character and temperament. We realise, as the story proceeds, that ultimately he knows no form of authority save the imposition of his own will. We watch him encounter danger after danger with his exhausted, dispirited, mutinous men. We realise that the various ideas he has for securing his wife to himself are all likely to be frustrated in the end because he is incapable of carrying any of them into effect. We feel sure that when the climax of the story comes he will start off well, and finish up by becoming a self-pitying bully from whom the wife will turn for ever. There is no need to sketch the story farther for us to see how a theme has been worked in. The author has not put a notice at the front to tell us the meaning of the events. He has placed a series of other events alongside the first series so that the interest he intends us to find in the first will be evident.

Every good story, short or long, requires a sound theme. Many of the best themes are, of course, drawn from character. Such are the themes of *Romeo and Juliet*, for example, from which the human interest of the play derives. Almost every character in the play contributes something which illuminates either the ecstatic love of Romeo and Juliet or the burning hatred of Montagues and Capulets, from the clash of which each of the two main interests comes to shine in a fullness of meaning. The themes are so clear that Shakespeare does not trouble to refer to them at the end of the play, being content merely to point the main one in two lines of paradox :

> "... Capulet ! Montague !
> See what a scourge is laid upon your hate,
> That heaven finds means to kill your joy with love ..."

Almost as frequently authors draw their themes from Nature or scenery.   One of Joseph Conrad's favourite means of showing forth the struggle within his main character was to place that character in a struggle with the forces of nature.

(iv) Characterisation

So far we have treated plot as if it were concerned only with events; actually it governs characters as well as incidents.   Indeed, character often governs the plot, so that we may divide plots into those of character and those of incident.   For instance, *Treasure Island* is mainly a novel of incident, *Weir of Hermiston* one of character, and *The Master of Ballantrae* balances between these two chief interests.   The fact is that a novel always loses when its characters are made to conform to its incidents.   If they are real characters, they will live, refusing to be jostled into situations to suit authors, but rather, as even our most unpremeditating writers have confessed, taking the plot into their own hands and demanding the situations their personal development requires.

Incident and character can never be really divorced in the making of a novel.   If they are separated you will notice that the author hides the fact by exceptional humour or some other quality.   As a rule, he depends on speed of action and suspense to carry you through the book before you feel its weakness.   That is fundamentally why you cannot read the best-selling " thriller " twice—there is nothing to go back for, no real characterisation, no evolution of plot from characters, no pressure of character on character. When a " thriller " does not depend on suspense and speed you will be aware that it has something more than other books which are perhaps more immediately exciting. It has left something which lingers in your mind, something almost good enough to go back and enjoy again. The extent to which plot and character are woven together is one test of a real novel. Motive must lead to incident, and incident to motive; the actions of the characters must lead to incident through human emotions, passions, habits, and fears. Only in this way can the novel fulfil its function of interpreting life to us who are so eager to know it as others find it or believe it to be.

The transition of thought from plot to character leads us to consider this feature of fiction, and especially of the novel. In reading a novel we wish to meet new people and learn what they are, as well as what happens to them. Consequently we have a real interest in noticing how an author presents them to us.

Perhaps we suspect that he has carefully got to know them thoroughly beforehand, compiling in his note-books every feature of their appearance, every detail of clothing, every small particular of gesture and accent and mannerism.

Whether this is the author's method or not, in any given book, there are certainly two ways in which novelists usually show us the people of their worlds.

One is to present them in flat—that is to say, under one
aspect, as Dickens frequently does.   Sairey Gamp is
"dispoged" of by her curious speech, her moist eye,
her faint aroma of gin; Mr. Boythorn by a loud, cheery
voice, a pet canary, and an upstanding figure.   These
flat characters live in a unique dimension of their own.
Memorable, amazingly alive, they are like talking,
posturing figures on canvas.

By contrast are the characters drawn in the round,
like Elizabeth Bennett, Becky Sharp, or Catherine
Earnshaw.   Here we have the whole person, so far as
human power can compass one fellow human and portray the reality.   It has been said of Hugh Walpole
that God is the principal character in each of his
books, and this is true in the sense that only God could
know so much about the other characters.   It is from
a similar omniscience that characters are drawn in the
round.   We know not only what they look like and
what they believe, but how they think and why they
think, what they hate and fear and desire.

Our first impression might be that characters in the
round are artistically better than those in the flat.
Against this we balance the fact of experience that
" flat " characters often reveal themselves to us better
than the others.   For instance, we know Micawber
and Heap far better than David Copperfield.

The fact is significant, for it helps us to understand
the novelist as well as characterisation, and also
because it shows us that we ourselves see people in the
flat rather than wholly.   How many people, real or

imaginary, do you know completely? Most people
you know only through a few aspects of them; the
daily help who appears to live on pickles and reminis-
cences of her brother-in-law, the broker who lifts his
head and pauses every time he is about to speak, the
old woman who looks like a wooden doll with a mop
of white hair above its brown old forehead—all these
people we know so well that we could almost imper-
sonate them. We know nothing of them beyond
certain aspects which seem to make up the whole
person. These people are usually more real than
people we know intimately.

That is why they are not only fully satisfactory in
fiction, but as truly artistic as the characters whose
every thought and act is described. They are the
equals of the rounded characters because the author
has presented their significant aspects to us. He has
given us all that is worth knowing.

That is the way in which authors usually work.
They stand before some phase of life and see what most
of us miss, an aspect we overlook, a significance we do
not perceive. And in that act of seeing they have
what is essential to fiction. Apart from exceptions,
usually unsuccessful, or successful only in spite of the
author's apparently unusual method, authors do not
arrange a set of characters and incidents and form them
into a pattern by imposing an artificial significance on
them. On the contrary, they see first one colour in the
carpet's design, as Hardy said, and then another. One
of those shows the rest in an interesting way. There

is authorship in fiction at its best; first a way of seeing things, and then the ability to show it to us.

Of the actual origin of characterisation in the author's mind we need say little here. However imaginative he may be, an author forms his characters from life and largely from himself. How his characters form themselves in his mind is a mystery; perhaps we shall guess near to its centre if we say the process depends on an acutely and sensitively developed perception of resemblances. From the people he meets and, no less, those he reads about, he notes details of behaviour and appearance that fit. Often he draws on his knowledge of himself, although this is the least conscious, as it may also be the most important, function in the process. All he observes passes through his experience and, occasionally as well as during the writing of his book, the details fuse together; the character emerges, sometimes more alive, more individual, and exacting than is comfortable for its creator.

He is busily engaged in presenting the new character to us. How shall he do it ? By talking about him, telling us what he is thinking, explaining his motives ? Or will he leave the character to reveal itself—a method slower and more subtle, dependent largely for success on the intelligence and experience of the reader ? Both methods may be used, of course, just as an author may use both the flat and round methods of portraiture. You will find great interest in noticing how fiction-writers portray their characters—

by direct statement, by their actions, by the conversation of other people, even by letters or diaries. Dialogue is necessarily highly important as a means of portrayal, and we shall deal with it separately.

A point worth noticing is the introduction of a character on its first appearance. Often a careful preparation is made so that you may, at the outset, gain an accurate idea of what is most significant about this person. Sometimes this takes the form of direct description, a method favoured by Sir Walter Scott; at other times there is a filling in of background, on which Dickens placed great reliance; again, instead of these methods, there may be dialogue revealing the character's appearance and mind, and this may occur long before the character enters the story. Notice how writers use different means of bringing their people before us, sometimes by natural preference and sometimes, or so it appears to us, more artificially and by choice.

In this bringing in of characters a remarkable disproportion is sometimes observable. Sir Walter Scott, for example, occasionally spends a whole page or more in building up a character who contributes almost nothing to the novel and disappears after one or two entrances. His own interest in delineating the person blinded him to the fact that his introduction could be likened to the disproportion of taking a page to describe a cab, which serves no function except to carry the heroine to a railway station. Usually, however authors observe a better proportion in this important task of bringing people onto the scene, and you will enjoy noticing how and when some preparation is made in this way.   Thomas Wolfe is a modern novelist whose disproportion is worth studying.

Once the character has been made known the author's task is to show us how he is affected by the incidents of the plot.   Admittedly many novels link their characters and incidents by artificial means, such as that a person was at a certain place when something happened, but excellence in a novel requires some deeper connection than that, since character and incident should not remain unrelated.   In real life we cause many incidents because we are individually what we are, with our misunderstandings, faultiness of judgment, anxiety about the future, affection, ambition, and almost innumerable other personal characteristics.   Many of these traits in turn are attributable to incidents, so that our lives are incomprehensible unless the observer knows what effects experience has had on us and how we come to behave as we do.   This analysis, well concealed, is set out in the characterisation of a novel in so far as the purposes of the book require any character to be understood by the reader.   The task can be fulfilled by " flat " delineation as well as by the " round " method.   It is not tedious, unless laboriously done, for a good deal is left to the reader's understanding; the author sketches in what is significant, and leaves the reader to complete the task by bringing to the characterisation both intelligence and human sympathy.   We may note, incidentally, the importance of a novelist's working inside his " experience " if he and the reader are to know his characters. This principle of fiction is closely tied to this aspect of novel-writing.

(v) Dialogue

Of dialogue little need be said, since its principles are not difficult to understand, but that little is supremely important, for the conversation taking place between characters is essential to the narrative. It is one of the chief links between them, the means by which they move each other to action and explain themselves to each other. The plot develops largely through conversation. By conversation, too, the author avoids the necessity of giving us prose sections in which he analyses his characters or comments on them, for he enables us to meet them at first hand. Apart from these uses, dialogue lightens a novel, makes it more dramatic, and so makes it easier to read with sympathetic attention.

You will have noticed, of course, that the dialogue of novels is not the conversation of daily life. The author has edited it, replacing inexact words and phrases, removing repetitions, and making it establish its points without prolixity or the backward movements and anticlimaxes observable in almost all real conversation. In doing this he has used care to avoid turning the dialogue into a monotonous piece of reading instead of an interesting few moments of listening. Good dialogue between well-drawn characters is always heard rather than read.

Dialogue is thus one of the tests of good fiction, for the writing of it is not easy. The easiest and best dialogue, from the reader's point of view, is often the most difficult from the author's, because only hard work makes it all it ought to be. And it ought to be several things.

For instance, it must be suited to both its speaker and his situation in any given stage of the story. It must reveal something both of himself and of the situation. It must, in general, promote the plot instead of leading the reader's attention away from it. At the same time it must be interesting, fresh, and natural. Moreover, through dialogue an author usually stirs our emotions and imagination. It is an excellent medium for humour, pathos, querulousness, cunning, and the lighter shades of characterisation.

To handle the feature of fiction-writing which has all this work to do is clearly a difficult task. It is a good thing to keep this in mind as we turn page after page of dialogue, reading lightly and happily, and perhaps failing to notice the subtleties that have gone into the lines we are reading. Dialogue should always be read attentively, so that we may have a just appreciation of an author and, more importantly, so that we may not miss any of his less obviously skilful work.

(vi) Background

Background is another feature of fiction-writing which repays any trouble we take to notice it. Usually it consists of scenic description, but the term is applicable to the description of any object provided the author's purpose is to suggest or heighten the emotional value of what he writes. Thus in *The Master of Ballantrae* Stevenson describes the duel between the Master and Mackellar against a background consisting of the stillness of intense cold. The feet of the duellists move silently on iron-hard ground; the flames of the candles stand stiffly in the air. Everything is taut with nervous excitement.

In this passage, as always in Stevenson's best books, background is only a means to the end of increasing in the reader the response which the main dialogue or incident is creating in him. This is the only right use of background, since fiction deals with character in action. It does not aim at description, except in so far as this may make character in action more effective in impressing itself on the reader.

This principle is often violated, and we need not wonder that it is when we recall how rarely it is stated and how often teachers of writing urge their pupils to " fill in the background ". They point out truly that vivid description increases interest, and they encourage the idea that it should be freely used. This is a misleading half-truth, for in the writing of fiction everything must be subordinated to the one end of exhibiting character in action. If the descriptive background does not do this it is irrelevant, and inevitably distracts the reader's attention. It may be that the description is excellently done and that the reader thoroughly enjoys it. This fact is also irrelevant, and the only relevant fact is that, while the reader has been enjoying the background, the story has been idle, losing power, and wasting to its ultimate loss.

The fault is remarkably prevalent, especially as many fiction writers today excel in descriptive writing. Time and again we meet long descriptions of towns or houses or people which interest us greatly. But they do not interest us in the story and are therefore out of place. By way of contrast notice Dickens's use of background—the fog that wreathes through every line which brings us nearer to the Court of Chancery in *Bleak House*, or the mud that almost founders the horses on the Dover road as we begin *A Tale of Two Cities*—mud which holds back the rider pursuing the coach as events hold back the characters in this novel of struggle.

We may sum up the matter by saying that if background is objective it should be removed, for its intrinsic value has nothing to do with its purpose, or want of purpose, in relation to the story. Only when it is subjective, when it aims solely at providing the incident it accompanies with a means of increasing that incident's effect, may background be used. You will find a study of this principle most interesting, especially if you trace it through an author's work. In Stevenson, for instance, you will always find a thorough understanding of it, and you will notice how, as his mastery of language and of the technical application of the principle improved, they reached their height of perfection in *Weir of Hermiston*, the unfinished novel that only Stevenson could have finished.

(vii) Indirect Suggestion

In Stevenson you will also find excellent examples of what I may call Indirect Suggestion, for which some space must be found here.   It is closely allied to background, for it is a concrete way of expressing things which makes the reader feel or see what is said. For instance, if asked whether I hate a man, I might say, " I hate him bitterly ".   Far more effectively, Stevenson has,

> " ' He hated the baron with a great hatred ? ' I asked.
> ' His belly moved when the man came near him,' said the Master."

This method of indirectly suggesting a description or a feeling is highly effective when rightly done, and you will be well repaid for any re-reading you may do in order to enjoy the artistry of it and the economy with which it is used.

The contents of this chapter, together with what has been written here about plot structure, will enable you to find far more interest and genuine excitement in fiction reading than is possible for a reader who has a less trained or less intelligent appreciation of books. This is highly satisfactory, yet it may be necessary to repeat the warning against judging the merits of a book too theoretically.   Even in science many things which are theoretically possible are practically impossible simply because material things may not work, for a variety of reasons, exactly as they do in theory. Dr. Jekyll discovered this as surely as do many inventors in real life.

In art the contrast between theory and practice is of a slightly different nature and far greater in degree. This is because whatever is possible or correct in theory is equally practicable, but the excellence of the component parts is variable. An author may excel in characterisation, dialogue, and in the invention of plots, and yet be unable to combine his plots into a unified whole. Another writer may be far more successful in plot management and be less able to bring us people we recognise—our other selves—in situations we can enter. In theory he may have the balance in his favour. In practice, would anyone seriously rank Wilkie Collins above Thackeray ? The excellence of some novelists more than atones for their weaknesses; in others there is more uniform excellence, but it is consistently on a lower level. What we have learned will help us to form our own estimates, and we should certainly judge for ourselves, provided we do not look at the technique so earnestly as to miss the real value of its results. Excellence of result is what really matters; an appreciation of how it is attained should not distract us from it, unless we have misunderstood what we know of theory.

Chapter Thirteen

The Theory of The Short Story

SINCE the *nouvelle* has not so far established itself as a regularly practised form of fiction in English, the only alternative to the novel which we need examine is the short story, which is in many ways a more excellent form of craftsmanship than the novel. Its brevity imposes on the author severe restrictions.

(i) Definition and Unity

The short story is best defined as a fictional narrative which may be read at one sitting and in which the author, in the words of Poe, " . . . having conceived, with deliberate care, a certain unique or single *effect* to be wrought out, he then invents such incidents—he then combines such events—as may best aid him in establishing this preconceived effect ".

Here we have the test of the short story—unity. Right from the opening sentence there must be one aim only; there must be one idea only to be established.

The source of the idea is irrelevant to this principle. It may come from a character and his peculiarities. It may arise from an incident. It may be discovered in an impression which the author decides to convey to us in narrative form. These are the three most fruitful sources from which short stories are derived, and many of the best writers of this form of fiction express preference for the last, including Poe, the supreme master of its theory and technique.

Whatever the origin of the story, the unity with which the story is constructed must begin with the first sentence and be preserved to the last.   Poe laid down a severe law, in which a little laxity may be allowed in practice, when he wrote :

" If his very initial sentence tend not to the outbringing of this (preconceived) effect, then he has failed in his first step.   In the whole composition there should be no word written, of which the tendency, direct or indirect, is not to the one pre-established design.   And by such means, with such care and skill, a picture is at length painted which leaves in the mind of him who contemplates it with a kindred art, a sense of the fullest satisfaction."

Thus there must be both singleness of aim and a single wholeness of effect.   If the story fails in either of these, it fails completely, nor can any merit it may contain make it anything better than a piece of good prose.

If it is objected that the classical severity of such principles is unnatural, one can only point to the results when they are ignored.   Our periodicals contain an abundance of short stories which are pleasurable and contain a good deal of merit in background, characterisation, or dialogue, but which we forget almost as soon as we have read them.   Their authors are notable for the bulk of their industrious output rather than for the intrinsic value of their work. Their concern is to give the public what is easily assimilated after it has been easily perceived.

By contrast are the stories of Poe, Stevenson, O. Henry, Bierce, Bret Harte, Hawthorne. We cannot forget what we have read once we have met *The Cask of Amontillado*, *The Merry Men*, *The Gift of the Magi*, *A Horseman in the Sky*, *Tennessee's Partner*, *The Maypole of Merry Mount*, because they secured one whole effect and it remains with us.

While we may and, indeed, must allow some relaxation of principle, lest art should become obvious " art ", the principles themselves must remain as they were expressed by masters of this form which came into full flower in the nineteenth century.

(ii) Implications of Unity

Following them into detail, we conclude that a short story's introduction must be of the same nature as the rest of the story. That is to say, it must be serious if it opens a serious story, comic if a comic story follows it. Apart from this, the opening may begin anywhere in the plot structure; it may offer us scenic description, a character sketch, or an incident. In other words, it may be of any nature, provided that it is suited to the nature of the story and is in all other ways in conformity with the unity of the story.

The main body of the story should be in accordance with the principles of fiction outlined in the last two chapters, and these must be applied as exactly as possible, since the space at the author's disposal is small. Every word counts; every detail must promote the single aim of the story; every paragraph must advance the one line of the story towards its final effect.

Above all this, there must be fidelity to life, in the sense that the characters and incidents must be convincing in the setting chosen for them, and there must be suspense. The reader's interest must be held every instant.

In the concluding stages of the story the Denouement is usually close to the Catastrophe, since it is inadvisable that the Resolution should, by any length greater than necessity requires, increase the risk of a falling off of interest. Anything elaborate between the supreme climax and the ending of the story will almost certainly weaken the effect of the story.

The securing of the story's one effect requires, further than these demands as to the story's structure, that character and dialogue should, in general, be nearer to what we meet in real life than they need be in the novel. The length to which the novel generally runs, being upwards of eighty thousand words, allows an author many means for securing his effects. In the short story he must rely mainly on character and dialogue, unless his story is removed from real life as in Poe's *The Fall of the House of Usher*.

The reason for this demand is that, in most cases, an author cannot get " inside the skin " of his characters if they are too ideal or imaginary, and in the short story he must live their parts if the people are to be, within the allowed space, wholly convincing to readers. Live characterisation is essential, and this is most likely to be achieved if the author works with characters recognisably real in themselves. Where dialogue is concerned, English as it is spoken rather than English as it is written should be the aim, without going to the extreme of faithful reproduction of dialect. The use of something as approximate to spoken English as clarity will allow makes the characters more individual, their speech more natural, and gives the story lightness, freshness, and the power to convince. Much of the striking effectiveness of Mary Lavin's work may be traced to the ease with which she meets these demands of the fictional form in which she excels.

In these principles and methods are found the secrets of short-story writing at its best. We need not proceed farther by remarking that the short story must be perfectly proportioned, since this fact is too evident to need statement. Clearly any story which suffers from want of proportion in its parts or balance in its characterisation and action must also suffer in loss of effect.

We may say, however, that all the essentials we have noted should be found in a state of fusion. In this blending of perfections lies the true perfection of the short story. No one characteristic should be so marked as to be readily distinguishable from the others. All should be blended, balanced, woven into each other, run smoothly through each other, so that single wholeness of effect may be achieved in technique as well as in narrative purpose.

Anyone unfamiliar with the short story would be wise if he were to make its acquaintance by reading Poe's work until he is familiar with it. That is an excellent beginning for both reader and writer. Perhaps in passing on to Hawthorne he may miss the austere application of theoretical principles. Presently, however, he will find that the principles are there as surely as in Poe's stories. And he may ask himself whether, because the technique is often less obvious in his work, Hawthorne is not the better short-story writer of the two. Whatever his opinion about this, he will have arrived at the degree of literary appreciation in which he can judge and value that art which seems most artless.

Appendix A

Aristotle and Style

In the Aristotelian view Style is not of the essence of writing, but is always something objective to the author. It may or may not be present in what he writes. Not easily definable from this point of view, Style may be said to be (as Schopenhauer states it), "the physiognomy of the mind". In other words, it is a manner of writing which an author may adopt or discard or change for another manner at will.

This manner of writing is regarded as a genus, which is divisible into species. These are usually given as seven in number, being according to author (e.g. *Homeric* or *Miltonic* styles), to time (as in *Elizabethan* style of Lyly), to language (as in *Gallic* or *Celtic* styles), to subject (as in *philosophical* style), to geography (as in *West Midland* or *Cockney* styles), to audience (as in *popular* style), and to purpose (as in *didactic* style).

Each of these species is capable of further sub-division until the individual writer is reached, who will be said to have his personal type of a certain manner of writing—e.g. Spenser may be said to have the Spenserian Elizabethan epic style. It is evident that any author may have several styles or manners of writing. In literary criticism the Aristotelian critic considers all the elements, as outlined above, which may go to form the " style " of an author.

The argument about the existence and nature of Style must remain confused because there is no definition of terms, and therefore little precision of thought, by which the Platonist or Aristotelian can keep his position clearly in mind. Many excellent critics will be found to speak from both points of view at different times. For example, both sides claim " Style is the man " as the complete summary of their position. The first step towards a methodical handling of the problem is the definition of terms, so that it will be evident when " Style " means *an inevitable literary result of inspiration* and when it means *a deliberately adopted manner of writing*. Until this step is taken and an adequate treatise on Style is worked out, readers must make what they can of the critical uncertainty which complicates the problems involved in a question which should have been at least properly formulated centuries ago.

Appendix B

Plays and Literature

To devote a chapter to appreciation of Plays is unnecessary, since from the literary point of view a play is a form of art governed by principles already dealt with in this book. Whether it is " good theatre " is for the dramatist to decide, not the literary critic. And this problem, it is worth noting, does not arise, for plays which are good to read are invariably suitable for stage production. From this remark we exclude, of course, poems written in dramatic form but not intended for presentation on the stage.

A play is not read primarily for its dialogue, nor for its plot, nor for its characterisation. It is read because, like any other literary form, it presents a section of life or experience under an aspect which gives it a certain significance. It may therefore be judged by ordinary literary principles, both in regard to its nature and its component parts of form or structure.

It differs from other literary forms in that it is general. That is to say, all poetry is personal, most prose (as distinct from mere writing) is chiefly personal, but the play is written for the many. It is addressed to a group wider even than the immediate audience, being rather for a class or a nation or mankind. The only apparent exceptions to this characteristic of the play will be found to be literary pieces which are devised, merely as an incidental, for possible stage presentation. They form, so to speak, the light opera of literature.

The general nature of the play inevitably affects it as an art form. It permits the widest generalisation of character, the presentation of a type, such as Hamlet, or of a vast section of life in a series of short expositions, such as we find in the expressionist playwright Toller. To this kind of presentation the play is particularly suitable, although it can be achieved less easily in other literary forms.

Apart from the consequences of this general nature of the play, literary work for stage production can be judged only by literary principles in so far as it is literature. And in this one exception it is to be criticised according to the fundamental principles of art, so that its examination lies outside the scope of this book.

INDEX

251

ADVERTISING & PUBLICITY   ALGEBRA   AMATEUR ACTING   ANAT
BOOK-KEEPING   BRICKWORK   BRINGING UP CHILDREN   BUSINES
CHESS   CHINESE   COMMERCIAL ARITHMETIC   COMMERCIAL AR
COMPOSE MUSIC   CONSTRUCTIONAL DETAILS   CONTRACT BRIDGE
SPEEDWORDS   ECONOMIC GEOGRAPHY   ECONOMICS   ELECTR
ENGLISH GRAMMAR   LITERARY APPRECIATION   ENGLISH RENASC
REVIVAL   VICTORIAN AGE   CONTEMPORARY LITERATURE   ETCHI
FREELANCE WRITING   FRENCH   FRENCH DICTIONARY   FRENCH
LIVING THINGS   GEOLOGY   GEOMETRY   GERMAN   GERMAN
GOOD CONTROL OF INSECT PESTS   GOOD CONTROL OF PLANT DISE
GOOD FARMING BY MACHINE   GOOD FARM WORKMANSHIP   GOO
GOOD MARKET GARDENING   GOOD MILK FARMING   GOOD PIG KE
GOOD ENGLISH   GREEK   GREGG SHORTHAND   GUIDEBOOK TO T
GREAT   BOLIVAR   BOTHA   CATHERINE THE GREAT   CHATHAM   CLEN
LIBERALISM   HENRY V   JOAN OF ARC   JOHN WYCLIFFE   LENIN   LOUIS
ROBES___   ___ ___ ___   ___ ___   HASTINGS
HOUS___   ___EPAIRS
WRIT___   **GIVE INSTRUCTION**   ___ND TOO
MECH___   ___LCRAFT
MOTO___   **TO A WISE MAN···**   ___FICIENC
PHYSI___   ___DESIGN
ADMI___   ___NG   R
PHRA___ ___OK   SAILING   SALESMANSHIP   SECRETA___ ___ACTICE
DEBAT___   SPELLING   STAMP COLLECTING   STUDE___ ___DE   S
TYPEWRITING   USE OF GEOGRAPHY   WAY TO POETR___   WRI
COOKERY FOR GIRLS   DOGS AS PETS FOR BOYS AND GIRLS   KNIT
PHOTOGRAPHY FOR BOYS AND GIRLS   RADIO FOR BOYS   RIDING
SOCCER FOR BOYS   STAMP COLLECTING FOR BOYS AND GIRLS   WO
ACTING   ANATOMY   ARABIC   ASTRONOMY   BANKING   BE
CHILDREN   BUSINESS ORGANISATION   CALCULUS   CANASTA   C
COMMERCIAL ART   COMMERCIAL CORRESPONDENCE   COMMER
CONTRACT BRIDGE   COOKING   CRICKET   DRAWING   DRESS
ECONOMICS   ELECTRICITY   ELECTRICITY IN THE HOUSE   ELOCU
ENGLISH RENASCENCE   ENGLISH RENASCENCE TO THE ROMANTIC
LITERATURE   ETCHING   EVERYDAY FRENCH   TO EXPRESS YOUR'S
DICTIONARY   FRENCH PHRASE BOOK   GARDENING   GAS IN T
GERMAN   GERMAN DICTIONARY   GERMAN GRAMMAR   GERMAN
CONTROL OF PLANT DISEASES   GOOD FARM ACCOUNTING   G
GOOD FARM WORKMANSHIP   GOOD FRUIT FARMING   GOOD GRA
GOOD MILK FARMING   GOOD PIG KEEPING   GOOD POULTRY KEE
GREGG SHORTHAND   GUIDEBOOK TO THE BIBLE   HINDUSTANI
CATHERINE THE GREAT   CHATHAM   CLEMENCEAU   CONSTANTINE   CO
ARC   JOHN WYCLIFFE   LENIN   LOUIS XIV   MILTON   PERICLES   PETER TH
USE OF HISTORY   WARREN HASTINGS   WOODROW WILSON   HOCKE
HOUSEHOLD ELECTRICITY   HOUSE REPAIRS   ITALIAN   JOINERY
MANAGEMENT   MATHEMATICS   HAND TOOLS   ENGINEERING
DRAUGHTSMANSHIP   METEOROLOGY   MODELCRAFT   MODERN DA
MUSIC   NORWEGIAN   PERSONAL EFFICIENCY   PHILOSOPHY   PHO
SHORTHAND   PLANNING AND DESIGN   PLUMBING   POLISH   PO

"BANNISTER'S CAFÉ"

a comedy in three acts

by

H. S. Gibson

Printed in the United Kingdom of Great Britain
and Northern Ireland

March, 1950

BELFAST:

H. R. CARTER PUBLICATIONS LTD.,

2 Marcus Ward Street

Sole Distributors in Great Britain: VAWSER & WILES (London), LTD.,
356/8 Kilburn High Road, London, N.W.6

A

"BANNISTER'S CAFE"

was first produced at

THE GROUP THEATRE, BELFAST,

on February 1st, 1949, with the following cast:

John Bannister .... R. H. McCANDLESS

Walter Bannister .... PAT MAGEE

Maria Bannister .... ELIZABETH BEGLEY

William McNinch .... JAMES YOUNG

Peter Dunnigan .... JACK O'MALLEY

James Chisholm .... JOSEPH TOMELTY

Sally Bell .... SHEILA CRAWFORD

Angela Carr .... MARGARET D'ARCY

Thomas Henry Kennedy .... JOHN F. TYRONE

The play produced by Harold Goldblatt

"BANNISTER'S CAFÉ"

a play in three acts

This play is copyright and must not be reproduced by duplication or in any other way.

CHARACTERS IN ORDER OF THEIR APPEARANCE

JOHN BANNISTER .... *A prosperous wholesale general merchant in the town of Carrigmore, North Antrim, aged 64. A widower.*

WALTER BANNISTER ...... *His son and only child, aged 25.*

MARIA BANNISTER .... *Spinster sister of John Bannister, who keeps house for him. Aged 61.*

WILLIAM McNINCH .... *Chief clerk in John Bannister's office, aged 27.*

PETER DUNNIGAN .... *A small farmer in the middle fifties.*

JAMES CHISHOLM .... *An agent and broker in the town, also in the early sixties.*

SALLY BELL .... *About 30. Another clerk in the office.*

ANGELA CARR .... *Daughter of a Belfast solicitor, aged 22.*

THOMAS HENRY KENNEDY *Also around 60. Owner of the Manor House, Carrigmore. A retired Ceylon tea planter.*

The time is early Spring of the year 1937. The scene throughout the action of the play is the private office of J. Bannister & Co., Wholesale General Merchants in the town of Carrigmore. The private office is situated on the other side of the yard from the general office and at the end of the yard are the stores. Over all is the dwelling house of the Bannister family, consisting of John Bannister, his son Walter and his spinster sister and housekeeper Maria. The door of the private office, opening to the yard, is down front (L.C.). Back stage is a window, giving a distant view of the bay and headland. Up stage (L.C.) is Walter's desk and (R.C.) his father's. A portable typewriter is on Walter's desk. The other essential furniture is a locker or cabinet containing the liquor and glasses used in Act Three. The rest of the office furnishings can be to the producer's taste. Stage movements, other than essentials, are left to the producer's discretion.

ACT ONE.

(When the Act opens, John Bannister *is seated at his desk. It is a bright Spring morning. The office door opens and* Walter *enters.)*

Walter *(breezily)*: Hard at it, Dad?

Bannister *(dryly)*: Somebody in the house has to work.

Walter: No left-handers!

Bannister: If the cap fits put it on. Where have you been gallivanting to since breakfast-time?

Walter: Having a look how the builders are getting on.

Bannister: Hmph—well?

Walter: Grand. At the rate they're going they'll be finished well within contract time.

Bannister *(grumpily)*: Which means I'll have to fork out the balance all the sooner.

Walter: If it wasn't for me you'd be a proper old stick-in-the-mud.

Bannister: Oh, talk's cheap. You're not risking the capital.

Walter *(lighting a cigarette)*: Listen—you know this town's just gasping for a first-class café. It beats me why nobody's thought of it before. As for risk, I can see none.

Bannister: I'm afraid that doesn't cut much ice with me. You've one of the best one-track minds I've ever come across. When it's set on anything you can't see an inch right or left.

Walter *(chuckling)*: You always backed dead certs, Dad.

Bannister: Well, I always counted the costs a good many times before I plunged. Then, as often as not, I didn't. Otherwise I'd still be in Bridge Street selling packets of pins and butter in quarters. And you'd have been running the messages with the backside out of your trousers. *(*Walter *laughs heartily.)* And that's not a joke, mind you. *(*Bannister *leans back in his chair and regards* Walter *fixedly for a moment before speaking.)* You're a puzzle to me, Walter. Sometimes I think I might as well have chucked all the money I spent on you down a grate. That posh school only seems to have put fool notions in your head.

WALTER (*lightly*): It took me out of Carrigmore for a while anyway.

BANNISTER: About all it did do.

WALTER: No, Dad. It taught me to see possibilities when I came back—even in Carrigmore.

BANNISTER (*contemptuously*): You and your possibiltiies. You go bouncing from one possibility to another like a pea on a drum. And every one's the right one—at the time.

WALTER (*facetiously*): You're a good preacher lost.

BANNISTER: Now you needn't try to side-track me, for you know I'm talking the truth. First you'd the notion o' being a doctor and how long did you stick that? One year and you got fed-up. Next you switched over to the law and it was the only thing for you.

WALTER: Now——

BANNISTER: I'm finishing what I'm saying whether you like it or not. Eighteen months at the law and damme if you don't go and get cold feet again at Christmas and tell me you're not going back.

WALTER: Now Dad, be fair.

BANNISTER: Be fair what?

WALTER: I told you there was a definite reason for that.

BANNISTER: Of course. There's always a reason for everything, unless a man's mad. My point is—what reason?

WALTER: Can't we skip that for the time being? I gave you my word I'd tell you in good time.

BANNISTER (*in exasperation*): I don't know why I'm so soft with you. It's not like me. If there'd been a few more in the family I'd likely have put the screw on you tighter. Anyway, now you are here, why don't you stick your back into the business? You're riding this new notion to death as you always do. I don't believe you could tell a damn thing about what's going on here.

WALTER: Anyone with half an eye could see this business would run itself.

BANNISTER: Run itself my foot. Do you think I've no competitors doing their best to collar my trade? Couldn't a young fellow like you go out after a bit of theirs? Take the mountain district out by Greenish—practically all in the hands of McKeever and not a reason in God's earth why it shouldn't be ours.

WALTER: Except that McKeever's a Greenish man and they're pretty clannish out there. And isn't it nice to see there's a bit of sentiment, even in business?

BANNISTER: Don't talk bunkum.

WALTER: And McKeever's only a small man in the trade and from all I hear has a pretty tough fight to keep his end up. You'd probably call me a fool for saying I wouldn't want to take the business from him.

BANNISTER: I certainly would.

WALTER (*shrugging his shoulders*): All depends on the viewpoint. Surely you've your fair share?

BANNISTER: You've a lot to learn, my lad. No man in business ever had his fair share till he's done his best to get it all. That's my idea of business.

WALTER: And a pretty lousy one, if you ask me.

BANNISTER: I'm not asking you. I'm telling you. The one rule in business is to hit the other fellow hard and anywhere, and no punches inside the law are barred.

WALTER (*shaking his head*): Not an ounce of imagination in that.

BANNISTER (*rapping the desk with his knuckles*): There's money —and it gets you a lot further than imagination. The workhouse is full of fellows with imagination—and the madhouse too.

WALTER: All things considered, it's maybe as well I don't take a greater interest in the business. You might soon be asking me to take less. And if you do want to concentrate on the money angle of things, a good first-class café is going to make it a damn sight quicker than peddling bags of cattle feed and the like.

BANNISTER (*testily*): I declare to God you rile me sometimes, with the blethers you talk.

WALTER: With profound respect, Dad, it's mutual.

BANNISTER: Well, remember this—the café idea is yours and it's up to you to make it go. I was daft letting you talk me into building a place that size in the like of Carrigmore.

WALTER: If you want reasons I'll catalogue them—from bedrock. Do you realise Carrigmore has natural advantages second to none and not one of the stick-in-the-muds——

BANNISTER: Including me?

WALTER: As you said a few minutes ago—if the cap fits put it on.
(*He goes over to the office window.*)   Take the sweep
of that bay, up to the cliff.   Could you beat it?

BANNISTER: Shire your head a bit.   You're talking like a Spring
poet.

WALTER: No.   Like a tourist guide-book.   Something Carrigmore badly needs.   But if you want to get right down
to the practical, it's O.K. by me.

BANNISTER: And you think you could?

WALTER: Just wait and see.   You'll find I'm talking turkey.
I know these Carrigmore people—content to dodge along
like this till the Resurrection if someone like me didn't
come back and waken them up.

BANNISTER: The one thing you're not bad at is blowing your
own horn.

WALTER (*enthusiastically*): Tell me, Dad—what's the greatest
asset Carrigmore has?

BANNISTER: Likely yourself.

WALTER: There's many a true word spoken in jest.   But just at
the minute I didn't mean that.

BANNISTER: That's very modest of you.

(WALTER *smacks the palm of the left hand with his
right.*)

WALTER: The beach.   Practically two miles of golden sand
scintill——

BANNISTER: Lord, you're off again.

WALTER: Dad, do try to be serious about this.

BANNISTER: Well, I like that   It's me that is serious.   It would
take me to be, with the money I'm gambling on this
thing.

WALTER: Good.   Well, to continue.   Here we are, seventeen
miles from a main line, with nothing but two or three
narrow-gauge trains running into the town in the day.
And such trains.

BANNISTER: Don't mention them.   It was the possibility
merchants in the town started that thing.   I lost £500
in it before it was taken over by the main line.

WALTER (*chuckling*): One of your dead certs that didn't come
off.

BANNISTER: Don't blame me.   Your Mother persuaded me against
my will.   She was a fine woman, with no head for
business.   You take after her, Walter.

WALTER: I'll bet you eat those words before long.

BANNISTER: I hope so, for the sake of my bank balance.

WALTER: Now listen—here are my reasons why there's good, sound common-sense in what I've got you to do.

BANNISTER: You'd do well up on a soap box. Well, as quick as you like, for I've got work to do if you haven't.

> (*The door from the yard opens and* AUNT MARIA *enters, dressed to go out. She is a woman about 61, with clipped speech and has a masterful manner. It is evident she has considerable power over even* JOHN BANNISTER. *She is inclined to be deaf.*)

AUNT M.: Don't forget the dinner will be at twelve-thirty sharp to-day, John. This is Bridget's half-day and I want to go to the Sale of Work this afternoon. I think I told you, Walter?

WALTER: Yes, Auntie.

BANNISTER (*muttering*): It's about six times you told me.

AUNT M.: What's that, John?

BANNISTER (*impatiently*): Nothing—nothing.

AUNT M.: I do wish you'd stop this irritating habit of speaking under your breath.

BANNISTER: For God's sake go and get yourself one of those wee gadgets for your ear or I'll have to start talking on my hands.

AUNT M.: It's funny I don't seem to have the same difficulty hearing other people.

BANNISTER: Not a bit. All they have to do is listen.

AUNT M.: I'm going up the length of Mrs. Colhoun's now.

BANNISTER: All right, Maria—go on—go on.

AUNT M.: And don't forget twelve-thirty.

BANNISTER: You're like a gramophone, with the needle stuck.

AUNT M.: I know your habit of going off somewhere just when the dinner's put on the table.

> (*Exit* AUNT MARIA.)

BANNISTER: It's easy knowing why women get murdered.

WALTER: Auntie's not a bad old stick when you humour her. The two of you are too much alike.

BANNISTER: It's a dispensation of Providence your Aunt Maria never married and reproduced herself. Have you any more to say?

WALTER: Oh, lots.

BANNISTER: Well, say it in shorthand.

WALTER: Very good. Now, Dad, if a study of humanity teaches
us one thing, it's this: there are always people looking
for the exclusive.

BANNISTER (*looking blank*): And what does that balderdash mean?

WALTER: Isn't it obvious? A certain type of folk won't touch
the trippery place with a bargepole, for even a day's
leave—let alone a holiday. Here, by and large, the day-
tripper from the city's just ruled out. The journey takes
two hours on the main line and another on the narrow-
gauge. Both ways, six hours. By bus it's worse, for it
goes round the world before it touches Carrigmore.

BANNISTER: Where's all this getting us?

WALTER: Patience, Dad, patience. You'll soon see. Now,
listen hard. You can come by car in less than two hours.
With my foot hard down I've done it in an hour and
thirty-five minutes, because you can by-pass the places
the bus has to go through. So there you have it in a
nutshell. When my idea's worked out and the café going
full swing, Carrigmore can cater for the private owner
and it'll simply jump on the map.

BANNISTER: If the wind o' your mouth meant anything you'd
be a genius. It's politics you should be in.

WALTER: It's practical politics for Carrigmore I'm talking.
These suburban people will just flock to a place that's
taboo to the plebs.

BANNISTER: To the what?

WALTER: Sorry, Dad. I forgot your Latin's a bit shaky. That
means " the common people."

BANNISTER (*dryly*): Oh, does it?

WALTER: And you can't deny there hasn't been a place to get
a decent meal up to now.

BANNISTER: Blethers. There's " Seascape " and there's " The
Sunshine Café."

WALTER: A glorified fish-and-chip shop and a Fadgee's, with
the stuff served up like a bucket of mash.

BANNISTER: What about the hotel?

WALTER: Dad, for Heaven's sake. Could you see old Minnie
or Annabell McMillen trying to cater for a crowd? Sure
nobody goes to the place but a few dried-up old mummies
year after year. I believe the skivvies have the devil
of a job sorting out their medicine bottles. Mark you
my words, when Bannister's Café, run on city lines——

BANNISTER : At city costs——

WALTER : And city prices—is going full steam, what I mean will
be sticking out a mile. When you take over the chair-
manship of the Rural District Council in a couple of
months you'll get the chance of your life to start a real
advertising campaign. And when it comes to that—I'll
be at your back.

BANNISTER : A comforting thought. It'll be a change from my
pocket.

WALTER : Dad—here's a very important point. When we get
this advertising under way the main thing we're boosting
is the beach. And why?

BANNISTER : God knows !

WALTER : Because we want them to take their cars there. Good,
firm sand, well above high-water mark. Just made for
the job. Slogans like this—" Park your car on the beach
and eat at Bannister's Café." Much more flowery, of
course.

BANNISTER : I wouldn't doubt that, with you.

WALTER : That beach is simply the corner-stone of my ideas.
The site of the Café is ideal, on the other side of the
road from the Manor House grounds. And that reminds
me. We'll soon have to see to the fixing of that lane
through the planting to take two-way traffic.

BANNISTER : It wouldn't be a bad notion to ask leave first.

WALTER : M'yes. I'll have to go along to see this man who's
bought the Manor House. It's an awful pity you didn't
take over that place when it was in the market.

BANNISTER : Do you think I'm John D. Rockfeller? Even I was,
I wouldn't have touched the property. I don't know
what it would take to put the house in order for a start.

WALTER : Yes, but if Carrigmore's developed, the land's bound
to become valuable.

BANNISTER (*contemptuously*) : Land? What are you talking
about? Half of it sandhills, facing the sea. Since the
old Colonel died a year ago there hasn't been a bid the
executors would touch from the ten townlands.

WALTER : What did this man Kennedy give for it?

BANNISTER : Nobody rightly knows. They wanted ten thousand,
but of course there's no harm in wanting. In the end
it was bought by private treaty.

WALTER: Well, the new tenant doesn't seem to be a man who'll give much trouble. Keeping to himself is his strong point. Did you ever hear what he was?

BANNISTER: Nothing very definite. Retired something or other from abroad and as odd as two left gloves. Beyond two or three of the shopkeepers, he's bothered with nobody. And even they say he's as close as a clam.

WALTER (*chuckling*): And, being Carrigmore, of course they've tried to pump him?

BANNISTER: Well, it's natural when a stranger comes to the town to wonder who and what he is. Anyway, they've found out he's a bachelor and the older they get the more kinks they develop. So look out for yourself.

WALTER: Thanks. I'll keep it in mind.

BANNISTER: By the way—did you hear anything about a young woman being seen around the Manor House several times lately? She comes in a wee closed car.

WALTER: No, who told you that?

BANNISTER: McNinch mentioned it first.

WALTER: I don't know where you'd be without that long nose of McNinch's. It's poked into a lot more than your cash books.

BANNISTER: Don't you say a word about him. If you took as much interest in the business as McNinch it would be better for you.

WALTER: We'll let that pass. Anybody besides McNinch?

BANNISTER: Lunty, the butcher, said something about her being a niece.

WALTER: Quite probable, isn't it?

BANNISTER: Maybe. And maybe not. I wouldn't trust some of these old bachelors in a hen-roost. The older they are, the younger their notions. And it's a bit funny this wee car always comes into the town by the back way through the Moss Road. Why all the secrecy?

WALTER: What does it matter anyway? Once I've fixed up about the lane to the beach he can run a harem for all I care.
(*Knock at the office door and enter* MCNINCH, *the book-keeper. He is a typical clerk, about 27, with spectacles.*)

MCNINCH: I'm taking the lodgment up to the Bank now, Mr. Bannister.

BANNISTER: All right. (MCNINCH *turns to go.*) Look into the bus depot and see if there's any sign of that stuff from McKeever for Blackstock of the Cross. I'm anxious to know if he's opened the account. Don't you know that clerk fellow in the depot?

MCNINCH (*unenthusiastically*): Yes.

BANNISTER: He could tell you.

MCNINCH: Is that all?

BANNISTER: Yes. Here. (*He gives* MCNINCH *money.*) Get me a bottle of stomach powder when you're passing the chemists. And be as quick as you can. I want to look into those statements with you.

    (*Exit* MCNINCH.)

WALTER: What's wrong with the faithful William? He looks a bit sour.

BANNISTER: Oh, never you mind about him. (*He rises.*) I want a word with the station-master about a breakages claim and I'll go through the back way. You may as well do something for your living, so sit down here and draft a letter to Willshire & Company about the new contract. The correspondence is on the current letters file. I want it on their books before there's any danger of the market moving up. (*He goes toward the office door leading to the yard and with his hand on the knob adds, as an afterthought.*) And—no big words.

    (*Exit* BANNISTER. WALTER *rises and sits down at the desk, picks up the papers, glances at them more or less casually, then throws them back on the desk. He puts his hands in his trousers pockets, tilts his chair back, puts his feet up on the desk, lights a cigarette and gives himself up to day-dreaming. There is a knock on the office door.* WALTER *almost upsets completely in an effort to recover his decorum, hastily picks up the papers and studies them intently.*)

WALTER: Come in. (*A worried-looking little man in the middle fifties enters.*) Ah, good morning, Mr. Dunnigan.

DUNNIGAN: Good morning, Mr. Walter. You'll maybe excuse me coming to the private office, but I wanted to make sure of seeing your Father.

WALTER: Sorry, he's just gone out. Anything I can do for you?

DUNNIGAN (*hesitantly*): It's—about my account. I got this
   month's statement and—— (*He fumbles in his breast
   pocket and produces the statement.*)

WALTER: Yes?

DUNNIGAN: It's this note at the bottom that's worrying me a bit.

WALTER: Uh-huh. Afraid it didn't go through my hands.
   What's it say?

DUNNIGAN (*apologetically*): Well, you see, the account's a bit
   overdue and——

WALTER: Let's have a look at it. (DUNNIGAN *hands over the
   statement which* WALTER *studies a moment and then
   hands back.*) M'yes—the old man must have been a
   trifle liverish when he sent you that billet-deux. Not
   exactly love and best wishes, Mr. Dunnigan?

DUNNIGAN (*rather flummoxed*): Er—no.

WALTER: Probably one of his off-mornings with the stomach.

DUNNIGAN (*blankly*): Eh?

WALTER: Flatulence, Mr. Dunnigan. Known better as wind.
   Blows him this way and that and plays hell with his
   innards. You know the saying—When the stomach's bad
   you're all bad—including the temper. Hence your note.
   Perfect sequence, isn't it? (*He grins at* DUNNIGAN, *who
   looks more puzzled.*) I never get too het up about his
   spasms, Mr. Dunnigan.

DUNNIGAN: But I'm not you.

WALTER: No, that's true. Still, don't worry too much. Things
   generally work themselves out if we've enough patience.

DUNNIGAN (*despondently*): Mostly the wrong way with me.

WALTER: Oh, we all hit rough patches now and then.

DUNNIGAN: You can't have much to worry you.

WALTER: You'd be surprised how many rough edges I've got
   at this minute. However, that's not your pigeon.
   Suppose you put me wise to the whole position and then
   we'll see if there's any daylight.

DUNNIGAN: I've struck it pretty bad for a while and I don't seem
   able to pull things straight. My land needs a lot of
   fertilisers and working out there at the beach and all
   that spells money. Money I haven't got.

WALTER (*sympathetically*): I know. Shortage of cash can be
   the very devil. You can't imagine the difficulty I have
   screwing it out of the old man at times. He holds on
   like a limpet.

DUNNIGAN: I—I suppose you hardly think you could persuade him to give me a bit longer to square this up?

WALTER (*heartily*): Of course. Damn it all, we can't see you hard up against it for the sake of—— Let me see that again. (*He scans the statement which* DUNNIGAN *hands over.*) Twenty-five pounds. How soon do you think you'd be in funds?

DUNNIGAN: With any luck a couple or three months would make a lot of difference.

WALTER: Say three, that'll be the odd one in for luck. Just leave it to me and I'll talk to the governor.

DUNNIGAN: Very decent of you, Mr. Walter.

WALTER (*very heartily*): Not at all, old man. Pleasure. (*He claps* DUNNIGAN *on the back.*) And my personal apologies for that rude message from my Fath——
   (*Just at this point the door opens and* BANNISTER *comes back into the office.* WALTER *looks sheepish and coughs to break the awkward silence.*)

BANNISTER (*gruffly*): What's all this about?

WALTER (*very suggestively*): Well—good morning, Mr. Dunnigan.

BANNISTER: Not so fast. What does all this mean?

WALTER: Just a little matter Mr. Dunnigan was enquiring about.

BANNISTER (*ominously*): Uh-huh. What little matter? (*He looks hard at* DUNNIGAN, *then at* WALTER. *Silence and tableau for a moment.*) Come on. You're not both dummies. All right, maybe I can guess. Your account, eh, Dunnigan?

DUNNIGAN: Yes.

BANNISTER: I suppose you're in to square it?

DUNNIGAN: Unfortunately I'm not.

BANNISTER: It will be—for you.

DUNNIGAN: Your son was saying I could maybe have a bit longer to——

BANNISTER: Oh, he did, did he? Well, never you mind about that. My son says a lot more than his prayers. In this business it's what I say. (*He glares across at* WALTER.)

WALTER (*feebly protesting*): Now Dad——

BANNISTER: Keep out of this.

DUNNIGAN: I could clear the whole thing in about three mon——

BANNISTER (*sarcastically*): I daresay you could. You've been going to clear it for the last six.

DUNNIGAN : And I meant to, only——.

BANNISTER : Did you ever hear about the road to hell being paved with good intentions, Dunnigan? Keep it in mind.

DUNNIGAN : If you come down on me it will ruin me——

BANNISTER : No sob stuff. It cuts no ice with me. Now, listen. You can have one fortnight more—fourteen days—to find that money, and not an hour more. And your account here's closed. That's all.

DUNNIGAN : Mr. Bannister !

BANNISTER (*holding open the office door*): I said that's all. (DUNNIGAN *goes out.*) (*Turning to* WALTER.) Now, what do you imagine you're doing? I'm beginning to think you're right about keeping out of the business.

WALTER : Sure the poor little chap's up against it.

BANNISTER : Walter—you're a born sucker. I think anyone could pull the wool over your eyes. If I'd my way I'd shake " Flit " over runts like that.

WALTER : Of course nobody can make much out of them.

BANNISTER : Your sympathy's wasted on a snivelling craytur like that. He's been running round girning about being hard up ever since I knew him and that's not yesterday. And not one to blame but himself.

WALTER : A very moot point.

BANNISTER : No. A fact. He was left quite a decent grocery in a wee way in Church Street, with a comfortable living in it. But that didn't satisfy him. (WALTER *takes out a cigarette and taps it on his case.*) Are you listening?

WALTER : Of course.

BANNISTER : So he sells the grocery business and decides to take up farming. God knows why, for he knows less about it than a dog does about its grandfather. (*The phone rings and* BANNISTER *lifts the receiver.*) Yes?—— Who?—— Yes, put him through——Good morning, Mr. Cleland—— Uh—huh——Sunday, the 17th? At the morning service? ——Certainly. Pleasure——Not at all, Mr. Cleland. Wife keeping well?——That's good. How's your father-in-law? ——Grand. Give him my kind regards——Right, Mr. Cleland. Good-bye. (*He hangs up the receiver.*) Mr. Cleland, the new Minister out at Cloughaninny. He wants me to be a special collector at the anniversay service on the 17th.

WALTER (*slyly*): You sounded as if you were going.

BANNISTER: Of course. His wife's a daughter of Mr. Bruddy, the managing director of Kenny's, the big importers. Wonderful how these ministers have a nose for the cash. Still, Kenny's are mighty useful people to keep in with.

WALTER (*with a cynical smile*): In fact a well-spent pound, Dad?

BANNISTER: Very. The father-in-law always comes down to anything special about the church. Not that the same old boy's any plaster saint. If rumour's right he still has an eye for a bit of skirt. Still, it'll do me no harm to be seen at this. Well—I was talking about this fellow Dunnigan.

WALTER (*meaningly*): A very different story, of course.

BANNISTER: Very. Where had I got to? Oh, yes—about him giving up the grocery business. Well, you'd have thought he'd look out for a decent place if he was determined to take up farming. But the demned idiot goes and buys that place beyond the Manor House grounds, marching with the beach, that has never been anything but a hopeless proposition. Pure sand. He might as well have chucked his money down a grate. I need hardly tell you he's been pulling the devil by the tail ever since. I should never have let him open an account here. Now you see the kind of man you're sympathising with.

WALTER: You've your idea and I have mine.

BANNISTER: If you'd had to battle through on your own you'd find it easier to know who pull their weight and who are passengers.

WALTER: Maybe my idea of weight-pullers and passengers wouldn't just fit in with yours, Dad.

BANNISTER: No. I daresay you'd have some fool notions on that too. Did you draft that letter to Willshire's?

WALTER: Sure I hadn't time. Dunningan came in just——

BANNISTER (*clicking his tongue*): Always some excuse. I think I'll get you to work alongside McNinch for a day or two and you'll see what can be got through. Now, for goodness sake, sit down and do that letter. The market's firming and I want the confirmation in their hands at earliest. (*He turns over the letter file till he comes to the ones he wants, then hands them to* WALTER.) There you are. You'll get all the data in those three letters. (WALTER *sits down and reluctantly commences to study*

B

the correspondence.   A knock comes at the door and
McNinch, *the clerk, re-enters.)*

McNinch : That's the stomach powder.

Bannister : Good.   You weren't long.

McNinch : No.   There was nobody in front of me at the Bank.

Bannister : Did you look into the bus depot?

McNinch : Yes, but I saw nothing there for Blackstock.

Bannister : You didn't ask the clerk fellow?

McNinch : He was engaged with somebody.

　　　　(McNinch *seemed ill at ease.)*

Bannister : All right.   Get out all those statements of unpaid
　　　accounts and I'll go into them with you after the dinner
　　　hour.

McNinch (*jerkily*) : Mr. Bannister?

Bannister : Yes?

McNinch : May I have a word with you?

Bannister (*after regarding him keenly*) : Go ahead.

McNinch : Alone?

　　　　(Bannister *again studies* McNinch's *face, then turns
　　　to* Walter.)

Bannister : You can finish that in the general office, Walter, and
　　　then give the letter to Miss Bell straight away.

Walter (*gathering up papers*) : Righto.

　　　　(*Exit* Walter.)

Bannister (*impatiently*) : Well, what's the need for all the
　　　secrecy?

McNinch : I'd like you to consider an increase in my wages,
　　　Mr. Bannister.

Bannister : I wouldn't doubt it.   It's a pity you got one not
　　　long ago.

McNinch : Half-a-crown nine months ago.

Bannister : You're one of mighty few that have got anything
　　　extra for many a day.

McNinch : I could tell you half-a-dozen who've got rises in the
　　　last three months.

Bannister : Don't believe all you hear.   Some people are better
　　　at blowing than anything else.   Prices have to be cut to
　　　the bone now to bring in any business.   No firm can
　　　afford adding to overheads these days.   No, as soon as
　　　I see any chance——

McNinch (*doggedly*) : Mr. Bannister—I've £2 17s. 6d. a week
　　　and that's not enough to get married on.

BANNISTER: Oh, so you're getting married? Well, I married on a sight less than that, my lad.

MCNINCH: Money was worth more then.

BANNISTER (*nettled*): Well, I've told you it's all this business can afford to pay you at the present.

MCNINCH: You can afford to sink a lot in the new business.

BANNISTER: What new business?

MCNINCH: The café.

BANNISTER (*angrily*): What the devil's it got to do with you how I invest my money? I'll take less of your cheek, McNinch.

MCNINCH: I'm giving you the chance of increasing my wages, Mr. Bannister.

BANNISTER (*with angry cynicism*): You're giving me the chance of increasing them? Did anyone ever see such decency? Watch your step, or I'll maybe take the chance in a way that won't suit you.

MCNINCH: What do you mean?

BANNISTER: Not so much of your questioning, young fellow, or I'll give you your cards.

MCNINCH: I'll save you the trouble by asking for them.

BANNISTER (*astounded*): Eh? What did you say?

MCNINCH: You can take a week's notice from Saturday.

BANNISTER (*flummoxed*): Oh, is that the way of it?

MCNINCH (*quietly*): That's the way of it. You know well my job's worth more than you're paying me, Mr. Bannister. I hoped you'd see that for yourself, but it looks as if I'll have to go on waiting.

BANNISTER (*temporising*): Isn't it a bit daft to throw in your hand for the sake of waiting a bit longer?

MCNINCH: Oh, I haven't just been sitting around till I came in here now.

BANNISTER: D'you mean you've got another job?

MCNINCH: I'm pretty sure of one.

BANNISTER: Where?

MCNINCH (*ignoring the question*): Do you want me to serve a week's notice?

BANNISTER: I see you're giving nothing away.

MCNINCH: Why should I?

BANNISTER (*bullying*): Don't be in such a hurry. And don't be so clippy with your tongue. You might need a reference, you know.

McNinch: I don't think so.

Bannister (*quite stumped*): Damned independent, aren't you?

McNinch: I wish I was. Then I wouldn't have to go begging for enough money to live decently.

Bannister: And how much more are you getting where you're going?

McNinch: That's my business.

> (Bannister *regards* McNinch *a moment longer in silence.*)

Bannister: Go back to your work and I'll think over this rise.

McNinch: I want to know one way or the other now.

Bannister: Well, you're not getting it one way or the other now.

McNinch: All right. Am I to serve the week's not——

Bannister (*shouting angrily*): No. Get your cards and your money to date and get out. (McNinch *quietly leaves the office.* Bannister *rings through to the main office.*) Tell Mr. Walter to come down here. What? It doesn't matter what he's finishing. Tell him he's to come at once. (*He bangs the receiver down angrily. Then rings through to the main office again.*) Miss Bell? Listen carefully, now. Make up McNinch's wages to date and give him his cards. Yes, I said McNinch. You're not deaf, are you? That's all.

> (*Enter* Walter *as he puts down the receiver.*)

Walter (*with a whistle of amazement*): Am I hearing right? Is the faithful William removing his pen and nose from your service?

Bannister: That's not funny. And I'm in no mood for listening to wisecracks.

Walter: Astounding! The model at whose feet I was supposed to sit. Truly this is Ichabod.

Bannister: If you can't talk sense, don't talk at all. Look you here now—this fellow's going and that means you're to do a bit of real work for a change. At least till I pick up somebody in his place.

Walter: What happened?

Bannister: Don't ask fool questions. I'm not having any whippersnapper of a clerk dictating to me.

Walter: All the same you don't seem to be viewing the nose's departure with whoops of joy, Dad.

Bannister: It always means a certain amount of dislocation getting another fellow into the way of the job at the busiest time. That's the thanks you get for taking a scut straight from school and training him. (*The door opens and* AUNT MARIA *enters*.) Heth, the gossip mustn't have been much worth this morning.

AUNT M.: I got a bit of news up the town there I thought you'd like to hear at once.

BANNISTER: It must have been good when it brought you back as quick as this.

AUNT M.: Maybe you'll not think it as good when you hear it. You know this man who's bought the Manor House?

BANNISTER } (*together*): Yes.
WALTER }

AUNT M.: You're not doing what you like with him, I'm telling you.

BANNISTER: What do you mean?

AUNT M.: Just what I say. He's put a big notice at the end of the lane to the beach.

WALTER: What kind of notice?

AUNT M.: Oh, very simple. " Cars not permitted "—that's all.

WALTER: Did you see it?

AUNT M.: No, but Archie Colhoun told me when I was up seeing his Mother.

BANNISTER (*to* WALTER): There you are now.

WALTER: Are you sure, Auntie?

AUNT M.: What?

WALTER (*louder*): I said are you sure?

AUNT M.: Didn't I tell you Archie Colhoun saw it with his own two eyes?

WALTER: Actually you didn't?

BANNISTER: This man's early throwing his weigh about. What about your big café now, my bucko?

WALTER: Oh, I'm sure it'll be all right when I explain things to him.

BANNISTER: You are? Well, I'm not. I've met this pig-headed kind before.

WALTER: Yes, I seem to have also. Anyway, there's no use moaning about it.

BANNISTER: There's a lot of use moaning about the money I'm throwing away.

AUNT M.: Well, there you have it. I'll go on in and see about the dinner.

(*Exit* AUNT MARIA.)

BANNISTER: Some of these windbags in the town have told him
   what you're after. You will go round gassing and thinking
   everybody's your friend.

WALTER: Possibly a bit of jealousy because I thought of the
   bright idea first.

BANNISTER: The cheek of some of these craglurs isn't ordinary.
   Hardly into the town till they're ruling the roost.

WALTER: Calm yourself, Dad.

BANNISTER (*snorting*): Calm myself? I like your nerve, atter
   getting me into this mess. Your tongue's been going
   like the clapper of a bell and every Tom, Dick and Harry
   in the town knows what we're after. Well, John
   Bannister never yet took a left-hander lying down and
   by Heavens——

WALTER: My dear Dad, that's only bull-neck talk. What's needed
   in a situation like this is diplomacy.

BANNISTER: Diplomacy be damned. Diplomacy won't stop those
   gurnets laying bricks at your " bright idea " and piling
   up costs against me.

WALTER: Whether you like it or not, this man is within his
   rights. Don't forget I was eighteen months at the law.

BANNISTER: I wish to God you'd stayed at it or anything else
   outside the town.

WALTER: We'll not argue the point at the minute. But get this
   clear—there's no right-of-way through that lane.

BANNISTER: Blethers. There's not a man, woman or child in
   the place doesn't know every blade of grass on it.

WALTER: Doesn't make a pick of difference. If I remember
   rightly, the gate was shut and padlocked on the last day
   of July every year. That simply meant they could have
   shut it all the time if they'd wanted. I'll just have to
   see this man and talk sense into him.

BANNISTER: I wish you joy of your job. But it's a nice thing
   to see a son of mine going with his cap in his hand to
   a craytur that never was heard of in the town till a couple
   of months ago.

WALTER: I'll not lose any sleep over that.

   (*The phone rings.*)

BANNISTER (*at phone*): Yes?——Mr. who?——Hmph, what does
   he want?——Right. Send him down. (*He puts up the
   receiver.*)

WALTER: Who is it?

BANNISTER: Chisholm, the agent. I wonder what this bucket of soft soap wants. (*Knock at the office door.*) Come in. (*Enter* MR. CHISHOLM, *a clean-shaven man in the sixties. Unctuous and oily sweet.*)

CHISHOLM: Ah, good morning, Mr. Bannister. 'Morning, Walter. (BANNISTER *merely nods.* WALTER *returns the greeting.*) Very glad to find you both in.

BANNISTER (*bluntly*): Anything in the business line I can do for you?

CHISHOLM: Yes, I would like a little chat about a certain matter, but I'll come to that shortly.

BANNISTER: As shortly as you can, if you don't mind. We're very busy at the minute.

CHISHOLM: Quite. I quite understand. (*Expansively.*) Well— I think you ought to know all of us in the town feel just as strongly as you and Walter must about this—what shall I call it?—dictatorship.

(*He looks from one to the other as if expecting some sign of appreciation.*)

BANNISTER (*dryly*): You might tell us what you're driving at.

CHISHOLM: I—I mean this notice that's been put at the beach lane.

BANNISTER: Oh!

WALTER (*filling an awkward pause*): Thanks, Mr. Chisholm.

CHISHOLM: Not at all, Walter. Pleasure.

BANNISTER: It's as cheap sitting as standing and less fidgety.

CHISHOLM (*sitting*): Oh, thank you.

WALTER: Then the townspeople appreciate we're trying to do something for Carrigmore?

CHISHOLM: You need have no doubts on that score, Walter. None at all. Personally I never lose an opportunity of telling them. No later than to-day I was saying I felt proud to belong to a community that has such public-spirited citizens, anxious and willing to invest——

BANNISTER: Not so strong on the " anxious and willing " part of it, Mr. This café business and all connected with it was my son's idea. Unfortunately it's being worked out with my money.

WALTER (*smiling*): You see, Mr. Chisholm, Dad wants to count his chickens before the eggs are laid, let alone hatched.

CHISHOLM: Well, Mr. Bannister, in my humble opinion there hasn't been anything so constructive done here in my time as the building of a really first-class café. Apart altogether from the attraction of summer visitors, th's is a market town and it will be a real boon to the country people.

WALTER : Of course my primary object is the attraction of summer visitors, Mr. Chisholm.

CHISHOLM : Yes, I can quite understand that, Walter. And the other will follow naturally. And in bringing a bigger public to Carrigmore the benefit will be felt by the traders generally. After all, nothing induces a buying frame of mind better than a well-filled stomach. (*He folds his hands and grins in oily fashion.*)

BANNISTER : Listen, Mr.—as I've told my son here more than once, talk's a cheap commodity. I haven't noticed much anxiety among any of the rest of you to put your hands in your pockets. You're pretty clear in your mind they're all going to benefit?

CHISHOLM : Yes, I do think so. Of course, you've rather anticipated the immediate need—from a publicity point of view.

BANNISTER : You think our guns are pretty well spiked at the minute?

CHISHOLM : Yes, by the closing of the right-of-way to the beach for cars.

WALTER : Not right-of-way, Mr. Chisholm. That's the crux of the whole matter.

CHISHOLM : I know, Walter. We'd all come to regard it as a right-of-way, till this notice forcibly reminded us that it isn't. It doesn't look as if much can be done about it, does it?

BANNISTER : You might be surprised, Mr.

CHISHOLM : I certainly would—and interested—if you can show me any way the rest of us in the town can help. Well— speaking for myself, you can most certainly count on me, Mr. Bannister. And on any influence I can have in other directions.

BANNISTER : Good.

CHISHOLM : And I repeat, as a Carrigmore man, I can't tell you how indignant I feel.

BANNISTER : Splendid. And, as you said yourself, knowing the benefit to the whole of Carrigmore, you'd be one of the first to help, if we can think of a way out of the mess?

CHISHOLM: Emphatically.

BANNISTER: Well, my son hasn't given up hope that he'll persuade this man at the Manor House to see reason. If he succeeds, it will mean the lane has to be got ready for cars. We can call on your help then, can we?

CHISHOLM: Just point the way.

(*Long pause.*)

BANNISTER: First turn to the left and the second building on your right.

CHISHOLM (*dubiously*): I—I don't follow you.

BANNISTER: You don't need to. I'm with the Northern Bank. Isn't your account with the Ulster? Second building on the right, round the corner.

CHISHOLM (*somewhat discomfited*): Er—yes. But what exactly do you mean?

BANNISTER: Just that if we can do anything about this lane it's going to cost money. And with the benefits you say you're all going to share, it shouldn't come out of my pocket only.

CHISHOLM (*confused*): Of course, when I mentioned benefits, I meant for the traders. You'll readily understand it wouldn't mean much, if anything, to a man in my line?

BANNISTER: I wouldn't readily understand anything of the kind, Mr. You're in general agencies and insurance. You're selling to the shops round here and these visitors will be buying your stuff from them. As far as I can see you're one who'll benefit most, for the repeat orders will come your way. With all this enthusiasm and indignation of yours you're the very man to head a subscriptions list and use all the influence you have to add to it. I'll promise to put my name to it. What d'you say?

CHISHOLM (*very confused*): M'yes. You see, Mr. Bannister——

BANNISTER: No hummin' and hawin', Mr. I'm a very plain-speaking man and I like straight answers to straight questions.

CHISHOLM: To be quite frank, I'm rather pressed for time at the moment.

BANNISTER (*dryly*): I'd never have thought it. What about the money part of it?

CHISHOLM: You see, in a business like mine one has continual requests for subscriptions for this and that. (*Putting his hand in his breast pocket.*) I could just show you——

BANNISTER: Don't bother. You'll pardon me saying the only thing you're generous with is the wind of your mouth.

WALTER (*embarrassed*): That's a bit of a left-hander, Dad.

CHISHOLM: Yes, I feel rather hurt.

BANNISTER: I was never much of a hand at gilding pills, Mr. And I'm not very partial to wind—whether it's in my stomach or my ears. (*Rising.*) What was it in the business line you were wanting to mention?

CHISHOLM (*rising too*): Perhaps this is hardly the best time to mention it.

BANNISTER: No time like the present, Mr. Fire ahead.

CHISHOLM (*hesitantly*): Well—I've taken on a new agency for a very good Sheffield cutlery house. I was wondering if and when the café gets going——

BANNISTER (*dryly*): Oh, I see. I can understand your indignation now, Mr. Just bring your samples round along with that subscription list and I'll have a look at them. Good morning.

CHISHOLM (*crestfallen*): Good morning. Good morning, Walter.

WALTER: Good morning, Mr. Chisholm.

(*Exit* CHISHOLM.)

BANNISTER: The place smells better with that out.

WALTER: You were a bit brutal with him, Dad.

BANNISTER: Handling hypocrites with kid gloves isn't my strong point. You're too ready to take people at their face value.

WALTER: But there are certain courtesies in life, especially under your own roof.

BANNISTER (*contemptuously*): Tcha— I've know that man for thirty years—since the days he came nosing round your Aunt Maria for a while, and he hasn't changed a bit.

WALTER: Oh, is he an old flame of Auntie's?

BANNISTER: Yes. They'd have been a nice pair to be tethered together. But I'll say she'd have squeezed some of the oil out of him.

WALTER: What ditched it?

BANNISTER: The late Mrs. Chisholm.

WALTER: She's not dead very long?

BANNISTER: A matter of eighteen months or so. I think the oil agreed with her stomach better than your Aunt Maria's. Not but what the man's miss was his mercy.

WALTER: You're not being very complimentary to Auntie, are you?

BANNISTER: No harm being honest inside the family.

WALTER: Dad, did you really mean you thought I'd pull it off with this old josser at the Manor?

BANNISTER: I really meant nothing at all. I wanted to get it out of that hypocrite that there wasn't an ounce of sincerity in all that blethers he was talking about indignation. It was just leading up to try and sell us cutlery.

WALTER (*slyly*): Then you think everything that's done as a means to an end is hypocrisy, Dad?

BANNISTER: I certainly do.

WALTER: Take care. What about the anniversary service at Cloughaninny?

BANNISTER (*looking hard at him*): What do you mean?
> (*The door opens and* AUNT MARIA *puts her head in.*)

AUNT M.: What did I tell you? Twenty minutes to one.

BANNISTER (*irritably*): All right. I'm coming.
> (BANNISTER *is waving her out as the curtain descends.* WALTER *is smiling as he follows* BANNISTER, *who turns and looks hard at his son as* WALTER'S *final remark dawns on him.*)

CURTAIN.

End of Act One.

ACT TWO.

(The scene is again the private office of John Bannister & Co. The time is evening, a week later. JOHN BANNISTER *is again alone in the office, seated at his desk, when the curtain goes up. He is intently studying some papers, with which he is obviously very dissatisfied. His displeasure is conveyed by repeated clickings of his tongue. The phone rings and he throws the papers from him with a gesture of disgust and lifts the receiver.)*

BANNISTER *(at phone)*: Yes?——Who?——Oh, Mr. McClatchy. Yes, put him through——'Evening, Mr. McClatchy. Anything I can do for you?——What?——Of course you've paid it——You've got the statement showing it still outstanding? *(He clicks his tongue disgustedly.)* Well, I'm very sorry, Mr. McClatchy——Yes, I know it's most annoying. Just hold a minute. I've the copies on my desk. *(He turns over the papers on his desk with extreme impatience, tossing them right and left till he comes to the one he wants.)* Yes, you're quite right. I have it here——Well, the position is that my managing clerk left a week ago and the fellow I've got in his place is just feeling his way yet——I know——Just tear it up and accept my apologies——Hello, Mr. McClatchy, I've a very nice parcel of——Oh, very good. Well, I'm really sorry about that blunder——Right, Mr. McClatchy. Good-bye. *(He slams down the receiver a moment, then lifts it again.)* Miss Bell? I want you here. *(He replaces the receiver. In a moment* MISS BELL *enters.)*

MISS BELL: Yes, Mr. Bannister?

BANNISTER: Have you not tried to show that brainless idiot how to make out statements correctly?

MISS BELL *(with frigidity)*: I've my own work to do, Mr. Bannister.

BANNISTER: There's McClatchy of Quay Road on the phone about getting a statement for a paid account. He couldn't have picked a worse man. Always prides himself he never has to be asked for an account and as touchy as be damned about it.

MISS BELL (*on her dignity*): Do you want to speak to the new clerk?

BANNISTER: No. Keep him out of my sight, till I cool down. In the mood I'm in I'd sack him on the spot.

MISS BELL: It was you engaged him, Mr. Bannister.

BANNISTER: You needn't harp on that. He seemed the best of a bad lot. Lord knows what the worst would have turned out. Anyway, couldn't you take an odd look over his shoulder?

MISS BELL: Yes, if I hadn't to do about two people's work as it is. Of course if you're not satisfied——

BANNISTER: Heavens, don't you be getting chips on your shoulder next. You're all that thin-skinned these days I can't look sideways at you.

MISS BELL: You can't blame me if he isn't able to do his work.

BANNISTER: Who's blaming you? I only asked you to try and put this numbskull on the rails. We'll maybe lose McClatchy's account over this.

MISS BELL (*on the verge of tears*): I haven't time, Mr. Bannister. And I never had anything to do with that work when Mr. McNinch was here.

BANNISTER (*with a gesture*): Now don't start blubbering.

MISS BELL (*sobbing*): Well, it's not fair.

BANNISTER: Oh, Lord—go on back to your work.

(*Exit* MISS BELL, *with her handkerchief to her eyes.* BANNISTER *picks up the papers again and resumes his tongue-clicking. In a moment or two* WALTER *enters.*)

WALTER: Well, Dad——

BANNISTER (*peremptorily*): Wait a minute.

WALTER: What's wrong?

BANNISTER: What's right? This creature I've taken on is about as much good as a cock sparrow. Most of this work will have to be done all over again. To crown it all, he's gone and sent a statement to McClatchy, of Quay Road, showing an account that's paid. The hardest man on our books to deal with and the best pay.

WALTER: And you said you'd find it easy to replace McNinch?

BANNISTER: Oh, quit yattering, would you.

WALTER: It strikes me the quicker you try to get McNinch back, the better; Miss Bell's as crotchety as a baby getting teeth these days.

BANNISTER : What d'you know about babies getting teeth? I'm
    just after asking her to take a look at this fellow's work
    and she's away out in a bucket of tears.

WALTER : You'll get her notice next.

BANNISTER : Aren't you the right Job's comforter?

WALTER : I know some of these women better than you think.

BANNISTER : You know everything. If you knew how to sit down
    and do an honest day's work in the office I wouldn't be
    spoon-feeding everybody in it. Well, I suppose you're
    back to add to the tale of woe? How did you get on?

WALTER : Not so good.

BANNISTER : I thought as much.

WALTER : I called at the Manor House after lunch-time. And,
    by the way, that little closed car was parked at the side.

BANNISTER : Hmph.

WALTER : An elderly woman—a housekeeper by the look of her—
    opened the door and I asked for Mr. Kennedy. She
    wanted to know who I was and then left me there.

BANNISTER : On the doorstep, like somebody selling brushes!
    Isn't that great? A nice come-down for the Bannisters
    in their own town.

WALTER : She came back and told me Mr. Kennedy wasn't free.

BANNISTER : I wouldn't wonder. You were likely spoiling sport.
    When these old fellows go like that, there's no holding
    them. Well, that's you up the gum tree.

WALTER : Oh, I don't give in as easily as that.

BANNISTER : Don't tell me you've hatched some new hare-brained
    notion?

WALTER : I've at least one card up my sleeve. When I left
    I went and saw Dunnigan.

BANNISTER : And what in Heaven's name did you go to see him
    about?

WALTER : It's time you put your thinking cap on.

BANNISTER : Quit this talking in riddles.

WALTER : I'm not talking in riddles. Don't you remember where
    Dunnigan's farm is?

BANNISTER : Heth, I ought to. I'm sure the postman's got
    corns on his feet carrying bills to it for me.

WALTER : And don't you remember the only other property that
    fronts the beach is Dunnigan's place?

BANNISTER : D'you mean you went to see Dunnigan about a way
    across his farm?

WALTER: Exactly.

BANNISTER: Sure there is none.

WALTER: I know that.

BANNISTER: Then what are you blethering about?

WALTER: Couldn't we cut one?

BANNISTER: And he'll let us do that for nothing, I suppose?

WALTER: Of course he won't.

BANNISTER: Meaning more expense?

WALTER: No use spoiling the ship for a ha'porth of tar. We're too far committed to neglect any way out.

BANNISTER: You've jockeyed me into this nicely. I'm going to be out a right penny before you've finished.

WALTER: Many a man makes a long-term investment.

BANNISTER: This one's elastic. It gets longer every time we talk about it.

WALTER: The wisest man on God's earth couldn't have anticipated this old fossil being so short-sighted about the whole thing.

BANNISTER: And I'll certainly admit you're not the wisest man on God's earth.

WALTER: Maybe not. But I imagine you'll find my head's screwed on tighter than you think.

BANNISTER: I'll live in hope. D'you know is Dunnigan's land free-hold?

WALTER: We'll find that all out in due course.

BANNISTER: I hope you didn't go and blab all this mix-up to that wee runt?

WALTER: Of course not. I just pretended I was out for a walk and looked in about what you did to him last week.

BANNISTER (*with his chin out*): What d'you mean?

WALTER: I just told him I was sorry for what had happened and that I'd still do my best for him. It'll get his sympathy for the other thing.

BANNISTER: I like your damn cheek.

WALTER (*unperturbed*): I'm glad you do. Because it was the only way to tackle it. We've got to get on the right side of this wee man by hook or by crook. By the way, I asked him to come along here this evening and see both of us.

BANNISTER: Well, heth it's the last straw, begging favours from a body like Dunnigan.

WALTER: He's the only one can get us out of this deadlock so I suggest you don't let him see that too plainly.

BANNISTER: I felt when I put my name to the building of that café I was daft. Now I know it. What with endless talking round this thing and neglecting my own work, I'm losing on both the swings and the roundabouts. When's this fellow coming?

WALTER: Any time now.

BANNISTER: What'll it cost to cut this way through his land?

WALTER: Well, I'd a good look round and at the narrowest part it's only about a hundred yards across to the beach from the county road. We don't need anything elaborate—a bit of cheap fencing on either side and a tar surface over screenings and the thing's done.

BANNISTER: If we're doing nothing else we're giving plenty of labour round the countryside.

WALTER: Bread cast on the waters, Dad.

BANNISTER: I've my doubts. (*Pause.*) Did Dunnigan give you any idea what he'd be looking for the bit of land?

WALTER: I didn't ask him. Driving bargains comes more naturally to you. That's why I asked him here.

BANNISTER: The land's no good anyway. If he got anything at all it'd be found money.

WALTER: I'm sure poor wee Dunnigan will be easy meat for you.

BANNISTER: It riles me having to be under a compliment to him for anything.

WALTER: Yes, I suppose it's a bit hard to stomach after being the other way round for so long.

BANNISTER: I'll offer him a cut-and-dried sum—take it or leave it.

WALTER: My dear Dad, you'll do nothing of the kind. I advised you before not to be bull-necked. Don't you realise Dunnigan's our only remaining hope? Forgive my harping on it, but you do need to learn diplomacy.

BANNISTER: I'm sick and tired of the whole thing. I've half a mind to go and buy the builders off that contract.

WALTER: What good would that do you? Would you leave the place there, more than half built? Or pull it down again? You'd be the laughing-stock of the town then all right. We can pull every one of these irons out of the fire yet, if we handle the thing right. And at the moment everything centres on Dunnigan.

BANNISTER: I'm sure the half of the town are splitting their sides already.

WALTER: That needn't worry us. He who laughs last laughs longest.

(*The phone rings.*)

BANNISTER (*at phone*): Yes?——Yes, send him in. (*He puts down the receiver.*) Here's this fellow now.

WALTER: Now, Dad, go easy.

BANNISTER: No soft talk out of you—remember that. (*Knock at the office door.*) Come in.

(*Enter* DUNNIGAN. *He appears much more assured and has lost his apologetic, cringing air.*)

DUNNIGAN (*brusquely*): Good evenin'. (*He takes a chair without waiting to be asked.*)

WALTER: Good evening, Mr. Dunnigan.

DUNNIGAN: You wanted to see me?

BANNISTER (*regarding him quizzically*): Not particularly. (WALTER *gives him a warning cough.*) My son here tells me he asked you to call in.

DUNNIGAN: Right. And here I am.

(BANNISTER *looks definitely puzzled.* This is a new DUNNIGAN.)

BANNISTER: Well—er—the fact is we wanted to see you about that—er—scruffy bit o' land of yours at the end of the beach.

DUNNIGAN (*belligerently*): Best bit o' land on my farm.

BANNISTER: God forgive you. (WALTER *coughs again and looks across at his father.*) It wouldn't grow weeds, let alone crops.

DUNNIGAN: It's my land and I'm the best judge of its worth.

BANNISTER: You must have changed a lot then.

DUNNIGAN: I might as well tell you I've made arrangements to get real good fertilisers since I was here last. You're not the only one in the trade, Mr. Bannister.

BANNISTER: You're welcome to go wherever you like for your stuff and the further from here the better.

WALTER: Dad, for Heaven's sake——

BANNISTER (*to* WALTER): Am I doing the talking or you?

WALTER: You are, and I wish you'd keep to the point. I asked Mr. Dunnigan——

BANNISTER: I know you asked him. Didn't I tell him that?

WALTER: Well, please confine yourself to why I asked him.

C

BANNISTER: Amn't I?

DUNNIGAN: Oh no, you're not. You're running down my land.

BANNISTER: Heth, you're getting very thin in the hide all of a sudden.

DUNNIGAN: That's as may be. But I'm not going to let you——

BANNISTER (*sticking out his chin*): You're not going to let me? (*He laughs cynically.*)

WALTER: For goodness sake will you both keep your wool on?

DUNNIGAN (*rising and addressing* WALTER): Any use me staying any longer, Mr. Walter?

WALTER (*conciliatory*): Of course. Sit down, Mr. Dunnigan. (*He produces cigarette case.*) Here—have a cigarette.

DUNNIGAN: Thanks, I don't use them. I'll have a draw at the pipe. (*He produces a clay pipe, with a tin top, from his waistcoat pocket, takes off the top and knocks the " dottle" into the heel of his hand. Then he takes a block of plug and a knife from another pocket, carves a slice or two and rubs it up along with the "dottle" and lights up. All the time* BANNISTER *regards him like a fascinated rabbit.* DUNNIGAN *blows a cloud of smoke and* BANNISTER *sniffs the air with very evident disgust.*)

WALTER: Now, Dad, forget all that and have a fresh go.

BANNISTER: Well—er—you know why you're here?

DUNNIGAN: I'm waiting to know, but I've a fair idea.

BANNISTER: My son estimated the width of the narrowest part of that waste lan——

DUNNIGAN: That what?

BANNISTER (*swallowing hard*): That land to the beach—at about a hundred yards.

DUNNIGAN (*very emphatically*): Oh, no. Divil the fear.

BANNISTER: That's what you said, Walter.

WALTER: Well—I admit it was a guess, but it seems about that.

DUNNIGAN: A hundred and fifteen yards and a couple o' feet. I measured it myself.

BANNISTER: That's a hell of a difference.

DUNNIGAN: Nothing like being dead right when it comes to land —or money. You'd be the first to agree with that, Mr. Bannister?

(BANNISTER *looks murderously at* DUNNIGAN, *but a warning glance from* WALTER *restrains him.*)

BANNISTER: Well, Dunnigan, my son and I are anxi——
    interested in cutting a way through to the beach from
    the road, wide enough to take two-way motor traffic.

DUNNIGAN (*slyly*): I see. What about the loanin' through the
    Manor grounds? After all, it's nearer.

BANNISTER: There are—certain difficulties about it.

DUNNIGAN: Are there so? Of course there might be certain
    difficulties about my land too.

BANNISTER: What kind of difficulties?

DUNNIGAN (*complacently*): Oh, different kinds. Financial and
    otherwise.

WALTER (*again conciliatory*): I'm sure there's nothing we can't
    talk over, Mr. Dunnigan.

DUNNIGAN: That's up to your father and you. I'm ready to listen
    to anything you have to say.

BANNISTER (*cynically*): Mighty good of you, I'm sure.

WALTER: Righto, Mr. Dunnigan. Well, the position——

BANNISTER: I thought I was doing the talking.

WALTER: I'm just trying to make things clear to Mr. Dunnigan
    for a minute. Then you can carry on.

BANNISTER: That's what I was trying to do.

DUNNIGAN: Oh no, Mr. Bannister. You were trying to dictate.

BANNISTER (*indignantly*): You wee——

WALTER (*coughing loudly*): Quite. You see, Mr. Dunnigan, as
    my father said, we're anxious to cut a way through from
    the county road to the beach that can take two-way traffic.

DUNNIGAN: I understand that all right.

WALTER: Splendid. Well, I think that spot on your farm would
    just be ideal. It's the shortest possible distance and it
    leads on to firm sand, well above high-water mark.

DUNNIGAN: So does the Manor loanin' for that matter. Of course
    I walked round that way coming up here and saw the
    notice.

WALTER: M'yes—spiteful bit of work, don't you think?

DUNNIGAN: Ach, I don't know. Every man has a right to do what
    he wants with his own property.

BANNISTER: You're a grand Carrigmore man, aren't you?

DUNNIGAN: I'm not such a mug as to believe you're doing all
    this just for the good of Carrigmore.

BANNISTER: You cheeky wee whippersnapper.

WALTER (*despairingly*): Listen here, both of you. We'll never
    get anywhere if you don't drop these personalities.

BANNISTER: All right. You do the talking for a while.

WALTER: I think it would be better. Now, we'll get down to brass tacks. Mr. Dunnigan, are you willing to part with a small slice of your land at that point?

DUNNIGAN: Maybe—if it's made worth my while.

BANNISTER: Worth your while?

WALTER (*protestingly*): Ach, Dad——

> (BANNISTER, *with his eyes on* DUNNIGAN, *silences* WALTER *with a gesture.*)

DUNNIGAN: Aye, I think that's what I said.

BANNISTER: How worth your while?

DUNNIGAN: That's up to you.

BANNISTER (*aggressively*): I mean, how do you mean worth your while?

DUNNIGAN: It's plain English, isn't it?

WALTER: You're not leaving the talking to me for long, Dad.

BANNISTER: I'm thinking it's as well I should handle this part of it. Now, Dunnigan, we're asking you for a bit o' land that hasn't grown as much as a potato for you since you took the place. (*Pointing with his forefinger at* DUNNIGAN.) You can't deny that.

DUNNIGAN: I thought I was asked here to discuss something. Not to go through a cross-examination. I don't choose to sit here answering questions about what I did or didn't do with my land before this. That's my affair.

BANNISTER (*almost apoplectic*): Well, damme——

WALTER (*warningly*): D-a-d. Quite right, Mr. Dunnigan. That *is* your affair.

DUNNIGAN: Yes, I think it is, Mr. Walter.

BANNISTER: Maybe. But there's no harm pointing out facts.

DUNNIGAN: Or what passes for them, to suit your argument.

WALTER: We all have our various opinions as to what Mr. Dunnigan's land is *per se*, but for our purpose that *is* beside the point, Dad.

BANNISTER: It's not beside the point. If I ask a man to give up a bit of good-growing early land he's going to lose a lot more than if I ask him for a few perches of sand.

DUNNIGAN (*triumphantly*): I just thought that was what you were aiming at.

BANNISTER (*chin out*): What d'you mean?

DUNNIGAN: You were were trying to talk me out of my price.

BANNISTER: Don't imagine I came in here on the last load of hay.

DUNNIGAN: Nor me either. So you're wasting your wind.

WALTER (*rising*): Mr. Dunnigan.

DUNNIGAN: Yes?

WALTER: I wonder would you mind going over to the general
office for a few minutes while I have a word with my
father alone? I'll give you a hail when we're ready again.

DUNNIGAN: Right you be, Mr. Walter. I'll just take a dander
round the yard. (*He struts out like a peacock.*)

WALTER: Thanks very much. We'll only be a minute or two.

DUNNIGAN: Oh, don't rush yourself. I'm in no hurry.

> (*Exit* DUNNIGAN, *a look of triumph on his face.*
> WALTER *carefully closes the door after him and comes
> over to his father.*)

WALTER (*earnestly*): Now listen, Father. If you don't watch
you're going to make a pig's breakfast of the whole
thing.

BANNISTER: I'd like to make a pig's breakfast of that wee runt.
Don't you see he's trying to stick his arm in us?

WALTER: And don't YOU see he's positively our last hope?
Whether you realize it or not, you're lording it over him
and that's getting his back up no end.

BANNISTER (*snorting*): That crab coming here to dictate.

WALTER: Now you see how well you like it. You can't get
used to the like of Dunnigan coming any way but with
his cap in his hand.

BANNISTER: Aye, certainly. What other way should he come in?
Doesn't he owe me twenty-five pounds?

WALTER (*impatiently*): Oh, for goodness sake forget about that
twenty-five pounds.

BANNISTER: I'll do nothing of the kind.

WALTER: Well, for the present at any rate. If you start
bringing that up we may call it a day. That would cost
you a sight more than twenty-five quid. If I call him
back, do you think you can keep your temper?

BANNISTER: And if I can't?

WALTER: Then it would be much better if you went out for a
while and left him to me.

BANNISTER (*contemptuously*): Left him to you? You? When
I came back you'd have him in as partner.

WALTER: Of course that's just tripe you're talking. Now, for
Heaven's sake keep on an even keel when I bring him in.
(*He goes to the yard and returns with* DUNNIGAN.) Now,

Mr. Dunnigan, my father and I have had a talk and I think we can come to an arrangement satisfactory to all of us.

DUNNIGAN: I'm glad to hear it.

WALTER ⎱ *(together)*: ⎰ You see, Mr. Dunn——
BANNISTER ⎰   ⎱ Well now, Dunn——

    (They both pause, looking at each other.)

BANNISTER *(to* WALTER*)*: Is it me or you?

WALTER: All right, fire ahead.

BANNISTER: It might be better and quicker for me to make you an offer, Dunnigan. Do you agree to that?

DUNNIGAN: There's no harm in listening.

BANNISTER: What would be your answer to ten pounds?

DUNNIGAN: It would be a rude one.

BANNISTER *(swallowing hard)*: D'you realise that would only be the beginning for us? After that we'd have to get a surface on the ground and fence it and, as likely as not, drain it.

DUNNIGAN: That's your affair.

BANNISTER *(persistently)*: And you won't touch ten pounds?

DUNNIGAN: No, I will not.

BANNISTER *(after a slight pause)*: Tell me what you would think a fair offer.

DUNNIGAN: Listen, Mr. Bannister—it's not what this land's worth to me as it sits. It's what it's worth to you. That's the way I'm looking at it, and you may as well know it right away.

BANNISTER: I thought as much.

DUNNIGAN: Then we needn't waste time talking round the thing. No man in Carrigmore would drive a harder bargain than yourself, or would be less likely to give way an inch once you'd made up your mind.

BANNISTER: We're not here to discuss what I am or amn't.

DUNNIGAN: That cuts both ways.

BANNISTER: You're a bit too ready with your tongue.

WALTER: Now, now—we're getting off the rails again. I think if you'd let us have your idea of a figure we'd get a bit forrarder, Mr. Dunnigan.

DUNNIGAN *(conclusively)*: Very well. I'll tell you what I want and I'm making no bones about it. *(Passionately, staring at* BANNISTER.*)* I came in here a week ago. All I was

looking was a bit o' credit to tide me over.   Any decent
man would have given it to me straight away.

WALTER: Oh come, Mr. Dunnigan, we're trying to get away from
all these personalities.

DUNNIGAN: I'm sorry, Mr. Walter, because I know you'd have
liked to give me a helping hand.   But it's a different
story with your father.

WALTER: MUST we go into all that again?

DUNNIGAN: I've got to.   I may tell you I've since raised the
twenty-five pounds and I could pay that account right now
on the spot.   (*He pauses and looks hard at* BANNISTER.)
But if you want that land, the first condition is that
I'm not paying it now.   I asked for a couple o' months
grace a week ago.   Now I'm fixing the time—SIX
MONTHS.

(*Pause and tableau.*)

BANNISTER (*regarding him fixedly*): I see.   Hmph.

DUNNIGAN: Good.   Do you agree?

BANNISTER: And you call that a fair do?

DUNNIGAN: You're a one to be talking o' fair do's.   (*Passionately.*)
Listen—I'm a wee man compared with you.   Somebody
to your mind that doesn't count.   A failure.   You were
a wee man yourself once, but you've forgotten all that.
And there's nobody as hard on my sort as the wee man
that's risen.   But I've got my feelings.   The last day
I called I asked for something that wasn't going to
mean a damn thing to you, one way or the other.   And
you threw me out.   I suppose you forgot it before the
door shut behind me?   WELL, I DIDNT.

BANNISTER (*laughing cynically*): I'm uneasy.   Well, I've list——

WALTER: Let him finish.

DUNNIAN: Now you want something from me.   Well, you can
have it, but by God at my price.

(*There is a short pause.*   BANNISTER, *with a curl on
his lip, regards* DUNNIGAN.)

BANNISTER: You're a right crooked wee crab, aren't you?

WALTER: Now, Dad——

BANNISTER: Shut up.

DUNNIGAN: And I'll thank you to keep a civil tongue in your head.

BANNISTER: And what if I tell you to keep your land and pay
my bill or I'll put a writ on you?

DUNNIGAN: Right. You think I'm bluffin'? (*He fishes a roll of notes out o fhis pocket.*) There you are. Don't think you're scaring me.

> (*There is a dramatic pause while their faces register their various reactions. On DUNNIGAN'S a look of triumph for his " one crowded hour." On BANNISTER'S a puzzled spleen at his discomfiture. On WALTER'S restrained admiration for DUNNIGAN'S stand.*)

BANNISTER (*to* WALTER): You'll better finish this. I'm going out for a minute. (*At the door he pauses and turns.*) Mind what you're doing. I've still to sanction it.

> (*He goes out, slamming the door. WALTER rises, goes to the door and looks out to make sure his father is out of earshot. Then he comes back to DUNNIGAN with outstretched hand.*)

WALTER: No disrespect to my father, but put it there, Mr. Dunnigan. You're the first man I ever saw leaving him without a word to say.

DUNNIGAN (*taking* WALTER'S *hand*): You tried to do the decent by me, Mr. Walter. I've no hard feeling to you.

WALTER (*shaking hands heartily*): Splendid fellow.

DUNNIGAN: I don't mind talking straight to you. You don't know what it's like to scrape a living begging favours from men who treat you like a doormat.

> (*There is a tremor in DUNNIGAN'S voice.*)

WALTER (*patting him on the back*): I know. But it's a long lane has no turning. Keep your pecker up. And if ever I can do anything to help you, don't hesitate to ask me.

DUNNIGAN (*moved*): Thanks.

WALTER: Now sit down and we'll have a quiet wee chin-wag about this thing. (*They sit down, facing out front. WALTER places his hand on DUNNIGAN'S knee in a very confidential fashion.*) I feel sure you'll not be the man to stick me when I tell vou this whole thing is MY pigeon, Mr. Dunnigan.

DUNNIGAN: But your father's behind it.

WALTER: Not really. Of course he's advancing me the cash to start, but I'll have to pay back every penny of it. Probably with interest.

DUNNIGAN: You don't mean it?

WALTER: I assure you, Mr. Dunnigan. Shylock was a third-rate amateur compared to Dad when it comes to the old pound of flesh business.

> (DUNNIGAN *looks blank*.)

DUNNIGAN: Shylock? Not a local man, is he?

WALTER: Er—no. Much further afield. I heard about him some years ago—when I was at school.

DUNNIGAN: Oh.

WALTER: So, in a way, we're both in the same box.

DUNNIGAN: I wouldn't say that altogether. There's a big differs.

WALTER: Tell you what—suppose we say fifteen pounds for that land?

DUNNIGAN: Oh, now, Mr. Walter.

WALTER: But wait a minute. We'll only regard that as a payment on account, due to the way I'm fixed. Then, when everything's going well, you come along to me at the café and I'll give you my word of honour there'll be a good handshake waiting for you. And I'll see you get your six months' credit on that account.

DUNNIGAN: You'll get him to put that in writing?

WALTER: I will. You'll have a memo to-morrow morning.

> (*There is a pause while* DUNNIGAN *thinks and* WALTER'S *gaze wanders anxiously from* DUNNIGAN'S *face to the door and back*.)

DUNNIGAN: I wouldn't do it for any man but yourself, but I know a decent man when I meet one.

WALTER (*seizing* DUNNIGAN'S *hand*): Stout fellow. I knew you'd be a brother in misfortune. And you can rely on my word.

DUNNIGAN: Yes, I think I can.

WALTER: Definitely. Well—I'll call over at your place and fix it all up. (*With great effusiveness he proceeds to usher* DUNNIGAN *out*.) Here, do have a cigarette.

DUNNIGAN: No, thanks. I never use them.

> (*Exit* DUNNIGAN. WALTER *closes the door, lights a cigarette and executes a triumphal war-dance round the office. As he is doing so,* BANNISTER *comes in. He enters quietly and at that moment* WALTER'S *back is towards him and for a moment* BANNISTER *silently watches*.)

BANNISTER: It's time I got a wall with spikes built round this place.

WALTER (*sheepishly*): Just limbering up the old muscles, Dad.

BANNISTER: Oh. I thought you'd the St. Vity's dance or something. Well—I saw that being going down the yard. How did you finish up with him?

WALTER: Top-hole. Indeed I flatter myself——

BANNISTER: You always do, but cut out the frills. How much did you settle with him for?

WALTER: Believe it or not—fifteen pounds.

BANNISTEx About twice as much as it ought to have been.

WALTER: You know you don't mean that. After all, you mentioned ten pounds as your rock bottom minimum.

BANNISTER: I didn't call it any fancy names like that. I wasn't anxious to waste half a day arguing, so I fixed what I thought a more than decent figure. But, of course, as usual you had to go one better with my money.

WALTER (*smiling*): Damn indigestible things, sour grapes, Dad.

BANNISTER: What are you blethering about?

WALTER (*good humouredly*): No matter. Now, Dad—I'm making out a memo and you're signing it. It's got to be in this evening's post.

BANNISTER: What is it?

WALTER: Something perfectly simple—just confirming the six months' further credit you're giving Dunnigan on his account.

BANNISTER: Well, I'm damned——

WALTER (*calmly*): Shush—don't fly off the handle. Merely a few words on paper and a flick of the pen at the bottom. Simple as ABC. I'll get Miss Bell to rattle it off in two shakes.

BANNISTER (*breathing hard*): If I said what——

WALTER: Right. Don't. You really must look after this blood-pressure of yours better, Dad.

BANNISTER: Who was the fellow in the Bible prayed about his son being a lunatic and sore afflicted?

WALTER (*ingenuously*): Can't quite recall. I'll look it up and tell you. Well—I am glad we've fixed this up with Dunnigan, because now we can go straight ahead. Better make out a cheque for fifteen quid, Dad.

BANNISTER: Before there's a sod cut? What do you think I am?

WALTER: If you asked me what kind of business man you are in making out that cheque, I'd say very far-sighted.

BANNISTER: I've a good mind to put it as a contra account against what he owes me.

WALTER: That would just be plumb daft. I don't think you realise the difficulty I had in getting him to accept fifteen pounds.

BANNISTER: Do you not know when you're being bluffed?

WALTER (*earnestly*): Dad—there was no bluff about that little man this afternoon. His very soul was smarting over what you did to him last week.

BANNISTER: If I had stayed any longer it wouldn't have been his soul. My toe was itching to get at his bottom.

WALTER: Thank Heaven you kept yourself from anything so insane as that.

BNNIASTER (*sarcastically*): Should we not send an apology for daring to say anything that wasn't flattering to him?

WALTER: I think that came better verbally.

BANNISTER: Came? Do you mean to say you——

WALTER: Of course. The family good name has to be restored by somebody. Blackguarding a man under the cover of your own roof is—well, rather outré, isn't it?

BANNISTER: Rather what?

WALTER: Beyond the pale.

BANNISTER: You've a neck on you.

WALTER: Possibly. I'm very conscious of its redness when you let your feelings off the leash.

BANNISTER (*going to his desk disgustedly*): I may as well get this pantomime over, much as it goes against my grain. (*He commences to write the cheque.*)

WALTER (*rubbing his hands*): Best job you've done for a long time, Dad.

BANNISTER: Rubbish. By the time Miss Bell's done that note it'll be as good as published in the " Chronicle."

WALTER: Well, if it eases your feelings anything I'll run it off on my portable and you can sign it. (*He crosses over to his own desk, where the typewriter sits.*) Here you are, Dad. Sign this. Now the cheque, please. (*Makes out a cheque and gives it to* WALTER.)

WALTER: Now we can make a start with cutting that road. I'll be on the job first thing to-morrow morning.

BANNISTER: You'll do no such thing. First, you'll give me a hand to put these statements right.

WALTER: Ach, Dad—you could do that yourself. Why not
    tackle it this evening?

BANNISTER: I've no time this evening. Half the day's been
    wasted already and the Lord knows who else will be
    ringing-up about mistakes besides McClatchy.

WALTER (*protesting*): I ought to be seeing about the labour for
    that job at once.

BANNISTER: Listen—it's months to the Summer, if it comes to
    that. Now I'm going down to Quay Road to see
    McClatchy. If he sits chewing that over in his mind,
    the Lord knows what he'll do.

WALTER: What the devil do I know about these statements?

BANNISTER: Any that have other than current items, put to one
    side, and we'll have a double check on them.

WALTER (*still protesting*): You see, Dad——

BANNISTER Of course I see. I see that if we don't curb that
    one-track mind of yours we'll be ending in the Bankruptcy
    Court. Now, sit down there and stop arguing.

> (WALTER, *with a gesture of futility, sits down and
> picks up some of the statements listlessly, while
> *BANNISTER* puts on his hat and leaves the office. After
> he exits,* WALTER *lifts the phone and rings through
> to the general office.*)

WALTER (*at phone*): Miss Bell?——I wonder would you be good
    enough to come down here a minute?——Thanks. (*He
    hangs up the receiver and in a moment there is a knock
    at the office door.*) Come in. (*Enter* MISS BELL.) Ah,
    Miss Bell. Do sit down. (*He carefully places a chair
    for her, and* MISS BELL, *rather embarrassed-looking,
    sits.*) Miss Bell, what do you think the best brand of
    chocolates?

MISS BELL (*looking puzzled*): I—beg your pardon, Mr. Walter.

WALTER: No, really—quite seriously. I'm anxious to know.

MISS BELL: Well, speaking for myself——

WALTER: Exactly. That's it, speaking for yourself—yes?

MISS BELL: I like " Carefree " best.

WALTER: Splendid. I saw a lovely two pound box in Miss Best's
    window. I'm going to get them for you.

MISS BELL (*very embarrassed*): No, no—really, Mr. Walter. If
    I'd known——

WALTER: Now, it's as good as done. I've simply been staggered
    with admiration for the way you've been looking after

things since McNinch went. And I know Dad thinks the same.

MISS BELL: You wouldn't have thought that if——

WALTER (*hastily*): Oh, I know. He never praises people to their face. But you should hear him when the two of us are alone. Oh, no—you're in tops with the old man, Miss Bell.

MISS BELL (*still embarrassed*): Well, I'm certainly glad to know that, Mr. Walter. But, about these chocolates——

WALTER: A personal pleasure, Miss Bell. I'll take no refusal. By the way, would you do something for me?

MISS BELL (*on guard*): What do you mean, Mr. Walter?

WALTER (*hastily*): In the way of business.

MISS BELL: If I can do anything——

WALTER (*very enthusiastically*): You certainly can. It's your dead accuracy that gets me. Now—this new fellow's a bit inclined to fluff things—decent chap in his own way, but ram-stam. I suggested to Dad before he went out that we get these statements gone into again carefully and set aside any that have—er— (*He is obviously trying to remember the phraseology.*) Oh, yes—any that have other than current items on them. For a double-check, you know. Very important, this double-check business. Don't you think so, Miss Bell?

MISS BELL: Yes, I suppose so.

WALTER: I knew you would. Well, the position is that I've some very urgent business to see to about the new café and I was wondering if you'd very much oblige me——

MISS BELL: By going over the statements?

WALTER: Exactly. I'm really worried about them and it'd relieve my mind no end.

MISS BELL: All right, Mr. Walter. You don't mind waiting for a little till I get my letters done?

WALTER: Not at all. Take your own time. And I'll have the chocolates for you to-morrow morning.

MISS BELL: Oh, that doesn't matter.

WALTER: Doesn't it? Wait till you see this box. Here you are, Miss Bell. (*He gathers up the statements as if they were hay and gives them to* MISS BELL, *who exits.* WALTER *lights a cigarette. After a moment there is a knock at the office door.*) Come in. (*Enter* MISS BELL *again.*) Yes, Miss Bell?

MISS BELL: Mr. Walter, there's been a young lady waiting in the general office till you were free. She wants to see you.

WALTER (*mystified*): Young lady? What's her name?

MISS BELL: She didn't tell me. She says she's an old friend of yours and wants to make it a surprise. Shall I send her in?

WALTER: I suppose so. (*Exit* MISS BELL. WALTER *fixes his tie and runs his hand over his hair. A light knock comes at the door.*) Come in. (*A pretty girl around* WALTER'S *age enters and carefully closes the door. At* WALTER'S *open-mouthed astonishment she smiles sweetly.*) Angela— well, I'm damned.

ANGELA: Probably. May I sit down, Walter?

WALTER (*placing a chair for her*): Sorry. I just can't get the hang of this. What are you doing in Carrigmore?

ANGELA: I'll tell you in a minute. May I ask a few questions first?

WALTER: Carry on. But my father may be back any time.

ANGELA: Oh, well, if he does you can take me out for coffee somewhere. Why did you not come back to Belfast after Christmas, Walter?

WALTER: Does it matter?

ANGELA: Yes, I'd like to know.

WALTER: I suppose you would. You always were fond of flattery.

ANGELA: What do you mean?

WALTER: You needn't look so innocent. You know jolly well, YOU were why I didn't come back. I'd hear about you being out with this one and that one and——

ANGELA: I didn't know we were engaged.

WALTER: We wern't, and it wasn't my fault. The last straw was the night you told me you had to stay in with your mother and I heard next day you were at the Opera House with Bobby Hayes.

ANGELA: And I was staying in that night, but Mrs. Hayes rang up to ask Mummy to make a fourth at bridge. You know Mummy would take hurdles to get at a bridge table. Of course that left me at a loose end, so Bobby asked me to go to the Opera House. Could anything be more simple?

WALTER: Angela, you could wriggle out of a strait-jacket.

ANGELA: I'm not wriggling out of anything. But you don't mean
to tell me you threw up the law because of that?

WALTER (*a little embarrassed*): Oh, we all have to do a bit of the
trial and error business till we get our real bent.

ANGELA: And you've got yours now?

WALTER: Maybe you wouldn't mind if I did a spot of questioning
for a change?

ANGELA: Not at all.

WALTER: May I ask how you came to be in Carrigmore?

ANGELA (*sweetly*): Certainly. I'm staying with Uncle Thomas
Kennedy at the Manor House.

WALTER (*sitting up with a jerk*): What? (*Slight pause.*) So you
were the young woman they talked about sneaking into
the town by the Moss Road?

ANGELA: Sneaking? Not at all. Can't I come the way I prefer?

WALTER: We'll let that pass. Well, this is the first I've heard
of Uncle Thomas.

ANGELA: Oh, no. I mentioned several times to you about
Mummy's brother, who was a tea-planter in Ceylon.

WALTER: Maybe you did. Somebody in Ceylon wouldn't come
into the picture very much anyway.

ANGELA: Well, Uncle Thomas gave up tea-planting about the
end of last year and decided to come home to Ireland.
He's a bachelor, so of course he came to us. He's always
had the idea of buying a place in the country when he
returned and it was just then we noticed the advert. for
the Manor House in Carrigmore.

WALTER: I see. It's all piecing together nicely now.

ANGELA: I'd heard a lot about the beauty of Carrigmore from
you, so I persuaded Uncle Thomas to make enquiries.

WALTER: Which he duly did and took it? By now he probably
feels he's been done brown.

ANGELA: Why?

WALTER: The place is a wreck.

ANGELA: Uncle got it a bargain and he's going to make all kinds
of improvements. When the contractors have finished
there won't be a nicer old house in the countryside.

WALTER: Are you housekeeping for him?

ANGELA: Oh, no. Mummy got him an elderly woman through
one of the agencies. You probably saw her when you
were up to-day.

WALTER: How did you know I was up?

ANGELA : She told me.

WALTER : I like the reception I got.

ANGELA : Well, I know Uncle Thomas was very busy when you
came.

WALTER : He must have been. Did his plans for improving the
place include the notice he's put up?

ANGELA : About cars going through to the beach?

WALTER : Yes.

ANGELA : That's what I've come to see you about.

WALTER : Oh. I did think he'd come to see the good sense
in my plans.

ANGELA : What do you mean?

WALTER : Aren't you going to tell me he's taking it down?

ANGELA : No. Why should he?

WALTER (*nonplussed*) : Then—what the deuce did you come to
talk about?

ANGELA : Well, I'm sure you realise Uncle didn't take a nice old
place in the country to have a procession of nasty, smelly
cars going through the grounds all Summer.

WALTER : How are you so well up in it all?

ANGELA : Oh, you've a few neighbours who like to talk.

WALTER : And who talked to you?

ANGELA : Oh, no—I'll not give them away. They were very
particular about that. But you said a lot to them first.
I'm sure that rather irritated Uncle Thomas.

WALTER : Might I ask how?

ANGELA : You had quite decided what you were going to do with
that lane before you asked his permission. Of course
your enthusiasms always did run away with you, Walter.

WALTER : Don't get up on a perch, Angela. Surely this old
josser—your Uncle--realises I'm trying to do something
to benefit the town?

ANGELA : Or yourself—according to most of the gossips. They
say they never knew John Bannister to spend a pound
without trying to turn it into two.

WALTER : Since when did I become John Bannister?

ANGELA : Oh, they all know your father's behind you.

WALTER : In one thing only—money. And if you ask me, he's
sorry he backed me when he sees those silly obstacles
put in my way.

ANGELA : You must allow Uncle Thomas his point of view.

WALTER : He can keep it, and I'll keep mine.

ANGELA: Then there's very little more you can do.

WALTER: Don't be too sure of that.

ANGELA: You can't force your way through the lane.

WALTER: I've no intention.

ANGELA (*intrigued*): Then I don't see . . . .

WALTER: Just wait.

ANGELA (*curiously*): Can you tell me how you're . . . .

WALTER: I could, but I won't.

> (*Slight pause, while* ANGELA *regards* WALTER *quizzically.*)

ANGELA (*wheedling*): You always tried to understand any explanation from me before, Walter. It's because I like you I went to all this trouble to make things clear. I don't want you to think Uncle Thomas just put that notice up to thwart you.

WALTER (*dryly*): Very good of you, I'm sure.

ANGELA: And you needn't be so beastly sarcastic.

WALTER: Did I ask you to come?

ANGELA (*indignantly*): Walter Bannister—such a horrible thing to say. (*She takes out her handkerchief and dabs at her eyes and nose.*)

WALTER: Angela.

ANGELA (*sniffing*): Y—es?

WALTER: You haven't changed your tactics a bit. Do you know what I'd like to do?

ANGELA: Apologise, I hope.

WALTER: Spank you, good and hard.

ANGELA (*bolt upright*): How dare you!

WALTER: I'm just being perfectly honest.

ANGELA: You're being perfectly horrible.

WALTER: Then I suggest we call it a day.

ANGELA (*rising and gulping*): Oh! (*She flounces over to the door and passes through, leaving it open.*)

WALTER (*calling*): Angela!

ANGELA (*turning back—curtly*): What?

WALTER: There's a shocking draught from that door.

> (ANGELA *bangs the door.* WALTER *gets up and walks about the office, his face thoughtful. He is lighting a cigarette. In a moment or two his father comes back into the office.*)

BANNISTER: Who was that young woman came out of the yard there?

WALTER: That, my dear Dad, is very much the lady in the case.

BANNISTER: What d'you mean?

WALTER: Sit down. It's quite a story. How did you get on with McClatchy?

BANNISTER: Oh, I smoothed his feathers with soft soap. What about the statements?

WALTER: Miss Bell's looking over them.

BANNISTER: Tut-tut—trust you to buck pass any real work. I suppose she'll be grouching about being put on.

WALTER: Not at all. I had her eating out of my hand in a couple of minutes. It's all in the approach with these women. Now, about this other girl.

BANNISTER: Well?

WALTER: First of all, she's the niece of that man at the Manor House. Secondly, I promised to let you know sometime why I didn't go back to the city after Christmas.

BANNISTER: You're talking like somebody daft.

WALTER: Well, in a nutshell, Angela was the reason—the girl you saw coming out the yard.

BANNISTER: Angela? Angela who?

WALTER: Carr. Her father's a solicitor in Belfast.

BANNISTER: You must be very thick with her?

WALTER: At one time I hoped I was going to marry her.

BANNISTER: Heth, this is news. Why didn't you tell me before?

WALTER: Because it all went haywire. The trouble about Angela is that she's always got her own way in everything, with everybody.

BANNISTER: Including you, I'm sure. I've told you before you're no hand at seeing through people. And you let a wisp of a girl make you throw up your job and everything. There's one born every minute, right enough.

WALTER: You can lay it on with a trowel, Dad, and I'll take it.

BANNISTER: In cold blood, do you see rhyme or reason in what you did?

WALTER: There's no cold blood, rhyme or reason in what any man does when he falls hard for a girl, Dad. I'm sure you were just the same at one time.

BANNISTER: Never. Women were sensible in my day, and knew their place. Not like these dressed-up dolls that are running about now. What did she come to see you about anyway?

WALTER: Well, according to her, her uncle didn't come here to allow a procession of cars to use the Manor grounds all through the Summer. She was very insistent I should see his viewpoint, and very annoyed when I didn't.

BANNISTER: So what?

WALTER: Status quo ante, Dad. In other words, we carry on with our little friend Dunn——

BANNISTER: Our little what?

WALTER: Now just you leave him to me and everything will be O.K. I'll call in with McDonnell, the surveyor, to-morrow and get him to run out to Dunnigan's place with me.

BANNISTER: What for?

WALTER: To get his advice about the best way to handle the job.

BANNISTER: More money. You'd think my pocket was a bottomless pit.

WALTER: Oh, he'll only charge a few guineas.

BANNISTER: And, of course, we pick that off the roadside.

WALTER: Listen, Dad, we simply must have that beach as a park for the cars. It's just as ideal as the town's hopeless. Honestly——

(*The office door opens and* AUNT MARIA, *obviously excited, enters.*)

AUNT M.: John!

BANNISTER (*tersely*): Well?

AUNT M.: Do you hear me, John?

BANNISTER (*louder*): I said " Well?"

AUNT M.: James Chisholm's across the way. He asked me to come over and speak to you.

BANNISTER: Heth, it's a change for him to lose his tongue. What does he want?

WALTER (*interposing*): Dad, I'll slip round to the Post Office with this letter for Dunnigan. Be back in a minute.

(*Exit* WALTER.)

AUNT M.: Listen carefully, John.

BANNISTER (*impatiently*): Go on, Maria—go on.

AUNT M.: James was up at the Manor House, seeing this man Kennedy—something about insurance——

BANNISTER (*sotto voce*): Aye, he'd insure the devil against his own flames if he could.

MUNT M.: I wish you wouldn't interrupt me, John. Well, it seems that in the course of conversation your name cropped up and Kennedy said he'd like to drop in and see

you here. James, being the kindly soul he is——
(BANNISTER *gives her a keen, eloquent look, appears to be going to say something, which he checks with a cough*) offered to introduce him to you, so Kennedy's come down with him.

BANNISTER: Hmph. Why has he to go through all this roundabout carry-on?

AUNT M.: You're that blunt I suppose he didn't know what way you'd take it, and maybe snub him. The manners can be far back in you when you like.

BANNISTER: Oh, quit your lecturing, Maria.

AUNT M.: I'll go over and send them in.

BANNISTER: Look here—this man's niece has been in this evening already and I'm not going to waste any more ti——

AUNT M. (*emphatically*): Then I'll go over and BRING them in. (*Snapping.*) And if you're rude to them I'll remember I'm a Bannister too. (*She exits on the last sentence and* BANNISTER, *with a sour look on his face, crosses to his desk and sits.* AUNT MARIA *returns with* CHISHOLM *and* KENNEDY *and precedes them into the office.* CHISHOLM *is obviously nervous about his reception;* KENNEDY *is the completely self-possessed Colonial; while* AUNT MARIA *is obviously trying to play up to* CHISHOLM.) Come in, gentlemen, and sit down. My brother will be very glad to see you.

(BANNISTER *gives her a searching look, which* AUNT MARIA *completely ignores.*)

CHISHOLM: Good evening, Mr. Bannister. May I introduce Mr. Kennedy?

KENNEDY: Afternoon, sir.

(BANNISTER *acknowledges the introduction with a curt nod and motions them to chairs with a gesture.* AUNT MARIA *takes a seat too, uninvited.*)

BANNISTER: Sit down. Well?

CHISHOLM (*doodling with his hat*): I was up at the Manor House transacting some business Mr. Kennedy very kindly put my way and——

KENNEDY: Maybe I'd better explain, Mr. Chisholm.

CHISHOLM: Oh, certainly—certainly.

KENNEDY: Well, Mr. Bannister, my housekeeper was apparently told by my niece that I was engaged when you called——

BANNISTER: When I called?

KENNEDY: Yes, just after lunch. She said a Mr. Bannister . . . .

BANNISTER: I have more to do with my time. That was my son.

AUNT M.: It's understandable Mr. Kennedy thought it was you, John.

BANNISTER: That's all right, Maria.

> (*Enter* WALTER.)

CHISHOLM: Walter—this is Mr. Kennedy. Mr. Bannister junior.

WALTER: How do you do?

KENNEDY: How do you do? I've just learned it was you who called this afternoon.

WALTER: That's right.

KENNEDY: And you were told I couldn't see you?

BANNISTER: That you were engaged. Wasn't that it, Walter?

WALTER: Yes, I think so. It's the same thing anyway.

KENNEDY: Quite.

BANNISTER (*belligerently*): Oh, no, it's not.

KENNEDY: In any case, it was a mistake; so I told Mr. Chisholm I'd like to come and see what you wanted. He very kindly offered to bring me along.

CHISHOLM: Oh, it was only a pleasure.

AUNT M. (*beaming at him*): I'm sure it was, James.

BANNISTER: Part of your enthusiasm and indignation, Mr.?

> (CHISHOLM *looks extremely uncomfortable,* AUNT MARIA *and* KENNEDY *puzzled. Slight pause and tableau.*)

WALTER: I suppose you know why I called, Mr. Kennedy? I gathered as much from Angela.

KENNEDY: Oh, you know my niece?

WALTER: Yes, I knew her in Belfast. She called here a short while ago.

KENNEDY (*in surprised tones*): Really? She didn't tell me she was coming.

WALTER: Oh! Then I've let the cat out of the bag.

BANNISTER: What does it matter anyway? Do you know why my son called to see you, sir?

KENNEDY (*unperturbed and smiling*): Not directly—as yet. I can only assume——

BANNISTER: Well, I'll clear the air. He called about that pig-headed notice——

AUNT M.: John—really.

BANNISTER (*exasperatedly*): Look here, Maria, if you can't . . . .

WALTER (*protesting*): Dad—Dad—keep on the rails. This is under our roof.

> (AUNT MARIA *has leaned forward, with her hand behind her ear, to hear* WALTER.)

AUNT M. (*emphatically*): Yes indeed, Walter.

> (CHISHOLM *does not risk anything but nodding agreement, till he suddenly catches* BANNISTER'S *eye on him and stops nodding with a jerk.*)

KENNEDY (*benignly*): It's quite all right. Yes, Mr. Bannister, you were mentioning this—er—pig-headed notice?

BANNISTER: And I wasn't trying to be funny, sir.

KENNEDY: Obviously not.

BANNISTER (*nettled*): Maybe you are?

WALTER (*hastily interposing*): Leave this to me for a minute, Dad.

CHISHOLM (*rising*): If you'll excuse me, I've a couple of calls before closing time.

> (*Assent on the part of* WALTER *and* KENNEDY. BANNISTER *merely looks at him.*)

AUNT M.: Certainly, James. I'll just see you to the end of the yard.

> (*Exit* CHISHOLM *and* AUNT MARIA.)

WALTER: Now, Mr. Kennedy, perhaps you know we're building a café?

KENNEDY: Yes, I've heard quite a lot about it from various people, and, of course, I've seen the men at it.

WALTER: That lane through the Manor grounds had a very vital part in my ideas for the improvement of the town. It was to take car traffic for parking on the beach.

KENNEDY: Quite. But as part of the Manor property, you'll realise the decision on that rested with me.

WALTER: Definitely.

KENNEDY: All I can tell you is that I had very real reasons for putting up that notice and I wasn't exactly a free-will agent in the matter. And I'm really sorry I can't do anything about it now.

BANNISTER (*explosively*): Don't bother shedding any crocodile tears over it, Mr. So far as we're concerned, you can keep the lane now till the grass is as high as the hedges.

WALTER (*embarrassed*): We needn't get hot under the collar about it, Dad.

BANNISTER: I'd just have this gentleman understand that people of substance in the town don't like strangers setting up as wee Popes.

KENNEDY (*smiling*): I quite understand, Mr. Bannister.

BANNISTER (*hotly*): Well, if you understand and are so sorry about it, why the devil don't you . . . .

WALTER (*interposing*): Please, Dad. It's alright, Mr. Kennedy, I've managed to make other arrangements.

KENNEDY: Oh! Might I ask in what way?

BANNISTER: No, sir, you mightn't.

WALTER: But I must say I find it hard to fathom your attitude to this thing, Mr. Kennedy.

KENNEDY: I'm sure you do. I can only hope it will all be made clear to you in due course. And there, gentlemen, I'm afraid we must leave it for the present. (*He rises and* WALTER *does so too.* BANNISTER *remains seated.*) Well, I'm glad we've met and (*to* WALTER) sorry for the misunderstanding when you called to see me. Good afternoon, gentlemen.

WALTER (*accompanying him to the office door*): Good afternoon.
    (BANNISTER *merely nods curtly. Exit* KENNEDY.)

BANNISTER: Well, that's the right hyprocritical cod. Another Chisholm.
    (*Enter* AUNT MARIA.)

AUNT M.: I think that was very nice of James Chisholm. Did you come any speed with that man, Walter?

BANNISTER (*very emphatically*): No, we came no speed. And when I'm talking business, less butting in from you, Maria.

AUNT M.: John—don't you imagine for one minute I'm going to sit and listen . . . .

BANNISTER: Who asked you to sit and listen?

AUNT M. (*her chin out*): And don't think you're going to shout me down either.

BANNISTER: There's divil all wrong with your hearing now.

AUNT M.: Nor my tongue, for that matter, and you'll get the length of it every time there's a display of ignorance like that you're after giving. My face just burned for that gentle creature, James Chisholm.

BANNISTER: Are you sure it was your face? I was waiting for you kissing him good-bye.

AUNT M.: Don't you dare to make such an insinuation, John Bannister.

BANNISTER (*shouting*): You may be my sister, but remember I'm boss here.

> (AUNT MARIA *advances close to him and* BANNISTER *involuntarily retreats.*)

AUNT M.: How dare you? You won't boss me.

> (*These exchanges follow rapidly and in crescendo.*)

WALTER: Auntie—Dad—for Heaven's sake——

RAPID CURTAIN.

End of Act Two.

ACT THREE.

(*The scene is the same, the private office of* JOHN BANNISTER *two weeks later. When the curtain goes up,* WALTER *and his Father are in conversation, just coming into the office together.*)

BANNISTER (*sourly*): And you were going to do it cheap—just pick a bunch of fellows from the Labour Exchange.

WALTER: Yes, that was my original idea.

BANNISTER: You'll never die of sticking in the one notion.

WALTER: When I talked it over with McDonnell he pointed out the danger of getting a botched job and offered to look after the whole thing for me.

BANNISTER: And you fell into the trap nicely.

WALTER: Trap?

BANNISTER (*emphatically*): Aye, trap. Can't you see McDonnell's trying to make a job for himself? Things have been a bit quiet in his line lately and a sucker like you's a gift from Heaven.

WALTER: Dad—you think everybody's out to do you.

BANNISTER: I don't think it. I KNOW it. The law of life is that everything living preys on something else. The only difference is that the animals are more honest about it. Did McDonnell say what it would cost?

WALTER: He said he'd get it done as reasonably as possible.

BANNISTER: That could mean anything. There'll be his own tee and likely a handsel for him in the contractor's charge.

WALTER: Dad, there's such a thing as professional etiquette.

BANNISTER: The greatest smoke-screen that ever was put up, son. I think I'll dander down and see McDonnell some time.

WALTER: For Heaven's sake don't, or you'll be getting his back up too.

BANNISTER: You'd think I wasn't paying for this to hear you.

WALTER: You'll get it all back with interest in time, once the café gets going. We've had enough complications, Heaven knows.

BANNISTER: Did you see any sign of that young woman or her uncle since?

WALTER: No, I haven't been looking for them. Now I've got Dunnigan's place, there's no need to.

BANNISTER: She's still here.

WALTER: How d'you know?

BANNISTER: I saw the wee car the other day when I was passing the Manor.

WALTER: Oh, she might be away twenty times over since then.

BANNISTER: I doubt it. I think that young woman has a purpose in being up at that place, whatever it may be. Maybe to watch the old uncle, or his money-bags.

WALTER: Not at all, Dad. Her people have pots.

BANNISTER: I never met any of those pots yet that couldn't hold more.

WALTER (*somewhat querulously*): Dad—I'd rather not talk about them, if you don't mind.

BANNISTER (*studying him keenly*): Oh. Still under your skin a bit?

WALTER: Cut it out, Dad. Where's Auntie?

BANNISTER: Isn't she in the house?

WALTER: She wasn't when I came through just now.

BANNISTER: What do you want her for?

WALTER: I met Mrs. Colhoun up at the Post Office and she asked me to give Auntie a message.

BANNISTER: Oh. And what's worrying Mrs. Colhoun?

WALTER: She just said to tell Auntie she was very anxious for the latest news.

BANNISTER: About what?

WALTER: Search me. I didn't ask her.

BANNISTER: Hmph. You're a funny fellow. By the way—what do you think's wrong with your Aunt these days?

WALTER: Wrong with her? How?

BANNISTER: She's too sweet. She hasn't been flying off the handle for days and she's actually gone and bought herself one of those wee ear gadgets—what I suggested. There's something radically wrong with your Aunt Maria when she does anything I suggest.

WALTER: Uh—huh. Hanged if I could say, Dad.

BANNISTER: She's always been a woman who spoke twice before she thought once. This last week or so you've got to come over things a couple of times before she answers you at all, even with her ear gadget. There's bound to be some reason for that, along with the extra sweetness.

WALTER: Well, she's said nothing to me that would throw any light on it.

BANNISTER: It never was an easy job undertsanding your Aunt.

WALTER (*smiling*): Why try, Dad? Just take her as you find her.

BANNISTER: Hmph—you're a right one to talk. You took that young woman as you found her, didn't you? People in glass houses shouldn't throw bricks.

WALTER: Very neat, Dad. Although I'm giving you that advice about Aunt Maria, for once I am inclined to agree with you: women are just about impossible to fathom.

BANNISTER (*dryly*): Isn't it nice to know we agree on something? Well—I wouldn't mind a lot if you got out of the way for a while.

WALTER: Oh! Why?

BANNISTER: I've somebody coming to see me.

WALTER: Any harm asking who it is?

BANNISTER: Boys, but you're curious.

WALTER: Part of the Carrigmore heritage, Dad.

BANNISTER (*defiantly*): Well—if you want to know—it's McNinch.

WALTER: What? You don't say so. So he wants back? That IS a victory for you, Dad.

BANNISTER: Did I say he'd applied to get back?

WALTER: Do you mean you sent for him?

BANNISTER: If I keep this other fellow on I'm going to lose half my customers.

WALTER: Congratulations! That's a spiritual victory of the first order, Dad. But—how do you think the humble pie will agree with your stomach?

BANNISTER: There's no humble pie about it. He seemed anxious enough to come when I sent for him. I doubt everything hasn't just gone according to plan about the new job. The wee rest will maybe have cooled him.

WALTER: Now, Dad, that's the old Adam coming up again. Sit on it.

(*The phone rings and* BANNISTER *answers it.*)

BANNISTER (*at phone*): Yes?——Right. Hold on a minute. It's for you, Walter.

WALTER (*taking receiver*): Yes?——Uh—huh I see. Very good. (*He hangs up receiver.*)

BANNISTER: Who is it?

WALTER (*ignoring the question*): Well—I'll push on out for a while and leave you to McNinch, Dad.

BANNISTER: Who was that on the phone?

WALTER (*enigmatically*): Who's curious now? See you later.

BANNISTER: Here——

WALTER (*as he exits*): Cheerio. And be nice to " The Nose."

> (*Exit* WALTER. BANNISTER *again takes up the papers on his desk and is studying them when a knock comes at the door.*)

BANNISTER: Come in. (*Enter* McNINCH.) Oh, it's you, McNinch. Sit down. And how are things with you?

McNINCH (*with affected nonchalance*): Not so bad.

BANNISTER: Have you not got your new job fixed up yet?

McNINCH: There's been a bit of delay about it, but I expect they'll be ready for me in about three weeks.

BANNISTER: Not so hot, eh? They seem to be a bit off-putting.

McNINCH: Oh, I think it'll be all right.

BANNISTER: Any idea why I sent for you?

McNINCH (*non-committal*): Your message didn't say.

BANNISTER: That's not answering my question, but no matter. Are you tied up with these people?

McNINCH (*steadily*): I'm tied up with nobody, Mr. Bannister, and from now on I don't intend to be. I've thought over this and read a few books in the last couple of weeks.

BANNISTER: I see.

McNINCH: It's clear to me selling your services is just like selling goods—look for the best market and no sentiment.

BANNISTER: Oh well, reading books'll not boil many pots. You liked your work here, didn't you?

McNINCH: It was alright. I don't suppose it would be much different anywhere else.

BANNISTER (*studying him intently*): Would you like your job back?

McNINCH: It all depends.

BANNISTER: On what?

McNINCH: What there is to induce me.

BANNISTER: Oh!

McNINCH: I got into a rut here, Mr. Bannister, and pulling your feet out of a rut's one of the hardest things in this world. But I pulled mine out and I'm not putting them back again. That's being honest and putting my cards on the table.

BANNISTER: Aye, they're certainly better there than in the Labour Exchange. How would three ten a week induce you?

McNinch: It wouldn't.

Bannister: It's a big increase on what you were getting.

McNinch: It's a decrease on what I'm going to get.

Bannister: If it comes off.

McNinch: Oh, I'm pretty sure it'll come off. Anyway, I'd sooner take the risk than start off on the wrong foot again.

Bannister: What would you take?

McNinch: Four pounds is the least I'd come back for, Mr. Bannister.

Bannister: You're asking plenty.

McNinch: I've seen you making five times it in five minutes over the phone, Mr. Bannister.

(Bannister *is obviously trying to keep a grip on himself and pauses before replying.*)

Bannister: You're still in the notion of getting married?

McNinch: Yes.

Bannister: When?

McNinch: As soon as I can get enough money gathered up.

Bannister: Well—you said you were putting your cards on the table, so I'll put mine beside them. This fellow I got in your place is hopeless. He just doesn't seem able to get the hang of the job and it's been one mistake after the other. I've neither the time nor the patience to be spoon-feeding him day and daily. (*The phone rings and* Bannister *lifts the receiver.*) Yes?——Who?——Tell him to hold on there a minute and I'll give you a ring through when I'm free. (*He puts up the receiver.*) Four pounds a week's a lot of money for a clerk, McNinch, but I'm willing to stretch to it rather than put up with this fellow any longer. Can you start at once?

McNinch: I think it's only fair I should tell the people I was going to first and let them look out for someone else.

Bannister: Alright. And make it as snappy as you can, for there's a pile of statements lying here to be gone through.

McNinch: And I may as well tell you, Mr. Bannister, if they're willing to rise to the same figure I'll have to think over this again.

(Bannister *looks fixedly at him before speaking.*)

Bannister: D'you mean you'd let me down?

McNinch: I don't call it that.

BANNISTER (*after a pause*): Go on—go on. And I'll be looking
  for you back here soon.

McNINCH (*as he exits*): I'll call back anyway.
        (BANNISTER *lifts the phone and rings through to the
        general office.*)

BANNISTER (*at phone*): Miss Bell—tell that man he can come in
        here now. (*He replaces the phone and in a moment the
        door from the yard is knocked.*) Come in.
        (*Enter* MR. CHISHOLM. *He appears to be nervous as
        he closes the door and takes the seat to which*
        BANNISTER *motions him.*)

CHISHOLM: Good evening.

BANNISTER (*curtly*): 'Evening. It seems you want to see me?

CHISHOLM: Yes, indeed. I hope I've called at an opportune
        time?

BANNISTER: One time's pretty much the same as another with
        me, Mr. What's worrying you?

CHISHOLM: I—er—called about several matters.

BANNISTER: If it's about that cutlery business, there's nothing
        doing.

CHISHOLM: I hadn't thought of bringing it up at all.

BANNISTER: I was wondering—now that you're as thick as thieves
        with that man at the Manor House.

CHISHOLM: I brought him down in all good faith and no one's
        sorrier nothing came of it.

BANNISTER: Oh, you'll be able to bear it when you take a look
        at his insurance policy. I suppose you'll hardly like to
        bring up the other thing now?

CHISHOLM: You mean the subscription list?

BANNISTER: The very thing.

CHISHOLM: I was just about to do so.

BANNISTER (*surprised*): Oh, really!

CHISHOLM: I had one of my principals up with me early this
        week, doing a round of our buyers. This particular man
        likes to round off the day with a few quiet drinks over
        a final chat. So we dropped into " The Globe " in
        Church Street.

BANNISTER: I didn't think you were a drinking man.

CHISHOLM: I rarely ever touch it, but it pays me to humour this
        man. We were sitting in the saloon bar and the door
        was slightly open. That little man, Dunnigan, who has

the farm at the far end of the beach, came in with a couple
of others and they seemed to be carrying a fair load by
the pitch of their voices.

BANNISTER: Empty vessels make most sound.

CHISHOLM (*smiling*): Not quite so empty on this occasion.

BANNISTER: What was he saying?

CHISHOLM: He was telling the whole bar about a deal he'd made
with you about a way across his land to the beach.

BANNISTER: The mouth. I warned my son the type of man he
was dealing with.

CHISHOLM: I thought over the matter afterwards and I could see
your point of view that this was going to benefit the
whole town and the leading people could fairly be asked
to take a hand.

BANNISTER: Financially, you mean?

CHISHOLM: Yes. So I made it my business to contact some of
these folk and put the whole case before them.

BANNISTER: How'll your friend Kennedy take that?

CHISHOLM: As it's not his land I don't see there's any issue.

BANNISTER: That's between you and him . Any results on your
calls?

CHISHOLM: A very fair measure of support. Quite a number
agreed it would help the trade of the town and are willing
to put their hands in their pockets.

BANNISTER: Not very deep, I'll warrant.

CHISHOLM: I've been agreeably surprised. At least four are
prepared to go the length of a five pound note.

BANNISTER: Who, for instance?

CHISHOLM: McMeel of the novelty shop was one.

BANNISTER: You don't say so! McMeel was actually willing to
part with five pounds?

CHISHOLM: He was. Oh, I can assure you it's quite correct.

BANNISTER: Then my son must be right. Anything that can take
five pounds out of McMeel's pocket short of forcibly
MUST be a winner.

CHISHOLM: I agree. Well—once the subscription list's complete
I suppose the best way would be to appoint a small
administrative committee to see that the job's done
properly?

BANNISTER (*after a short pause—awkwardly*): You haven't
collected any actual money yet, Mr.?

CHISHOLM: Oh, no. I've merely tapped possible sources. But I've no doubt they'll redeem their promises when I approach them for the cash.

BANNISTER: Do nothing about it yet, Mr. As I told you before, the whole thing's my son's idea and he may want to keep control of this new road he's cutting in his own hands. Anyway, I'll let you know when I have a word with Walter.

CHISHOLM: I see. Well, I hope you recognise I'm trying to make good my offer to help in any possible way?

BANNISTER (*increasingly awkwardly*): Oh, yes, certainly—certainly. Well—anything else you wanted to see me about?

CHISHOLM (*very hesitantly*): Er—yes. It's only because I know you've an extremely good servant that I'm proposing—er—what I'm going to propose.

BANNISTER (*mystified*): Eh?

CHISHOLM (*floundering*): It all happened one evening lately at Mrs. Colhoun's, or, rather, after it.

BANNISTER: What on earth are you getting at, Mr.?

CHISHOLM: It's so very difficult to explain, but Maria asked me to see you——

BANNISTER: Maria?

CHISHOLM: Your sister Maria.

BANNISTER: What about her?

CHISHOLM: I've asked her to marry me.

BANNISTER: You've WHAT?

CHISHOLM: Believe me, I know it must be a very big shock to you, and I appreciate the fact.

BANNISTER: You weren't in for a few drinks to-day as well?

CHISHOLM: Oh, no, I'm quite serious.

BANNISTER: Well, I'm damned. This IS a surprise. I've been wondering what was the matter with my sister these last few days, but I can see it all now.

CHISHOLM: Yes. She was very worried about how to break it to you and in the end she asked me to do it. These sensitive souls are like that.

BANNISTER: Hmph.

CHISHOLM: Of course this is the revival of an old affair between Maria and me and it just shows how the passage of time and events sometimes brings people together again.

BANNISTER: Well—I suppose you know your own minds. You're no chickens.

CHISHOLM: Oh, yes. I must say I'm very grateful to Mrs. Colhoun for being the means of Maria and I meeting again. Of course I realise it means a big break in your household.

BANNISTER: Don't let that worry you too much. As you said, I've one of the best servant girls in the town and I'm sure she'l be well able to look after things for me.

CHISHOLM: I'm glad to know that, and I assure you I'm very grateful. And it'll please Maria.

BANNISTER (*extending his hand*): Well—congratulations, Mr. When are you thinking of getting the job done?

CHISHOLM: My place is being painted and papered, at Maria's suggestion, so it'll not be till that's finished.

BANNISTER (*with a grim chuckle*): It looks as if she's the tabs on you already. It's your blood on your own head, Mr.

CHISHOLM: Oh, I feel quite confident Maria and I will get on well together.

BANNISTER: Aye, of course it's not as if it was love's young dream, or anything like that. (*Rising.*) Well—if you look in in the course of a week or two we'll maybe be able to talk about the cutlery for the café.

CHISHOLM: That's very kind of you. I'll bring along the catalogues. Now, if you don't mind, I'll go across and tell Maria everything's fixed up satisfactorily.

BANNISTER (*accompanying him to the door*): Certainly. You know your way?

CHISHOLM: Oh, yes. And again thanks very much.

BANNISTER: Not at all. The pleasure's mine, Mr.

> (*Exit* CHISHOLM. BANNISTER *returns to his desk and resumes work with his papers. There is a look of satisfaction on his face. The phone rings.*)

BANNISTER (*at phone*): Yes?——Who? (*He frowns.*) No, I'm not free. (*He hangs up the receiver. In a moment or two a knock comes at the office door.* BANNISTER *looks over frowningly at it.*) Well?

> (*The door opens and* MR. THOMAS KENNEDY *enters, closing it after him.*)

KENNEDY: Good afternoon, Mr. Bannister.

BANNISTER: I said I wasn't free, sir.

E

KENNEDY: Yes. And you must absolve the typist. She passed on your message.

BANNISTER: It's not usual to barge into a man's office here, whatever it is where you come from, sir.

KENNEDY (*imperturbable*): No, and I must beg your pardon.

BANNISTER: It's less usual in a place where you're anything but welcome. I'm a very plain-speaking man, sir, and after your attitude here the other day your room's a lot better than your company.

KENNEDY: I shouldn't be at all surprised.

BANNISTER (*more nettled*): Now that you know it you'd think you'd close that door again, with yourself on the other side.

KENNEDY: I'm quite sure you think I should.

BANNISTER: You would't like me to put it a bit plainer?

KENNEDY: No. And when you know what brought me here I fancy you'll be quite glad you didn't.

(BANNISTER *regards him keenly for a moment without speaking.*)

BANNISTER: What do you want?

KENNEDY: To ask you a question first.

BANNISTER: Go ahead.

KENNEDY: Do you understand women, Mr. Bannister?

BANNISTER: I think you fancy yourself as a funny man, sir. (*Emphatically.*) Well, I don't.

KENNEDY: Please believe me, I'm perfectly serious. What's more, in a minute or two you'll find me giving you a perfect explanation of how that notice went up and is now coming down, and why I couldn't say more than I did on the afternoon I called here. I repeat, Mr. Bannister, do you understand women?

BANNISTER: Well, sir, allowing you really mean what you're saying, I'll give you a straight answer. No man, living or dead, ever understood or ever will understand women.

KENNEDY (*leaning across the desk*): Shake hands.

(BANNISTER *takes his hand with a certain reticence.*)

BANNISTER: What led to that question?

KENNEDY: There's a story to that, that now involves us all and has a very direct bearing on my visit here to-day, so perhaps you'll put up with it.

BANNISTER: I can listen when it's necessary.

KENNEDY: Good, Well, I imagine you've heard something of my background before I arrived in Carrigmore?

BANNISTER: Your niece told my son the day she was in.

KENNEDY: I thought so. Incidentally, it's she who prompted my question about women.

BANNISTER: Oh, is that so?

KENNEDY: When I came back from Ceylon I stayed for a while with my sister, Angela's mother, and they all knew I had the notion of buying a place in the country. One day Angela came to me with the Press advertisement about the Manor House here and told me she knew quite a lot about Carrigmore from somebody who lived in it.

B3NNISTER: Likely my son.

KENNEDY: That's perfectly clear now. Well, she infected me so much with her enthusiasm that before I knew where I was she had me up here, over the place and in the agent's office discussing terms. I might tell you, Mr. Bannister, that this niece of mine is an only child and a very masterful young woman, who has possibly had more of her own way than most.

BANNISTER: And possibly more than's good for her.

KENNEDY: Quite. I admit that.

BANNISTER: I've had some little experience of that side of things. However, go ahead with your story.

KENNEDY: Well, sir, if I might digress for a minute, I've been a hard-headed business man for the greater part of my life, but I've found that a scheming young person who's of my own flesh and blood can pull the wool over my eyes and mould me to her will like a piece of putty.

BANNISTER (*with feeling*): Shake hands again, sir.

(KENNEDY *shakes hands, looking rather surprised.*)

KENNEDY: I take it you agree with me?

BANNISTER: I couldn't agree with you more.

KENNEDY: Good. Now, Mr. Bannister, I'll pass to the vexed question of that notice on the beach lane.

BANNISTER: That's what I want to hear. And, as a man who calls a spade a spade, I may tell you, sir, I took a poor view of that, you being a stranger to the town.

KENNEDY: And perhaps I can understand that—NOW. Any way, I'll just ask you to try and put yourself in my position. If you had a niece, the daughter of a very favourite sister, who came to you and said the putting up of that

notice would help more than anything in settling an affair
of the heart that had gone wrong—what would you do?

BANNISTER: I'd be inclined to advise her to see a mental specialist.
Then—maybe—in fairness to you, I'd say to myself she's
a woman and the ways they take to get at a thing are
beyond the wit of men.

KENNEDY: Exactly. And if the niece in question had grown
into a very attractive young woman, who knows how to
bring all her charm to bear on a susceptible old bachelor
uncle——

BANNISTER: Then I'll admit, sir, your guns would be pretty well
spiked.

KENNEDY: That's the position in a nutshell, Mr. Bannister.
I just HAD to agree to the notice going up, though I didn't
care tuppence if all the cars in Ulster went up and down
that lane from January to December. In fact, when
I came to see you here I had the greatest difficulty in
hiding that from you all.

BANNISTER: I certainly couldn't understand your attitude.

KENNEDY: In my heart I sympathised with the boy's ideas
completely, but I'd given my word to Angela that
I wouldn't let him talk me into taking the notice down.
Now, of course, it's perfectly clear what she was aiming
at.

BANNISTER: What was that?

KENNEDY: An excuse to come along here and meet your son
again in a way that saved face. Of course the old ogre—
that's me—had sternly refused to listen and that gave her
the opening she wanted to do the fairy princess act.
All this, by the way, secretly, and then she'd try to pull
things straight.

BANNISTER: Isn't it wonderful the wiles of these young women?
Do you really think she'd all that worked out in her mind?

KENNEDY: I'm certain of it. In fact, Mr. Bannister, I'm
convinced the whole business of persuading me to take
the Manor House, put up the notice and everytnihg else
had one object and one only, to patch up this love affair
between Walter and her.

BANNISTER: But I was led to believe the interview between them
here didn't just go the way she wanted.

KENNEDY: My dear sir, that only added fuel to the flame. I got
it all out of her afterwards. It seems she'd always been

able to wheedle anything out of Walter and wind him round her little finger. She came back just full of the change in him, how masterful he'd become and how much more she admired him for it, and he was the only chap she wanted and God knows what else. That brought us to this afternoon, when she telephoned and asked him to come out and see her and surrendered completely.

BANNISTER: So that's where the phone message came from. The young snipe wouldn't tell me. If you ask me, the love's not one-sided.

KENNEDY: I quite agree. In fact I'd ample evidence of that before I left for here. Indeed, they asked me to come and tell you first and they'd follow later.

BANNISTER: Well, I think this very special occasion demands recognition. Do you take a drink, sir?

KENNEDY (*smiling*): I've been known to, Mr. Bannister.
(BANNISTER *opens the door of a locker and brings out a bottle, two glasses and a water croft.*)

BANNISTER: Liqueur Irish meet your taste?

KENNEDY: Excellently. I used to dream about it in Ceylon. We got nothing but wishy-washy Scotch there.

BANNISTER: Water?

KENNEDY: Always—with Irish. Just a little, please.

BANNISTER: It's changed every day by the office-cleaner, so it's quite fresh.
(*He dispenses two very liberal drinks and hands one to* KENNEDY.)

KENNEDY: Well—your very good health, Mr. Bannister.

BANNISTER: And yours, sir. It looks, from what you tell me, we're soon going to be relatives of a sort.

KENNEDY: And the prospect's very pleasant to me, having met your son.

BANNISTER: Yes, he's a right lad. Like your niece, he's just had a wee bit too much of his own way.

KENNEDY (*smiling*): They'll probably be a good brake on each other, with the odds on Walter.

BANNISTER: As it should be, and I don't say that because he's my son. I've no use for bossy women, single or married.

KENNEDY: I agree. I wouldn't go so far as to say that's why I'm still single, but it always weighed with me.

BANNISTER: You were wise, sir. To my mind there's no more
contemptible sight than a man wriggling under the thumb
of a woman.

> (*The door to the yard opens and* AUNT MARIA *puts her
> head in.* BANNISTER *is in the act of drinking and
> hastily, as if by reflex action, tries to conceal his glass
> below the level of his desk, while the whiskey goes
> " the wrong way " and starts him coughing violently.*)

AUNT M.: Oh. I'm sorry, John. (*She withdraws.*)

BANNISTER: You've met my sister? Sixty-two next month and
she's just got engaged for the first time. Your friend
Chisholm's the happy man.

KENNEDY: Really? I must congratulate him.

BANNISTER: Aye, God help him. Wait till she gets into her
stride. She's as full of giggles and blushes now as if
her age was the other way round. Women again, sir.

KENNEDY: How will you manage when she gets married?

BANNISTER: First-class, sir. I've a grand servant girl and she'll
be tickled to death to get her head in running the house.
(*The whiskey is working.*) (*Sotto voce.*) And I'll be the
boss again beyond that door, what I haven't been for
twenty years. How d'you like that whiskey?

KENNEDY: Grand stuff.

BANNISTER: Twenty years old if it's a day. Another dram? (*He
makes a gesture towards the bottle.*)

KENNEDY: I've plenty at the moment, thanks.

BANNISTER: How does this café idea of my son's appeal to you?

KENNEDY: Now that I can speak my real mind, I think it's
first-class.

BANNISTER: So do I, in my heart of hearts. Of course I had
to throw a certain amount of cold water on it with
Walter. It doesn't do to let these young fellows think
they know everything.

KENNEDY: The truth is, I envy him.

BANNISTER: How d'you mean?

KENNEDY: Starting a new enterprise. Doing something creative
—having youth on his side—all the best things in life
within his grasp. To tell you the truth, Mr. Bannister.
I put myself on the scrap-heap and I'm finding it a damn
uncomfortable spot.

BANNISTER: Yes, I think the old tag's right: It's better to work
out than rust out. Why did you throw in your hand?

KENNEDY : Because we're never too old to build castles in the
air. I've been the most of thirty years in the East—a
long time in a hot climate. I've made a lot of money,
Mr. Bannister—far more than I'll ever need. Out there
I used to dream about those " soft " Irish days Stanford
wrote about, a pleasant thought when the heat's
shimmering, and see myself the owner of a nice property
here. Well—you know the rest; I needn't go over it all.

BANNISTER : And it hasn't panned out as you thought?

KENNEDY (*after a moment's thoughtful hesitation*) : No, it hasn't.
I'm beginning to realise it IS better to travel hopefully
than arrive. No matter how nice leisure seems in prospect
—well, when you've worked hard all your life and get it,
it's——

BANNISTER : Dead Sea fruit, eh?

KENNEDY : To a great extent, yes.

BANNISTER : Well, well, well—it's a waste of good whiskey to
let you get down in the lip like this. Maybe we can do
something about it.

KENNEDY : Oh, don't worry. It's good ot you to let me get it off
my chest anyway.

BANNISTER (*emphatically*) : Oh, I'm not talking through the
whiskey, good and all as it is. When I say " do something about it " I MEAN do something about it. Listen,
sir—I've worked hard all my life, too. I've built this
business from nothing till its annual turnover's one of
the biggest in the county. I could sell it to-morrow
for five figures and not a wee one in front either. But
would I?

KENNEDY (*smiling*) : Somehow I don't think so.

BANNISTER : And you're right. Don't imagine it hasn't got its
problems, but that's maybe where you could come into
the picture.

KENNEDY : Oh. In what way?

BANNISTER : I'm a man who either likes people or doesn't, sir.
What you've told me to-day has changed my opinion of
you more than a bit.

KENNEDY : For the better, I hope?

BANNISTER : Definitely.. I can see you're a business man and
we've a lot in common. We've something more in
common—a new family in the making that's your flesh

and blood on one side and mine on the other. Am
I right?

KENNEDY: You couldn't be more so, Mr. Bannister.

BANNISTER: Good. Here—what about that glass of yours?
It's nearly empty.

KENNEDY: Now, now—it's half full.

BANNISTER (*lifting the bottle*): Come on. God never made half
things, Mr., and who are we to improve on Him?

> (*He pours another liberal whiskey into* KENNEDY'S
> *glass.*)

BANNISTER: Any more water?

KENNEDY: Just a spot.

BANNISTER (*with the water croft*): Say when.

KENNEDY: Thanks. That'll do.

> (BANNISTER *replenishes his own glass.*)

BANNISTER: I'll come to the point now. I've been having a lot
of trouble over staff. I needn't bore you going into the
" whys and wherefores " of it all, but I lost my chief
clerk for a bit. I'm hoping to have him back this very
evening, but there's a deal of leeway to be made up.
And Walter's that full of this café business I can't look
for much help from him.

KENNEDY: Once he's married, all that'll change, Mr. Bannister.
It's wonderful how the sight of a row of nappies in front
of the fire steadies a young fellow up.

BANNISTER (*laughing*): That's certainly good—coming from a
bachelor. Well, sir, the day you and I see that sight
I'll broach another bottle.

KENNEDY: I'll hold you to that.

BANNISTER: With a heart and a half. Meantime, how would the
idea of giving me a hand in here appeal to you?

KENNEDY: Very much indeed.

BANNISTER: Right. There's a big bit of development in this
business yet and you're a man of experience. As to
money——

KENNEDY: We needn't fight over that. I've told you already
I've more than I need. And both yours and mine will
probably reach the same place eventually.

BANNISTER: Shake hands, sir. You're a man after my own heart.
You don't talk round a thing. I think you and I should
get on well together.

KENNEDY: I'm sure of it.

BANNISTER (*rising*): D'you know—I was born and bred in this wee town and to me there's no place like it. I'm no musician, but if there's one line sticks in my head it's this——

> (*He sings, very unmusically, one line of " There's no place like home." Just as he is finishing there is a knock at the door and* McNINCH *enters. He looks at the scene in amazement.*)

McNINCH: Sorry, sir. I didn't know you were engaged.

BANNISTER: It's all right. This is my chief clerk, Mr. Kennedy.

KENNEDY: How d'you do?

McNINCH: Pleased to meet you.

BANNISTER (*with a mellow smile*): Well—are you still my chief clerk, McNinch?

McNINCH: Yes. I've fixed it up. I can start now.

BANNISTER: Good.

> (McNINCH *turns to go.*)

BANNISTER: McNinch.

McNINCH (*turning*): Yes?

BANNISTER: My son's just got engaged to Mr. Kennedy's niece this evening.

McNINCH: Indeed, sir? Maybe you'll give him my congratulations?

BANNISTER: He'll be here soon and you can give them to him yourself. But just to celebrate it, there'll he ten shillings on that wages figure we agreed.

McNINCH: Thank you, Mr. Bannister.

> (*Exit* McNINCH.)

BANNISTER: Grand clerk, that fellow. Couldn't catch him out on anything. Well, as I was saying, there's no place like your own home town. And Carrigmore doesn't need to take any back seat for scenery. Just come here. (*He moves to the window and* KENNEDY *follows.*) As my son said to me the other day, take the sweep of that bay up to the cliff. Could you beat it?

> (*His left hand is on* KENNEDY'S *shoulder, his right, holding his glass, points. In the middle of the sentence the door opens and* WALTER *and* ANGELA *stand looking at the scene smiling.*)

WALTER (*chuckling*): Rank plagiarism, Dad. You know that's my copyright.

> (BANNISTER *and* KENNEDY *turn.*)

BANNISTER (*cheerfully*): So there you are. This is a quick one you've worked on me.

WALTER: No interfering with Fate, Dad. What about the traditional blessing?

BANNISTER (*extending his hand to* ANGELA): Well, young woman, welcome to the Bannister family.

ANGELA (*shyly*): Thank you, Mr. Bannister

BANNISTER: Well—we're going to be a woman short in it one of these days, so you've chosen a good time.

WALTER: What d'you mean, Dad?

BANNISTER: I mean, son, your Aunt Maria's entering the holy estate of matrimony.

WALTER: W-h-a-t?

BANNISTER: Yes, she's just beaten you by a short head in this engagement business.

WALTER: And——

BANNISTER: Who's your new uncle? Oh, a very nice, precise gentleman, Mr. Chisholm.

WALTER: Well, Auntie certainly HAS been a dark horse. Or should I say " mare "?

BANNISTER (*chuckling*): I don't think she'd worry WHAT you called her. She's walking round in a kind of moon-struck daze. But what are we all standing like pelicans for? Get chairs for yourselt and Miss——

ANGELA: Angela, please, Mr. Bannister.

BANNISTER: Alright, Angela. (WALTER *brings two chairs forward*.) Your uncle and I have had a wee celebration all on our own and I think I cay say we've got to know each other very well without anybody's help. Isn't that so, Mr. Kennedy?

KENNEDY: Yes indeed, Mr. Bannister.

BANNISTER: Some of the things we've decided can keep for the time being. The one thing that CAN'T keep is to tell you young people we're very pleased you've fixed things up.

WALTER: Very nice of you, Dad. Thanks a lot.

ANGELA: That goes for me too, Mr. Bannister.

BANNISTER: What will Angela drink, Walter? We've a few toasts yet.

WALTER (*looking at* ANGELA): Sherry?

ANGELA: Just a small one, Walter, please.

BANNISTER: There's a bottle in the locker there and the wine glasses are in the far corner. I suppose you'll have whiskey?

WALTER: Yes, Dad. I need it after that shock about Auntie.

BANNISTER: You can get it yourself. And not too big a one, for I'm sure your head's floating already. (WALTER *gets drinks for* ANGELA *and himself.*) Are you all right, Mr. Kennedy?

KENNEDY: Plenty yet, thank you.

BANNISTER (*suddenly*): Damn it, Walter, with all this excitement I clean forgot.

WALTER: Forgot what?

BANNISTER: What about the road through wee Dunnigan's place now?

WALTER: Oh, I've thought all that out, Dad. We'll go ahead with it.

BANNISTER: But—sure you won't need it?

WALTER: Oh, yes, we will. We're going to make the Manor lane the entrance way to the beach and Dunnigan's the exit. Much better arrangement every way you look at it. No traffic jams and no bumping and boring. Everything running smoothly.

BANNISTER: I suppose you'll have your own way, no matter what I say.

WALTER: I couldn't think of letting the poor little devil down now any way.

BANNISTER (*to* ANGELA): Take a tip from me, young woman, and keep your hands on the purse strings. This lad has too soft a heart.

ANGELA (*smiling*): Oh, I'll watch him, Mr. Bannister.

KENNEDY: Dunnigan—that's the little fellow came up to see me, Angela? The one you had the chat with?

ANGELA: Yes. Pathetic little creature, I thought.

BANNISTER: Was he blarneying you too?

ANGELA: No. He's really a very honest little man, Mr. Bannister. Shall I tell them, Uncle?

KENNEDY: By all means.

ANGELA: I had a few casual talks with him and he told me he was trying to pull things straight after an awful spell of bad luck. I was really sorry for him. One day, not long ago, he came to me with a rather extraordinary request. He wondered if I could persuade Uncle Thomas

to lend him twenty-five pounds—JUST FOR TWO
HOURS. He said he couldn't just tell me why, but he'd
give his word of honour to return the money in two
hours. Indeed, he offered his place as security for its
return.

(WALTER *and* BANNISTER *are looking intently at each
other, a smile playing round* WALTER'S *lips.*)

KENNEDY : And she persuaded me to lend him the money and,
sure enough, back he came with it well under the two
hours. Extraordinary business altog——

BANNISTER : Well, I'm damned.

WALTER (*laughing*): Dad, I TOLD you that wee man had a bent
in life somewhere. Now I KNOW it. He'd have made
his fortune at poker. (KENNEDY *and* ANGELA *are looking
puzzled.*) Listen, you folks, that twenty-five pounds
worked the best bluff's Dad's ever got put across him.

(BANNISTER *is still thinking it out, then, suddenly,
under the mellowing influence of the whiskey, he bursts
out laughing too.*)

BANNISTER : We'll not waste time telling you it all now. Walter.

WALTER : Yes, Dad?

BANNISTER : I think we ought to have your Aunt Maria over.
And there's just a chance your new uncle might be there
too. You can tell them the news about yourself

WALTER : Surely, Dad.

(*Exit* WALTER.)

BANNISTER : Mr. Kennedy—let me give you a drop more in that

KENNEDY : Very little, now, Mr. Bannister. You've been mighty
liberal with it already.

BANNISTER : Oh, we'll never have a day like this again. Have
you enough sherry, Angela?

ANGELA : Plenty, thanks, Mr. Bannister.

(*Enter* AUNT MARIA *and* MR. CHISHOLM *with* WALTER.
AUNT MARIA *has her ear gadget prominently displayed
and is obviously using it to please her brother. She
is very benign and keeps glancing across at* CHISHOLM
during the conversation. WALTER *brings chairs for
them.*)

KENNEDY (*to* AUNT MARIA *and* CHISHOLM): May I offer my very
hearty congratulations? (*He shakes hands with both
and* AUNT MARIA *simpers and looks at* CHISHOLM.
BANNISTER *turns to them.*)

BANNISTER: This is Walter's fiancée, Miss——

ANGELA: Just Angela still, Mr. Bannister.

    (AUNT MARIA *and* CHISHOLM *shake hands with her and there are mutual congratulations.*)

BANNISTER: A drop of sherry, Maria?

AUNT M.: Thank you, John.

BANNISTER (*to* CHISHOLM): Whiskey, I suppose?

CHISHOLM: Thanks, Mr. Bann——

BANNISTER: Oh, John'll do. (*He dispenses the drinks.*) Well, Kennedy, you and I have a toast to ourselves. "To the engaged couples." (KENNEDY *and he drink the toast; tableau with the others.*)

WALTER: Thanks, Dad, on behalf of all of us.

KENNEDY: Now, ladies and gentlemen, I have a toast we can all drink, to an institution that did a lot to bring this happy day nearer for at least one of the engaged couples. I ask you, ladies and gentlemen, to drink with me to " BANNISTER'S CAFE."

(*Tableau.*)

CURTAIN.

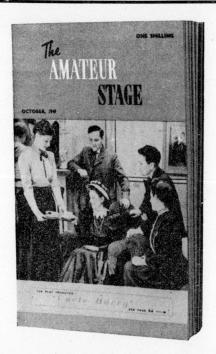

"THE AMATEUR STAGE"

The Monthly Magazine for the Amateur Player, Producer and Playwright.

First-class Articles by Prominent Writers on Every Aspect of the Amateur Theatre.

Club Drama : Youth Drama : Religious Drama : Opera : Management : Production : New Plays, Books, etc., etc.

1/- monthly from your newsagent

(or by direct subscription 12s. 6d. a year,
6/6 half-year, post free).
Specimen copy 2½d. from the Publishers.

VAWSER & WILES (London), LTD.,
356/8 Kilburn High Road, London, N.W.6